W9-DBZ-817

THE
ETHNIC
MOMENT

THE
ETHNIC

THE SEARCH FOR EQUALITY IN THE AMERICAN EXPERIENCE

MOMENT

PHILIP L. FETZER

M.E. Sharpe
Armonk, New York
London, England

E
184
/84
A /
E8355
1997

Library of Congress Cataloging-in-Publication Data

The ethnic moment : the search for equality in the American experience /
edited by Philip L. Fetzer.
p.   cm.
Includes bibliographical references (p.   ) and index.
ISBN 1-56324-926-X (hardcover : alk. paper)
1. Minorities—United States—Social conditions.
2. Equality—United States.
3. United States—Social conditions—1980–   .
4. Racism—United States.
5. Sexism—United States.
6. United States—Race relations.
7. United States—Ethnic relations.
I. Fetzer, Philip L.
E184.A1E8355   1996
305.8'00973—dc20
96-20612
CIP

Printed in the United States of America

The paper used in this publication meets the minimum requirements of the
American National Standard for Information Sciences—
Permanence of Paper for Printed Library Materials,
ANSI Z 39.48-1984.

BM (c)   10   9   8   7   6   5   4   3   2   1

For Elizabeth and Jim

Think where man's glory most begins and ends,
And say my glory was I had such friends.

      —Yeats, *The Municipal Gallery Revisited*

Equality and justice, the two great distinguishing
characteristics of democracy, follow inevitably from the
conception of men, all men, as rational and spiritual beings.

—Robert Maynard Hutchins,
Democracy and Human Nature

Attempt the end, and never stand to doubt;
Nothing's so hard but search will find it out.

—Robert Herrick, *Seek and Find*

Contents

Preface

Success is counted sweetest
By those who ne'er succeed.
To comprehend a nectar,
Requires sorest need.

    —Emily Dickinson, "Success"

The Pueblo people have a saying: "Always tell a story from the beginning." For me, the beginning of this anthology began in the summer of 1959. I was on the way home from a month-long bus trip through Mexico. I was fifteen. We had traveled to Mexico City and Guadalajara as part of an Episcopal church–sponsored "Summer Works Project." We stopped briefly in Tucson. I walked into town with a friend (an African American) while he went to a barbershop. We sat down and waited. The barber refused to give him a haircut. It was nothing personal, he explained, only other businessmen in town would get mad at him if he did. I was stunned. I don't recall how my friend reacted. For me, it was an awakening—the beginning of social consciousness.

Growing up in the 1950s in South Pasadena, an all-white suburb of Los Angeles, I received a "good education." But I never knew about racism. I never knew about poverty. I was completely ignorant of the fact that for millions of Americans, *equality* was a term that had little or nothing to do with their lives.

⌒

In 1961, the summer after my senior year, I went to Haiti on another church project. We helped rehabilitate some local schools. Just about everyone in Haiti is black. I am white. The bus drivers were black. The police were black. All the shopkeepers were black. I became alive to the fact that when one is in the distinct minority, particularly as it relates to race, one is conscious of this fact *every* moment of *every* day.

⌒

In the fall of 1961, I began my college career. I was attending Princeton, one of the finest universities in the country. Three years later, representatives of the Student Nonviolent Coordinating Committee came on campus to recruit students for voter registration work in Mississippi and other Deep South states. Four of us, three undergraduates and one grad student, drove to Jackson for a brief "training" session before we went to our assigned towns. Busy registering people in the Mississippi Freedom Democratic Party (MFDP), I met a woman who worked in the fields, picking cotton. She said that she was paid $3 a day for ten hours' work. I walked through the little town, Shaw, in northwest Mississippi, and found out that the paving on roads in the town stopped where the houses of black Americans began.

⌒

My education about equality—political, economic, and social—and about "equality of opportunity" occurred outside the classroom. I know that we talk a lot about equality in the United States. I know that we read about it. I know that we study the concept and discuss its implications in courses in philosophy and political science and history. Now, I think one has to live it to learn it, to know what it means.

The book represents an attempt to *humanize* the concept of equality. It seems to me that one may be able to understand equality more fully through the stories that people tell about their lives than through abstract discussions.

The first chapter, "Thinking about Equality," briefly describes the historical evolution of the concept of equality. Philosophers and religious thinkers both contributed to our early understanding of the term. Contemporary approaches to the way in which the word *equality* has been applied—legal, political, economic, equality of opportunity, and social equality—are then presented. After this chapter comes the heart of the book, autobiographical essays, each of which brings a new perspective, a personal perspective, on equality.

In part I, the authors describe critical experiences in their lives that awakened in them a new and deeper understanding of equality. In the first of these essays, Morris Dees explores the meaning of legal equality in an excerpt from his book *A Season for Justice*. Both as a young man growing up in rural Alabama and later as a trial lawyer, Dees became conscious of the way law can be used to deny or affirm the "equal protection of the laws." The essay clearly demonstrates that *effective* legal representation is the *sine qua non* for those who might otherwise be denied the chance to exercise their rights in the judicial system.

Betty Friedan shares the conflicts between aspirations for gender equality and the desires of young women like herself to take the "acceptable" and "secure" path of marriage and family in "The Way We Were—1949." Although she was educated at one of the outstanding liberal arts colleges in the country, Betty Friedan discovered that she was not going to be considered for certain positions of responsibility, not because she lacked the ability, but simply because she was the "wrong" gender. Friedan's article plainly reveals her personal experiences with the ways in which social equality, equality of opportunity, and economic equality are interrelated.

The opportunity to teach political science and history at Spelman College in the 1950s gave Howard Zinn the chance to educate young women for whom a degree was "a matter of life and death." He also had the opportunity to become actively involved in bringing about social change in Atlanta, one of the largest cities in the South. In an excerpt from *You Can't Be Neutral on a Moving Train*, Howard Zinn describes his firsthand experiences in the state capitol and the local libraries—places where the myths and realities of equality were brought into sharp focus.

The Voting Rights Act of 1965 is considered by many to be the most important piece of legislation ever adopted to give substance to the concept of political equality. Julian Bond was prevented from exercising his political rights because of the irrelevant characteristic of race. In "A Participant's Commentary," Bond discusses how he became involved in the civil rights movement, including sit-ins, as well as his legal efforts to breathe life into "the Act."

As a young girl, Donna Lopiano wanted to pitch for the New York Yankees. She had more talent than most young people who held such aspirations. The fact that she was female precluded achieving this goal. As we learn in "Growing Up with Gender Discrimination in Sport," Lopiano channeled her disappointment and anger into a career, first as director of women's athletics at the University of Texas and later as head of the Women's Sports Foundation. "I do what I do today," she writes, "because I do not want any little girl to feel the way I felt or go through life wondering if she could have realized her dream."

In "Equality Requires a Fight for Recognition and Meaning," Michael Lerner discusses the effects of his religious upbringing. Judaism tells a "story of the way that inequality had in fact been overcome . . . our task was to tell this story about the possibility of overcoming inequality." Lerner believes that aspirations toward societal equality cannot be realized unless the individual's needs for "authentic recognition" and "meaningful work" are met.

Taking his family back to Clarinda, Iowa, for Decoration Day, Gayle Pemberton's father celebrated something very personal—his own imagination—that had taken him out of that segregated town and away from poverty. In "Another 'Theme for English B,' " Pemberton focuses on the need for blacks and whites to exercise their imaginations if they are ever to see one another as individuals and not stereotypes.

In part II, each contributor describes how he or she came to know the meaning of equality at an early age. Congressman Henry Gonzalez grew up in San Antonio, Texas. He was active in local government and became a member of the House of Representatives in 1961. In "From Participation to Equality," he focuses on the experiences of people who, as a result of their ethnicity and poverty, had difficulty even receiving clean water from the city. Later on in his essay, Gonzalez discusses the undemocratic aspects of the ways economic policy is made in the United States with special emphasis on the role of the Federal Reserve System, or the Fed, as he calls it.

Michael Parenti tells about growing up in an Italian immigrant family in New York City in the 1930s and 1940s. "La Famiglia, La Famiglia" is a story of the pleasures and perils of leaving the old country and living in what some people called "a slum." People's willingness to work hard did not guarantee them a decent wage or a steady job. Disparities in the treatment of individuals based on ancestry were obviously in conflict with the idea of equality of opportunity that is part of everyday political rhetoric in the United States.

In "Grampa's Indian Blood," a Native American storyteller, Joseph Bruchac, tells how he developed his understanding of equality through observing his grandfather, Jesse Bowman. In order to survive the widespread hostility toward Indians, Bowman called himself French Canadian. Joseph Bruchac learned about the rights of children from his grandfather. Non-abusive child raising "was always deeply part of the Abenaki Indian culture," writes Bruchac.

Is it true that "Prejudice Is a Curable Disease," as William Winter maintains in his essay? In the "factory neighborhood" where he grew up, he writes, "we kids were color-blind." It wasn't until his family moved to a "nicer neighborhood" that he began to hear words like "dago" and "wop." During a lengthy career as a radio correspondent for CBS, Winter also learned about racial and ethnic stereotyping in Asia. Ahmed Sukarno, the first president of Indonesia, told Winter that he expected no help from the United States in the war for independence against the Dutch because "we're Asians" and not white Europeans.

Alice Brooks grew up poor in Chicago. In "A Dream Deferred," she first describes her early life—a life full of violence and physical abuse. In the early 1960s, she joined the navy and was sent to Memphis. Totally "unprepared for life as an adult in the South," Brooks faced overt racism, not the subtle kind she had previously experienced. Her story is an extraordinary testimony to the persistence and faith needed to overcome the hurdles of racism and sexism that continue to confront millions of women throughout the country.

Reading and editing the stories that appear in this anthology has led to one conclusion: *the search for equality begins when one first becomes aware of inequality.*

Acknowledgments

This project was considerably enhanced by others who shared both their time and their talent: I want to thank my colleagues from the California State University System who, during a workshop on scholarly and professional writing in the summer of 1991, gave me my first public encouragement for the idea that became the basis of this book. Several members of the English Department at California Polytechnic State University, San Luis Obispo, provided welcome assistance: Professor John Harrington made helpful suggestions on my prospectus; Professor John Hampsey introduced me to Howard Zinn. California Polytechnic State University, San Luis Obispo, also provided me with a sabbatical leave during the fall of 1994 to continue editing and working on revisions of the first chapter.

Stan and Terry Hoffman are dear friends who provided me with the opportunity to visit with William Winter. I also wish to thank Don Reisman for his assistance and encouragement along the way.

Special thanks is owed to Marsha Epstein. Marsha provided invaluable assistance in the world of computers. There is no telling how much time she saved me.

My brother James Fetzer, professor of philosophy at the University of Minnesota–Duluth, carefully read my first chapter with a keen eye for errors in logic and structure. Jim's willingness to share his extensive knowledge in publishing was certainly pivotal to the success of this project.

ACKNOWLEDGMENTS

This book would not exist were it not for the individuals who so generously contributed their essays. To Morris Dees, whose life epitomizes a commitment to equal justice before the law; Betty Friedan, a pioneer for gender equity; Michael Parenti, who has labored long in the vineyard of political and economic fairness; and Howard Zinn, who both in his life and in his writings has demonstrated sensitivity and commitment to social justice, I want to express my deep thanks and appreciation for allowing me to use pieces previously published.

I wish also to thank Julian Bond, for sharing his personal experiences on voting rights and his legal battles for fair political representation; Alice Brooks, whose life provides inspiration to all who face gender discrimination and sexual abuse; Joseph Bruchac, a Native American storyteller who learned about equality from his grandfather; Congressman Henry Gonzalez, whose public commitment to political and economic equality is without peer; Michael Lerner, for his recognition of the psychological sources of inequality; Donna Lopiano, a lifelong activist against gender discrimination in sports; Gayle Pemberton, an astute observer of the ignorance that provides fertile fields for ethnic stereotyping by both blacks and whites; and William Winter, who reminds us that prejudice and bigotry are not confined to any one economic class or nation.

I wish also to thank Peter Coveney, executive editor at M.E. Sharpe, for his enthusiastic support of the project. He is a good editor to work with. Others should be so fortunate.

Finally, for her intelligent and candid advice on virtually every aspect of the book throughout the seemingly endless travails leading to publication, I want to thank my wife, Elizabeth.

Friendship is the most special gift of life. To those I have listed, as well as the many others who have provided sustenance during difficult times, I wish to express how much you have meant to me.

THE
ETHNIC
MOMENT

Thinking about Equality

Philip L. Fetzer

General Definition

Certain terms or concepts have eluded precise definition even though they have existed for millennia. Indeed, the interpretation we give to words may vary substantially from century to century. *Equality* is such a word. Discussions of "equality" may often be confusing. Suppose one says, "Everyone should be treated equally."

What is meant by such a statement?

Most people are likely to agree that equality includes fairness and impartiality. There is also a general consensus that equality describes a *relationship* among or between people. Additionally, equality is a term that may be either factually based or express a subjective judgment. If "economic equality" is the issue, monetary information can be provided. Voting requirements can be examined to determine whether impartial standards have been applied if one is discussing "political equality." Questions about "equal opportunity" or "social equality" are more problematic. For example, on what basis could one validly claim that equality of opportunity exists for applicants to a particular college?

Complete Equality?

A possible definition of equality might include (1) equality of ability or (2) equality of achievement. But a basic aspect of genetics is that people are born with a wide range of abilities. These inequalities of ability *inevitably* lead to inequalities of achievement.

In his satirical short story "Harrison Bergeron," Kurt Vonnegut effectively illustrates that even if it were possible to create a society based on equality of ability, it would not be *desirable* to do so. A society without differences of ability would generate no leaders, no great works of art or literature, no new ideas. The society would quickly stagnate. Vonnegut writes:

> The year was 2081, and everybody was finally equal. They weren't only equal before God and the law. They were equal in every which way. Nobody was smarter than anybody else. Nobody was better looking than anybody else. Nobody was stronger or quicker than anybody else. All this equality was due to the 211th, 212th, and 213th Amendments to the Constitution, and of the unceasing vigilance of agents of the United States Handicapper General. (Vonnegut 1988, 7)

How does the Handicapper General do her work? She enforces laws that require Harrison's father, who is more intelligent than most people, to wear a "mental handicap radio in his ear" that emits shrill sounds every twenty seconds. Attractive people must wear masks. Gifted ballerinas must wear weights. The absurdity of attempting to eliminate differences in skills through artificial devices is clear.

It is logical, for example, to choose members of a high school football team based on differences in one's ability to run, pass, kick, or tackle. The differences in *ability* are clearly relevant to the selection. Yet it would not be defensible to

4

make such a choice on the basis of one's race, ethnicity, or political views, since none of these characteristics relates to the ability to succeed in football. Similarly, a defensible principle of equality would *not* require a potential employer to hire an individual as a bookkeeper who knew nothing about bookkeeping, while it would prohibit rejection for the position on the basis of gender.

One may consider "equality of achievement" as well. Given the vast differences in abilities known to humankind, it is difficult to construct an argument in favor of equal achievements. Without artificial barriers such as those satirized by Kurt Vonnegut, it is clear that some individuals will always achieve more than others *in every comparable aspect of life.*

Equality of ability and equality of achievement, therefore, must be rejected as inadequate and irrelevant to a defensible principle of equality. One's skills, and the products of those skills, are interrelated. Without such differences, all significant achievements in society would not occur and could not flourish.

Historical Evolution

The concept of equality appears to have originated from two distinct sources: philosophy and religion. Aristotle was one of the first philosophers to discuss the concept. He believed that "internal warfare" within states found its source in people's desire for "what is fair and equal." Revolutions begin, he believed, when "those who are bent on equality . . . believe that they, having less, are yet the equals of those who have more." At the same time, those who desire inequality will rebel if they believe they are "not getting more but equal or less" (Aristotle 1964, 191, 192). Aristotle seems to have been referring to some form of *economic equality.*

In the third century B.C., the Stoics thought that every

person had an equal ability to reason in spite of differences of race, culture, or class (Thompson 1949, 6). Belief in the ability of each person to act virtuously was another aspect of Stoicism (Russell 1945, 254). Rationality and knowledge of "the good" were traits that human beings were supposed to have in common. The Stoics favored a form of *social equality*.

Thomas Hobbes, John Locke, and Jean-Jacques Rousseau all believed that man was equal in the "state of nature." Before society was organized with a government and laws, Hobbes argued, nature had made men "so equal" that no one could claim any benefit to himself that another was not equally entitled to (Hobbes 1968, 183). Locke took a somewhat different slant. While men were "naturally" in a state of equality, this was not an equality based on ability or status but only the "equal right that every man has to his natural freedom" (Locke 1952, 31). Rousseau thought that there was general equality in the state of nature. Nevertheless, "from the moment it appeared advantageous to any one man to have enough provisions for two, equality disappeared" (Rousseau 1950, 271). Hobbes and Locke, therefore, discuss equality from the standpoint of *rights*, while Rousseau focuses more on the economic aspects of the term.

In the nineteenth century, Alexis de Tocqueville concluded that Americans were strongly committed to *political equality*. "But for equality their passion is ardent, insatiable, incessant, invincible," he stated. "They will endure poverty, servitude, barbarism; but they will not endure aristocracy" (Tocqueville 1989, 97). Tocqueville apparently saw no inherent conflict between poverty and equality, perhaps because he directed his attention to politics rather than to the distribution of wealth.

Western religions also supported the concept of equality. Christians were taught that all people are children of one Father. The Old and the New Testaments both support *social equality*. In the Parable of the Good Samaritan, for example,

Christ spoke to those who did not help strangers, the poor, the hungry and thirsty. "Verily I say unto you, Inasmuch as ye did it not to one of the least of these, ye did it not to me. And these shall go into everlasting punishment."

Although biblical Hebrew has no word for equality, Judaism teaches that there is to be *one law* for both the stranger and the citizen. *Equality before the law* was "divinely ordained" (Rackman 1967, 154). The Catholic philosopher Jacques Maritain (1941, 265) also argued for social equality based on religious values.

Contemporary Meanings

Rights

In 1776 Thomas Jefferson wrote: "All men are created equal. They are endowed by their Creator with certain inalienable rights. That among these are life, liberty and the pursuit of happiness." Since all men manifestly are *not* born equally intelligent, with equal athletic skills, or equal artistic talents, what did Jefferson mean? He seemed to be arguing for some kind of equality of rights. But since slavery was then in its prime, and women as well as Native Americans had few rights, it is clear that the meaning of equality was more abstract and theoretical than substantive in late eighteenth-century America.

In 1789 leaders of the French Revolution wrote: "Men are born and remain free and equal in rights." The Universal Declaration of Human Rights states in part: "All human beings are born free and equal, in dignity and rights" (Abernethy 1959, 312).

The relationship between equality and rights is primarily based on the belief that there are certain fundamental rights that every person has. If there is a conflict between the exercise of a fundamental right and other rights, then the former

7

takes precedence over the latter. Under this view, for example, the *liberty right* of a restaurant owner to refuse service to a customer on the basis of race would be denied because it would conflict with the *fundamental right* of the individual to be served without regard to irrelevant characteristics such as race. Lack of funds or rude behavior, in contrast, would be reasonable grounds for denying service.

But there is a major difficulty with this interpretation. Who decides which rights are "fundamental" and which are not? In the abortion debate, for example, those who believe that the right to life is basic are divided from those who view privacy as the primary right.

A major problem in evaluating equality of rights is that rights might be "equal in name," while the ability to exercise such rights is significantly "different in fact" (Tawney 1931, 94). The right to travel across a country may be considered fundamental. Yet it is clear that some people cannot make such a trip because they do not have the money. In what sense are rights equal in this situation? One response might be that whereas all people have a *theoretical right* to travel, only those with sufficient funds have the *effective right* to do so.

Legal Equality

Equality is commonly associated with legal traditions in many countries. "Equal Justice under Law" occupies a prominent place on the Supreme Court building in Washington, D.C. Equality and justice are closely linked in the minds of many. The Fourteenth Amendment, adopted in 1868, requires each state to provide its citizens "equal protection of the laws" (Goldman 1991, 896).

Numerous landmark decisions of the Supreme Court are associated with aspects of equality. In race relations, the doctrine of "separate but equal" was accepted by eight justices in

Plessy v. *Ferguson* in 1896 but was rejected sixty years later in *Brown* v. *Board of Education*. Equality is also the basis of leading cases affecting the rights of the accused. *Gideon* v. *Wainwright*, for example, established the right to counsel for people who could not afford one. *Miranda* v. *Arizona* provided the right to remain silent and the right to be informed that anything one says while in custody can be used against one. "Due process of law" is likewise directly linked with the concept of equality. Indeed it has been argued that uniform application of legal rights is, in fact, "the true meaning of equality" (Tawney 1931, 97).

The relationship between equality and law in the United States would seem to be quite strong. The reality, however, may be different. While the country's laws are written by those who are economically secure, the nation's prisons are occupied almost exclusively by those who are not. A number of studies have established that the greater the wealth a person has, the greater the tendency of juries and judges to approve of his or her actions (Patterson 1978, 33). The rich are able to avoid going to jail for wrongs that they may have committed. The poor are not so fortunate. As Anatole France (1949, 113) noted: "The law, in its majestic equality, forbids the rich as well as the poor to sleep under bridges, to beg in the streets, and to steal bread."

Not only does *class* appear to be a salient feature in who goes to prison, but *race* plays a significant role in punishment for criminal offenses. Afro-Americans and Latinos, for example, are disproportionately represented in our jails and prisons (Krikorian 1996, 1). In *McClesky* v. *Kemp*, the Supreme Court dismissed the evidence in a massive study demonstrating that race is a significant factor in who receives the death penalty and who does not. Morally irrelevant characteristics such as race or class obviously conflict with the idea of "equal justice before the law."

Political Equality

One scholar has recently argued that "in a democracy, political equality means the equal capacity to make judgments about political ends" (Hudson 1994, 219). The relatively low level of political information that most adult Americans appear to have raises some question as to the appropriateness of defining political equality in such terms. A public opinion survey taken in the midst of the 1994 midterm elections, for example, indicated that barely 30 percent of those surveyed even knew the name of their local congressperson. It is apparent that we are no more equal in political intelligence than we are equal in mathematical or verbal skills.

Equality of participation might be a better way of defining political equality. The political worth of every person is recognized to the degree that he or she is able to participate effectively in the process that determines who will make political decisions affecting him or her. Of course, political equality did not exist when the Constitution was adopted. Denial of voting rights based on gender was not removed until the adoption of the Nineteenth Amendment in 1920, while Native Americans did not gain citizenship rights until 1924. And finally, it was not until 1965 that the federal government fully committed itself to protecting voting rights regardless of race or ethnicity.

Even though the right to political participation has expanded in this century, the *rate* of participation in elections has declined. In each presidential election from 1960 to 1988, for example, the voting rate dropped. Voting in the United States is the lowest among industrialized societies with competitive elections. Turnout in the Bush–Dukakis election was less than half of those eligible—the lowest it had been since the 1920s (Wilson 1989, 10).

10

Furthermore, although restrictions on voting rights have diminished, class-based aspects of campaigns have not. The United States has the fewest restrictions on the use of private funds of any democracy. Those individuals and families with the greatest monetary resources exercise disproportionate influence on all significant aspects of the political process. The 1994 campaign for the U.S. Senate from California featured nearly $40 million in spending. Since the ability to compete in elections is closely related to the ability to raise and spend significant amounts of money, those without this ability cannot participate on the basis of equality in the election process.

Voting, the central component of any reasonable definition of political participation, tends to correlate closely with income levels. The higher one's financial resources, the more likely one is to vote, and vice versa (Verba 1985, 17). The *equal interest* every person has in the outcome of political processes can never be realized as long as some people, "merely by virtue of [their] possessions," can affect the course of political debate and action, while those with lesser resources cannot (Tawney 1931, 172). The idea of political equality does not correspond with the evidence of declining participation rates and the upper-class bias in political campaigns.

Economic Equality

Economic equality does not exist in the United States. Instead, the American economy is characterized by wide disparities in wealth. While 1 percent of the people control 40 percent of the nation's stocks, bonds, savings, and property, and 10 percent of the people own nearly 90 percent of the wealth, nine out of ten Americans have no significant financial assets (Parenti 1988, 10). Moreover, income disparities grew considerably during the 1980s, with average incomes of the top 1 percent of households increasing sharply while falling considerably for the bottom fifth of the population (Rich 1991, 34). Top corporate executives earned as much as 120 times the salary of the average employee in their companies in 1990.

Economists Paul Samuelson and William Nordhaus have used a visual image to describe the distribution of resources in the United States: "If we made an income pyramid out of a child's blocks, with each layer portraying $500 of income, the peak would be far higher than Mount Everest but most people would be within a few feet of the ground" (Samuelson and Nordhaus 1995, 359). It is not difficult to understand why this is the case when one considers two facts: (1) inheritance is the single largest source of wealth in the United States (Parenti 1988, 10), and (2) the poor pay a significantly higher percentage of their income in taxes than the rich (Moffat 1991, 1).

Education, long thought to be the main source of social mobility, does not effectively serve this purpose. It is true that the longer one is in school, the more income one is likely to earn. Nevertheless, the length of time one may spend in school strongly correlates with family income. Both future education and future income can largely be predicted by knowing the current resources of an individual's family. As one author noted: "To put it bluntly, with respect to equality, education is either ineffective or irrelevant, or both" (Patterson 1978, 27).

Public criticism of economic inequalities is muted at best. A recent study indicated that "American leaders" were opposed to significant equalization of income distribution (Verba 1985, 253). These leaders found nothing to criticize in salary ratios of better than eight to one between top executives and unskilled workers at the same firm. Indeed, few Americans believe that government should play an active role in reducing such wage differentials (Verba 1985, 24).

Access to high-wage jobs and job promotions continues to be characterized by inequality for both racial minorities and women. A 1991 study by the Urban Institute concluded that a strong antiblack bias exists among large numbers of potential employers. The report stated that employment discrimination "continues to cripple black male job-seekers" even in situations where whites and blacks are of "nearly identical" experience, education, language skills, and age (Fulwood 1991a, 1).

Once hired, women and minorities are generally excluded from jobs that lead to managerial or executive positions. "Networking," mentoring, and opportunities to participate in policymaking committees tend to be reserved for white males. Former Labor Secretary Lynn Martin characterized this form of artificial limitation as a "glass ceiling" in a news conference held in the summer of 1991 (Hawkins 1991, 1).

The lowest-paying jobs are almost exclusively held by women. As one author noted: "Inequality on the basis of sex is a constant in all societies at all times. . . . Even if the woman is equally educated, even when she is working, she is rarely able to make a comparable salary to that of her husband" (Kendrigan 1984, 47). Gender discrimination is a major factor in the lower earnings for women in all job classifications.

Equal Opportunity

Given the obvious political and economic inequalities in the United States, is there still room for egalitarian values? One leading candidate is the concept known as "equality of opportunity." Equal opportunity has been characterized recently as the "dominant ideal for American leaders" (Verba 1985, 72). The term implies an equal start in the race for economic success. After the "race" begins, ability, talent, and effort theoretically differentiate the winners and losers.

Equal opportunity sounds appealing. But what is the reality? It is manifestly *not* the case that we all begin with an equal start in society. An example provided by John Gardner (1961, 13) in his study of public education, *Excellence*, illustrates the point: "When a New York social worker asked a Puerto Rican youngster whether there were any books in his home, the boy nodded proudly. 'The telephone book,' he explained."

Differences in family wealth at birth are the single strongest predictor of future financial success in the United States. In a 1991 study of the lives of two young boys in Chicago, *There Are No Children Here*, Alex Kotlowitz demonstrates that for countless young people in our urban areas the idea of equal opportunity is a myth. In many big cities *surviving* into adulthood is a significant achievement. While everyone needs an income that allows for life's necessities, the rhetoric of equal opportunity allows us to ignore the fundamental facts. The wage gap is *widening*, not narrowing. Access to public colleges and universities is declining with tuition costs rising and financial support for middle- and lower-income students shrinking.

Economic opportunities are not and have never been equal. Irrelevant factors such as gender, class, and ethnicity deny large numbers of individuals the chance to make use of their native abilities. In the United States, privileges based on economic power allow the few to close off opportunities for the many. To move toward genuine equality of opportunity, then, would require major changes in the political and economic affairs of the country, as well as a significant reduction in social inequalities.

Social Equality

The meaning of "social equality" rests on an ethical concept: the dignity of each human being (Johnson 1956, 275). The basic tenet of social equality is that no person has the right to better treatment in his or her daily life than another based on irrelevant characteristics such as gender or ethnicity. Denial of access to political and economic power has been especially noteworthy for members of certain ethnic groups as well as for women and people at the low end of the economic scale.

Furthermore, it is essential that human beings are seen as "ends in themselves," that they are "subjects of claims" and not simply objects to be acted upon (Benn 1967, 67). Social equality is achieved to the degree that a society recognizes that each person's right to the development of individual potentialities is equal to that of any other person.

Jacques Maritain (1941, 262) believed that we can discover humanity's common core through social equality: "If you treat a man as a man, that is to say if you respect and love the secret he carries within him and the good of which he is capable, to that extent do you make effective . . . his equality with yourself."

Social *inequalities* are found throughout society. In the family, for example, the role of those who run households is commonly undervalued compared to that of individuals who are wage earners. While the job of keeping the family organized on a daily basis through activities such as shopping, cleaning, cooking and, most especially, raising children, falls disproportionately on women, social or economic recognition for such activities does not necessarily follow. Additionally, the division of labor associated with marriage usually places a double burden on women in the United States: most need paid employment outside the house in order to help maintain the living standards of past generations, but their household responsibilities do not decline proportionately to compensate for their additional duties.

Disparities in wealth generate attitudes that favor social

inequality. The rich take their wealth and advantages for granted, while they expect justifications or explanations from those who seek similar benefits for themselves. An example occurs in a scene from the movie *Roger and Me.* The director, Michael Moore, interviews two women on a golf course. One of them offers her view that people recently laid off by General Motors could *easily* find a job "if they weren't so lazy." A *New Yorker* cartoon makes a similar point. A king is standing in his castle with one of his aides. Far below the castle walls, an angry group of riders approaches the gate. The king wonders why they are there. The aide says: "What they are seeking, sir, is a lifestyle more similar to your own."

One of the single best measures of social equality is life expectancy. In 1910 black Americans could anticipate living about fifteen years less than their white counterparts. This gap steadily declined until 1984 when the difference was 5.6 years. Four years later, the disparity had begun to widen again. An Afro-American born in 1988 could expect to live a little more than sixty-nine years, while a white was likely to live well beyond his seventy-fifth birthday. Factors that contribute to this difference include the effects of urban violence on young blacks, poverty, and lack of access to quality medical care (Fulwood 1991b, 5).

Why is social equality so difficult to achieve? Some political theorists believe that inequality is an *inevitable* result of human relations in society. In *Leviathan,* for example, Thomas Hobbes (1968, 161) described human nature in the following way: "I put for a generall inclination of all mankind, a perpetuall and restlesse desire of Power after power, that ceaseth onely in Death."

In Hobbes's view, people are chronically insecure. They cannot be certain of "the power and means to live well . . . without the acquisition of more" (Hobbes 1968, 161). For Hobbes, power can be understood only in relation to what others have. Many human beings seem to be on an unending quest for power that can be measured in wealth, possessions, reputation, or friends. In short, we are constantly seeking advantages over other human beings. By this argument, inequality is "natural" and equality is "unnatural" in human relations.

Some contemporary philosophers have reached similar conclusions. For example, in *Equality*, John Wilson (1966, 162) argues that "we positively prefer to treat the other person as an enemy, or as a superior, or as an inferior: at any rate, not as an equal." Or, as another contemporary thinker stated, we "devote ourselves to striving for superiority" (Ryan 1981, 4).

John Stuart Mill believed that long-term relationships based on equality could be sustained only by those with special moral sensitivity: "It is only the highminded to whom equality is really agreeable," he wrote. "A proof is that they are the only persons who are capable of strong and durable attachments to their equals" (Elliot 1910, 383).

Because anyone can maintain unequal relationships, they are found in all parts of society. Hierarchical structures commonly occur in both families and the workplace, institutions that are central to most individuals' everyday existence.

Not only does equality demand high ethical standards, but it requires psychological maturity as well. The central problem is that each person "tends to prefer himself simply because he is himself" (Stace 1937, 256). Most of us tend to defend or accept behaviors in ourselves that we may find intolerable when practiced by strangers.

Equality

Philosophers and prophets, economists and politicians, poets and academics, all have reflected on the meaning and significance of equality. The difficulties that challenge aspirations for political, economic, and social equality are enormous. Are we capable of discarding the "loathsome mask," which places us, as Shelley wrote, in superior or inferior classes, tribes, or nations?

Let us suppose that our ultimate objective is social equality. How might this be achieved? Social equality depends on attitudes that recognize each human being as an end in herself or himself, not an object to be exploited for one's own purposes. Because of the difficulties of maintaining socially equal relationships, legal equality would be necessary to enforce this value.

Legal equality without economic equality, however, seems extremely difficult to achieve. Imagine that O.J. Simpson had been poor at the time of his trial. Would he have received the same quality legal assistance that he did?

At the same time, economic equality as a desirable objective is strongly opposed by most Americans. Politics also appears to reflect these economic inequalities. The vast majority of successful candidates for public office are those of exceptional independent wealth or those who have access to individuals or organizations that generate huge sums of money.

The obstacles to equality would seem to be insurmountable. Is there a commonality in our lives that would allow us to overcome such unpropitious circumstances? Ironically, one universal in human experience that could provide us with the opportunity to place a higher priority on social equality is suffering. Ursula LeGuin illustrates such a perspective on our "common humanity" in *The Dispossessed:*

> It is our suffering that brings us together. . . . We are brothers. We are brothers in what we share. In pain, which each of us must suffer alone, in hunger, in poverty, in hope, we know our brotherhood. We know it, because we have had to

18

learn it. We know that there is no help for us but from one another, that no hand will save us if we do not reach out our hand. (LeGuin 1974, 284)

We spend much of our lives isolated and alone. How can we overcome this feeling of alienation? Social equality in human relations is important, in part, because it can help us transcend these feelings of loneliness and isolation.

In the essays that follow, individuals tell stories of equality as they have experienced it. These writers come from many different backgrounds and circumstances. Some are women. Some are men. Some are people of color. Some are not. What they share is the knowledge and understanding of our common humanity, of the pain that helps us recognize and truly *know* one another, of the methods we have used to survive the "slings and arrows of outrageous fortune." The degree to which we are able to treat one another equally in our daily lives is both a reflection of the kind of society in which we live and of the kind of society in which we *wish* to live. As one modern philosopher has stated: "A society that ranks human individuals as lesser or greater beings proves itself only semicivilized" (Hofstadter 1955, 112).

If liberty has a substantive meaning in our lives, then surely it means that we can choose "equality" if we want to, in whole or in part: legal, political, economic, or social. How do we treat those who are "different" from us in gender, ethnicity, economic condition, or social status? Ranking people as "greater" and "lesser" is a denial of equality. It is diametrically opposed to the *spirit* of the Declaration of Independence.

It is hoped that through these stories readers will come to recognize their lives in the lives of others. And that their understanding of the meaning of equality will be enhanced. Let the story begin!

19

Bibliography

Articles

Fulwood III, Sam. 1991a. "Hiring Study Finds Strong Anti-Black Bias." *Los Angeles Times,* May 15, A1.

———. 1991b. "Black–White Life Span Gap Is Growing Again." *Los Angeles Times,* July 31, A5.

Hawkins, Beth. 1991. "Career-Limiting Bias Found at Low Job Levels." *Los Angeles Times,* August 9, A1.

Krikorian, Greg. 1996. "Study Questions Justice System's Fairness." *Los Angeles Times,* February 13, A1.

Moffat, Susan. 1991. "The Richer They Are . . . The More Taxes They Pay." *Los Angeles Times,* July 25, D1.

Rich, Spencer. 1991. "Them That Gots Get More of It." *Washington Post Weekly,* July 29–August 4.

Books

Abernethy, George L. 1959. *The Idea of Equality.* Richmond: John Knox Press.

Aristotle. 1964. *The Politics.* Baltimore: Penguin Books.

Benn, Stanley I. 1956. "Egalitarianism and the Equal Consideration of Interests." In Pennock and Chapman 1967, 61–78.

Blackstone, William T., ed. 1969. *The Concept of Equality.* Minneapolis: Burgess Publishing.

Block, W.E., and M.A. Walker, eds. 1981. *Discrimination, Affirmative Action, and Equal Opportunity.* Vancouver: Fraser Institute.

Brecht, Arnold. 1959. *Political Theory.* Princeton: Princeton University Press.

Bryson, Lyman, et al., eds. 1956. *Aspects of Human Equality.* New York: Harper and Brothers.

Carr, Edward Hallett. 1964. *The Twenty Years' Crisis, 1919–1939.* New York: Harper and Row.

Cauthen, Kenneth. 1987. *The Passion for Equality.* Totowa, N.J.: Rowman and Littlefield.

Edsall, Thomas. 1984. *The New Politics of Inequality.* New York: Norton.

Elliot, Hugh S.R. 1910. *The Letters of John Stuart Mill.* Vol. 2. London: Longmans, Green.

Feinberg, Walter, ed. 1978. *Equality and Social Policy*. Urbana: University of Illinois Press.

France, Anatole. 1949. *Crainquebille*. New York: Heritage Press.

Gardner, John. 1961. *Excellence*. New York: Harper and Brothers.

Goldman, Sheldon. 1991. *Constitutional Law Cases and Essays*. 2nd ed. New York: HarperCollins.

Hobbes, Thomas. 1968. *Leviathan*. Baltimore: Penguin Books.

Hofstadter, Albert. 1955. "The Career Open to Personality: The Meaning of Equality of Opportunity for an Ethics for Our Time." In Bryson et al. 1956, 111–42.

Hudson, William E. 1994. *American Democracy in Peril*. Chatham, N.J.: Chatham House.

Johnson, Charles S. 1955. "Equality of Opportunity." In Bryson et al. 1956, 273–83.

Kendrigan, Mary Lou. 1984. *Political Equality in a Democratic Society*. Westport, Conn.: Greenwood Press.

LeGuin, Ursula K. 1974. *The Dispossessed*. New York: Avon.

Locke, John. 1952. *The Second Treatise of Government*. New York: Bobbs-Merrill.

Lucash, Frank S., ed. 1986. *Justice and Equality Here and Now*. Ithaca: Cornell University Press.

Maritain, Jacques. 1941. "Ransoming the Time." In Abernethy 1959, 262–72.

Parenti, Michael. 1988. *Democracy for the Few*. 5th ed. New York: St. Martin's Press.

Patterson, Orlando. 1978. "Inequality, Freedom, and the Equal Opportunity Doctrine." In Feinberg 1978, 15–41.

Pennock, J. Roland, and John W. Chapman, eds. 1967. *Equality*. New York: Atherton Press.

Rackman, Emanuel. 1967. "Judaism and Equality." In Pennock and Chapman 1967, 154–76.

Rothenberg, Paula S. 1988. *Racism and Sexism*. New York: St. Martin's Press.

Rousseau, Jean-Jacques. 1950. *The Social Contract and Discourses*. New York: Dutton.

Russell, Bertrand. 1945. *A History of Western Philosophy*. New York: Simon and Schuster.

Russell, William F. 1936. *Liberty vs. Equality*. New York: Macmillan.

Ryan, William. 1981. *Equality*. New York: Pantheon Books.

Samuelson, Paul A., and William D. Nordhaus. 1995. *Economics*. 15th ed. New York: McGraw-Hill.

Shelley, Percy Bysshe. 1959. *Prometheus Unbound.* Seattle: University of Washington Press.

Stace, Walter T. 1959. "The Concept of Morals." In Abernethy 1959, 255–61.

Tawney, R.H. 1931. *Equality.* London: Allen and Unwin.

Thompson, David. 1949. "The Problem of Equality." In Blackstone 1969, 1–13.

Tocqueville, Alexis de. 1989. *Democracy in America.* New York: Knopf.

Verba, Sidney. 1985. *Equality in America.* Cambridge: Harvard University Press.

Vonnegut, Kurt, Jr. 1988. *Welcome to the Monkey House.* New York: Dell.

Wilhoit, Frances M. 1979. *The Quest for Equality in Freedom.* New Brunswick, N.J.: Transaction Books.

Wilson, James Q. 1989. *The 1988 Election.* Lexington: D.C. Heath.

Wilson, John. 1966. *Equality.* New York: Harcourt, Brace and World.

Cases

Brown v. *Board of Education,* 347 US 483 (1954).

Gideon v. *Wainwright,* 372 US 335 (1963).

McCleskey v. *Kemp,* 481 US 279 (1987).

Miranda v. *Arizona,* 384 US 436 (1966).

Plessy v. *Ferguson,* 163 US 537 (1896).

Part I

Moments

Morris Dees graduated from the University of Alabama where he also received his law degree. After a successful career in marketing and publishing, he cofounded the Southern Poverty Law Center and currently serves as its chief trial counsel as well as chair of the Executive Committee of Teaching Tolerance. He is a recipient of numerous awards, including Trial Lawyer of the Year from Trial Lawyers for Public Justice. He is the author of *A Season for Justice* and *Hate on Trial.*

A Season for Justice

Morris Dees

In this excerpt from A Season for Justice *(1991), Morris Dees describes his early life in Alabama and the influence of his father on his decision to become a lawyer. He also explains how a stranger was the first one to challenge him about his commitment to equal rights for people regardless of race. The effects of the 1963 Birmingham bombing that killed four young girls, his experience representing Vietnamese fishermen harassed by the Ku Klux Klan, and the "most important case" of Dees's life are all portrayed.*

I. Becoming a Lawyer

December 1936
Mount Meigs, Alabama

If it hadn't been for my daddy, Morris Seligman Dees Sr., I don't think I'd ever have found myself mixed up with Louis Beam and the Knights of the Ku Klux Klan. It was Daddy who insisted I study law. As a teenager, I fancied myself a preacher. Our family had helped build the Pike Road Baptist Church—a red brick structure that sat next to the school about five miles from our house in Mount Meigs—and Rev-

erend Russell, who came out from Montgomery to preach
once a month, put the fear of God into me early.

His work was complemented by my fifth-grade teacher,
Miss Margaret Waugh. Ancient and afflicted with palsy, always outfitted in black dresses with high white collars, her
hair pushed into a permanent bun, Miss Waugh made us
memorize a different Bible verse every week and warned us of
the evils that lay outside God's shrine:

> Tobacco is a filthy weed and from the devil doth proceed.
> It picks your pockets and burns your clothes
> And makes a smokestack of your nose.

I was an impressionable boy (to this day I've never smoked
a cigarette), and by the time I was in high school, I could
quote many a Scripture and was speaking at Baptist summer
youth revivals. I seemed to have a knack for swaying a group,
so the ministry seemed a logical calling. But Daddy, who
could sleep through church services despite the hard pine
pew, had his eyes wide open when it came to supporting
oneself on the wages of a country preacher. "Bubba," he said,
"you can be a preacher anytime. You can do that on Sundays.
But you need to do something you can make a living at."

Fine, I thought, then I'll be a farmer. That seemed to come
as natural as preaching, and I had plenty of experience. From
the time I could lift a hoe, I had worked in the cotton fields.
In junior high I grew and sold watermelons. In high school I
had my own cotton patch and a chicken, pigs and cattle
operation that was netting me five thousand dollars a year by
graduation. The Future Farmers of America named me Star
Farmer of Alabama and awarded me a scholarship to Auburn
University. But, again, Daddy had other ideas. He had been a
cotton farmer all his life, and he was convinced it would be
even harder for me to make a living off the land than it

would be to make a living off the Word. "You be a lawyer, Bubba," he said. "No boll weevil ever ruined a law book."

There was nothing I liked more than sitting out front of Pinkston's store with Daddy—unless it was going raccoon hunting in the oak and palmetto swamps along the Tallapoosa by our land with T.J. Hendricks, a black farmer who lived down the road; or riding my bike to Mam Maw's house and being invited to spend the night in her big featherbed; or hiking the mile and a half to Solomon's Pond and fishing for bream with Momma and an old superstitious woman we called "Rat," who claimed her secret for success was that she spit on her hook and worm before she threw in the line attached to her cane hoe; or swimming naked with Little Buddy Orum in the hole under the Western Railroad of Alabama trestle; or terrorizing Mount Meig's spinster postmistress, Miss Theus Raoul, by riding my pinto pony down Pike Road faster than she was driving her 1932 Chevy; or working behind the counter in my uncle Lucien Dees's country store; or listening to Johnny Ford, an aged black hand, play the blues on an old guitar using the neck of a broken Red Dagger wine bottle to slide over the strings; or greeting Big Jim Folsom, our populist governor, when he came out to our house on Sunday afternoons. . . .

Daddy had come to know the governor through Charles Pinkston, who'd spent a lifetime cultivating political contacts instead of cotton. Daddy knew about being a lawyer from watching Mr. Pinkston: You practiced law for a while, met the right people, got a chunk of state business or got appointed to an office or got elected judge, and had a guaranteed source of income for life. Daddy figured he could help me find cases, and in fact he brought me my first client.

"Bubba," Daddy said one morning at the breakfast table, "I want you to go up to Shorter and see if you can't get Clarence out of the trouble he's in."

I put down my fork. "Well, what kind of trouble is he in?"

"The state trooper stopped him coming from Shorter to Waugh over in Macon County, and they got him for driving while intoxicated and resisting arrest."

I thought I'd heard Daddy wrong. Clarence Williams was a humble black man in his mid-thirties who lived on our land and drove a tractor for us (we had finally graduated to tractors). He had nine children and was not the hard-drinking type. "Clarence? Intoxicated? Resisting arrest?"

"That's what they say. You see what you can do."

After breakfast, I went over to Clarence's shack. The eleven people in Clarence's family lived in two rooms, sharing four iron-framed beds, mattresses stuffed with corn shucks. The boards for the shack had come from the run-down plantation home we had demolished when we built our new house. The inside walls were covered by old magazine pages attached with flour paste. They were a feeble attempt to keep out the damp winter winds that snuck through the boards and roared through the open windows. You could see the tin roof above the uncovered pine ceiling beams. There was no running water or electricity. Oil lamps lit the drab interior. Heat was supplied by a single fireplace and a wood cook-stove that sat in a corner of the small, sloped kitchen at the rear.

Clarence's children, dressed in ragged hand-me-downs, played aimlessly in the dirt yard alongside the shack. Clarence, a strong-muscled man with an impassive face, put on his old felt hat and met me at my truck.

"Clarence, tell me what happened."

Clarence usually spoke in a slow drawl. This morning he hurried his words. "Bubba, you know my car ain't nothing but a piece of car, and I was driving along there and this tire rod came loose and it ran off and hit that concrete median up there on the road and it knocked me dizzy, and the state trooper came along and he opened the door of my car and he

28

pulled me out and he said, 'Nigger what you doing drunk?'
And I said, 'Boss, I ain't drunk.' And I got out and staggered
'round, and next thing I know that state trooper shoved me
in the back of the car and hit me upside my head with a
blackjack and took me on up to jail in Tuskegee."

It seemed like an open-and-shut case to me. "Shoot, Clarence, we can beat that. You c'mon with me."

We got in my truck and drove a few miles up the road to
Shorter where the "Honorable" Judge Metcalf Letcher held
his court. Actually, Judge Letcher was a justice of the peace,
and his courtroom was the little country store he owned and
operated on U.S. 80.

Clarence took his hat off as we opened the screen door and
entered the "courtroom." A sloped wood floor ran narrowly from
front to back, framed by shelves of packaged and canned goods
and household and hardware products: cigarettes, Bruton snuff,
King Edward sardines, mule harnesses, and plow points.

Judge Letcher stood behind a counter at the back of the
store by a big brass cash register. An old Coca-Cola sign was
nailed to the wall behind him. The judge was cutting a
pound of yellow cheese for a customer while a state trooper
drank a bottle of Nehi Orange.

"What you want, son?" the judge asked me.

I looked at the floor nervously. "Well, I came up here to
represent Clarence."

The judge handed his customer the cheese and rang up the
transaction on the cash register. He didn't bother to make eye
contact with me, but asked, "What about?"

"Well, you know, he's not guilty."

The judge turned to the trooper "Well, Officer, tell us
what he did."

The trooper drained the Nehi Orange and then told his
story. He insisted that "the boy" had been drunk and had
tried to resist arrest.

When he finished, I spoke up. "Well, Judge, you know that's not right."

The judge was barely paying attention. Another customer squeezed by me, placing a loaf of bread on the counter.

"Clarence," I continued, "tell 'em what you did."

Clarence started talking and the judge kept trading. Shoot, I thought. This is important to Clarence. He makes five dollars a day driving a tractor. He's got nine little ones. He can't afford to lose his driver's license, can't afford to pay a fine.

When Clarence finished, I made a little closing argument summarizing our view of the case. I felt good. The facts were on our side, and besides, I was the son of Morris Dees Sr. White folks. I ought to be able to come in and vouch for Clarence and get him off.

After I thanked the court for its patience, Judge Letcher hit the counter with his gavel. "Guilty. One-hundred-and-fifty dollar fine. Bubba, you tell your daddy he can send three dollars a week up here. That'll be all."

I looked at Clarence apologetically. He just shrugged.

When we got back to the farm I rushed to the tractor shed. "Daddy, you know it just ain't right. I know Clarence, and Clarence is not guilty."

"Did you tell 'em everything, Bubba?"

"Yes, I told 'em everything. Can't you call the judge up there and do something about it?"

Daddy shook his head. "Nope. Judge Letcher's kind of tough. Besides, story is he keeps two sets of books, one for the state and one for himself, and that he makes a pretty penny on these fines."

"Well, that's just not right." I kicked the dirt. "It's not fair."

Daddy smiled. "Well, if you don't like it, why don't you go to law school."

I was sixteen at the time, still in high school. I'd always

figured that if you told the truth, you'd receive justice. but that hadn't happened in Shorter. I thought about this for a while, and it occurred to me that maybe telling the truth wasn't enough. Maybe it was *how* you told it. I figured if I was going to be a good lawyer, I'd better know how to tell the truth. I found a book with the speeches of Thomas Jefferson and Abraham Lincoln and memorized them. When I thought I had them down pat, I went out to an empty cotton field, climbed up on an old tractor wagon, and delivered them, my only audience the red-tailed hawk gliding lazily in the blue sky above.

II. Learning about Civil Rights

When I was worried about collection matters and getting our practice off the ground, the civil rights movement was taking flight. I wasn't yet on board. In fact, I was remarkably oblivious considering that Montgomery, as the state capital and Martin Luther King Jr.'s base of operations until 1960, was often in the center of things. On May 4, 1961, when a group of blacks and whites started a trip through the South to test the Supreme Court's recent rulings outlawing segregation in bus terminals, I didn't pay too much attention. As their journey continued, I did realize that the Freedom Riders, as they called themselves, were encountering hate and violence. Less than two weeks into the trip, they were beaten by a mob in Anniston, Alabama. After that, they were attacked in Birmingham, then in Montgomery, where more than a thousand angry whites beat them without police intervention.

While I didn't applaud this brutality, I never raised my voice in protest. Later, when Claude Henley, a rural neighbor charged with assaulting a television reporter during the riot, asked me to defend him, I didn't think twice.

Claude, a thirty-five-year-old used-car salesman, was a big old country boy with a potbelly and a fat cigar that seemed permanently attached to his mouth. He was a defendant in two cases—a civil suit filed by the federal government and a criminal proceeding instituted by the city of Montgomery. He had clearly been involved in some of the action. A picture of him kicking a newsman had appeared in *Life* magazine after the riot. The assault charges brought by the city didn't worry Claude as much as the federal government's suit, which also named the city of Montgomery's police department and several other individuals, including Bobby Shelton, as defendants for their roles in the attack on the Freedom Riders.

Sitting in my office, in red-and-blue-checked slacks, a short-sleeved white shirt, and a brown tie, Claude took a puff on his cigar and blew the smoke my way, making me wish he'd heard Miss Margaret Waugh's "filthy weed" lesson. He said that John Blue Hill, a prominent local attorney, had asked for fifteen thousand dollars to represent him. I had been thinking about charging five hundred dollars.

"I'll take your case for five thousand dollars," I said.

He agreed.

The federal lawsuit took aim at the police department for its failure to protect the marchers after it realized the trouble in Anniston and Birmingham would probably occur in Montgomery as well. Claude was just a small fish. While the picture in *Life* wouldn't help with our assault defense, it would help in federal court. It demonstrated that Claude hadn't been where the marchers were, but instead a block away, beating up a reporter.

The Justice Department had brought in some big guns for the federal case. I sat at the defense table with Shelton, who was dressed in a blue seersucker suit and white socks, and other Klansmen and their lawyers. They were neither penitent nor worried. They just passed the time making racial cracks.

When the Justice Department's John Doar came over to our table, I asked him what he wanted from Claude. He said

A SEASON FOR JUSTICE

he just wanted Claude to agree to be enjoined from future disruptions. That was fine with us. We told the judge, Frank M. Johnson Jr., and we were out of the case.

In the hallway, two young black men, part of the Freedom Riders group, approached me. "How can you represent people like that?" one of them asked. "Don't you think that black people have rights?"

I was startled. This was the first time a black person had ever confronted me. "Yes, I do," I said sincerely. "I agree with you a hundred percent." Then I walked off.

Claude and I parted on the street. I didn't let him see that I was shaken. My actions, my morality had been challenged. Did I deserve to be challenged? I didn't see representing Claude Henley as a racial thing. To make some money, I was taking a case that just happened to be tied up with the Freedom Riders. My God, it wasn't that I was interested in the Klan! I was interested in making five thousand dollars representing a neighbor and keeping him out of trouble.

But looking in the face of my accuser, I felt the anger of a black person for the first time. He saw me as an enemy representing the Klan, just as years later Louis Beam and his compatriots would see me as an enemy opposing the Klan. Here I was feeling that I was friends with blacks, remembering that I had spoken up for Emmet Till and Autherine Lucy, and all of a sudden this young man was doubting me. I vowed then and there that nobody would ever again doubt where I stood. It took me a couple of years to make good on that promise.

III. Awakening

September 1963
Birmingham, Alabama

The four little girls were in the basement of Birmingham's Sixteenth Street Baptist Church straightening out their fancy white dresses when the dynamite bomb exploded. The church

33

shook. Walls crumbled. Ceilings fell. The people upstairs coming into the holy place for a special Youth Sunday celebration screamed, then raced outside. The girls in the basement didn't even have time to scream; Addie Mae Collins, Cynthia Wesley, and Carole Robertson, all just fourteen years old, and Denise McNair, only eleven, were killed instantly.

This wasn't the first Birmingham bombing. Ministers' homes, a black-owned hotel, and other churches had been destroyed. But there had been nothing as evil as the dynamiting of children during Sunday school. After the bombing, the aptly named white supremacist Connie Lynch told a Klan gathering that the bombers deserved medals. The four little girls who had died "weren't children," he said. "Children are little people, little human beings, and that means white people. . . . They're just little niggers . . . and if there's four less niggers tonight, then I say, 'Good for whoever planted the bomb!' "

Less than three weeks earlier, Dr. King had given his famous "I Have a Dream" speech in Washington, D.C., to the largest civil rights gathering in history. Now he spoke to eight thousand mourners at a joint funeral for three of its victims. 'The innocent blood of these little girls may well serve as the redemptive force that will bring new light to this dark city," he said. "Indeed, this tragic event may cause the white South to come to terms with its conscience."

Ninety miles away in Montgomery, I felt the reverberations for the bombs, and as Dr. King prophesied, I came to terms with my conscience. Beverly and I were still good Baptists. We said our prayers together every night. We belonged to the Pike Road Baptist Church—the church my family had helped build, the church of my parents and grandparents, the church that had given us a Bible without names in front to commemorate our marriage. When I had returned home from law school, I had been named superintendent of the Sunday school.

34

On Sunday, September 22, 1963, I stood before the congregation. Before saying anything, I looked over the assembled: our friends, our neighbors, the parents of the children with whom my boys went to school, the people who owned the stores where we traded, the people to whom I had always been "Bubba."

"Brothers and sisters," I said, "there's another Baptist church that needs our help."

"Tell us, Bubba," someone said.

"It's a church that has had a tragedy."

The congregation, my friends, nodded approvingly. I wasn't surprised. These were good-hearted, charitable people. They weren't the type to turn down fellow God-fearing folk in a time of need.

"Where's the church?" someone asked.

"You've heard of it," I said. "It's the Sixteenth Street Church in Birmingham where those four little girls were killed last Sunday and the church was destroyed."

The blood drained from my friends' faces, the nodding stopped. The members of the Pike Road Baptist Church quickly fell into two camps—those who were angered by the suggestion and those who were too shocked to be angry. I couldn't make out their whispers, but I could read their expressions.

I pulled a check from my pocket. "I'm giving this to help the church rebuild," I said. "I hope you all will either write a check of your own or give what cash you can."

An old woman sitting in the back of the church stood up. "This ain't none of our business, Morris Jr.," she said. "This ain't nothing we want to get involved in."

The nodding began again. I felt I had to go on. "I'd like you to join me in a little prayer for the girls before we go to our classes," I said.

There was a deathly silence.

"Please, won't you join me in a prayer? We all have children of our own. No matter how you feel about—" My words hit their frozen hearts and fell to the floor. Head bowed, I prayed silently. Soon, I heard a rustling and then some footsteps. I looked up. Beverly stood beside me, and we prayed together.

We stayed up there at the front of the church . . . and stayed, nobody joining us. I prayed and prayed, and when I finally looked up, just the two of us were left in the sanctuary. Everyone else had left for Sunday school.

Years later, Beverly would look back on this day and say, "That was the beginning. You knew your life was going to change and you had to go on with it."

More than a quarter century after the fact, it seems like such a small gesture. Asking for a contribution, praying for the souls of little girls hardly seems extraordinary, certainly not worthy of self-congratulation. I hadn't gone to Washington, D.C., for Dr. King's march; I'd never marched, period. I hadn't stood up to Bull Connor in Birmingham. Just a silent prayer, an act consistent with Christian teachings, praying for the souls of other Christians. *Children.* And yet my good friends and neighbors could not free themselves from the slavery of the southern tradition and, forgetting about color, do the Christian thing.

It was the Christian thing. I remembered one of Reverend Russell's sermons. On Judgment Day, a man consigned to hell had asked God why. God had answered: "When I was hungry, you failed to give me food. When I was without clothes, you didn't give me any. When I was sick, you didn't come to visit me." Reverend Russell had rightly told us this meant that we had to minister to the sick, to feed and clothe those in need. I'm not one to put words into the Lord's mouth, but the logical extension was *When I was denied the*

basic rights for things like education, you did nothing. When I was
without the right to participate in government, you denied me the
right to vote. But the white southern preachers didn't complete
that circle. They turned the civil rights movement away from
their doors.

IV. Klan Watch in Action

[Dees sold his publishing company in 1969 and began to
practice law full-time. That same year he and a friend, Joe
Levin Jr., cofounded the Southern Poverty Law Center. The
Center provided legal assistance and representation to people
who couldn't afford to defend themselves. He organized "Klan
Watch" as a part of the Center's activities in 1980.—Ed.]

In April of 1981, we filed our second suit—in Houston,
against the Texas Knights of the Ku Klux Klan, Louis Beam,
and his cohorts. The case against Beam was typical of many of
the cases the Center took on. Colonel Nam and the Vietnamese
Fishermen's Association didn't find us. We found them. . . .

"Thank you for coming," the colonel said as we sat down in
his living room. Then he let me have it. "The elders of our
community have asked me to talk to you, Morris. We want to
thank you for representing us, but we have decided to drop
our lawsuit."

I was stunned. The climate was certainly frightening.
Thatcher's camera and Beam's gun had unnerved all of us,
and rumors were floating that the Klan intended to kill Colonel Nam and me. But the hearing was only a week away. If
the colonel and his friends could just hang tough. . . .

"Colonel, we've got Beam on the ropes now. We've taken
all these depositions. We've got a good case here. I think we
can win," I said.

"I understand," the colonel said. "But what can a court injunction do? If they want to shoot you in the night, they can."

I explained again that if the court ruled in the refugees' favor and then anyone violated that order, he would go to prison for contempt. Of course, I realized that if a Klansman shot someone, the fact that he might go to prison would provide little consolation to his victim. But I truly believed that with the court looking over their shoulders, the defendants would be less likely to bother, much less shoot, the Vietnamese.

"Morris, this is not my decision alone," said Colonel Nam. "The elders feel there is bad blood. They say if we don't stop now, the Americans will be mad at more than the fishermen, be mad at all of the Vietnamese businessmen." He explained that the Vietnamese business community—owners of restaurants, flower shops, convenience stores, and other establishments—feared economic repercussions if the case went forward and the Vietnamese were portrayed as threatening to the Americans.

As much as I wanted to fight Beam and the Klan here and now, my obligation was to my clients. If they wanted to drop the suit, I'd drop the suit—but not without trying to persuade them that it was in their interest to continue.

"Colonel, I'd like to talk to those people who made the decision. I'd like to meet with the elders."

The colonel looked surprised. He got up from his chair, walked over to the window, and stared out over the channel for a long time. "I'll see what I can do," he said.

I couldn't tell whether his heart was with the elders or with me.

A priest led me down a church corridor to a small meeting room. Forty Vietnamese elders, some dressed in suits and ties, some in traditional Vietnamese clothing, sat in two wide rows of folding chairs. I joined Colonel Nam and an interpreter at a table in front.

"Sometimes lawyers are called counselors," I began. "I'd

38

like to give you my counsel tonight." I was so excited. I was speaking too fast. The interpreter signaled for me to slow down. I took a deep breath.

"I don't really know what your vision of America was before you came to live in this country, how you thought you'd be treated here. But I'm ashamed at the way you have been treated. In the United States all citizens are supposed to be treated equally, regardless of race, creed, or color. It doesn't matter if you're black or Jewish or Vietnamese, whatever, our Constitution provides for equal treatment under the law.

"Unfortunately, just because something is written down on a piece of paper, even if that paper is the Constitution, doesn't mean that everyone is gong to respect it and abide by it. When I was growing up in Alabama, Constitution or not, black folks were second-class citizens. They had to fight for their rights. Dr. Martin Luther King Jr., and others gave up their lives so their brothers and sisters could have their lawful rights. One of the groups that wanted to keep the blacks in their place was the Ku Klux Klan, the same Ku Klux Klan that wants to drive you to pack up your bags and get out of town. I sure hope you don't think these people, people like Louis Beam and others hiding in their hoods, represent America. Because they don't. The Klan is nothing but your basic group of criminals and outlaws.

"I know the Klan, and I know that if our fishermen leave without putting up a fight, Louis Beam and his crew will not stop. You've heard the talk. Some folks are saying the Vietnamese shouldn't even be allowed to live on the coast. It may be fishermen that feel the heat now, but you can be sure that if they get the fishermen to give up today, they'll go after the rest of you tomorrow. 'Why should the Seven-Eleven be run by a foreigner? Why aren't there any Americans employed at the flower shop? This is hurting American business.' That's what they'll say. You have just as much right to be here as Louis Beam or Gene Fisher. That is what America is really about. That's what the people who came to this country over two centuries ago as immigrants just like you had in mind. That's the vision of America you have to believe in and fight for. You have—"

A slow, rhythmic clapping had begun. It wasn't terribly loud, but it was steady. I had no idea what it meant. The expression on the faces of the elders hadn't changed. It was just that now they were clapping—slowly, steadily. Were they trying to get me to sit down? Was it meant as a jeer? Were they behind me?

I looked at Colonel Nam. He, too, was clapping, but his face was as impassive as the faces of the elders. I looked at the interpreter, a young Vietnamese-American who was a pilot for Pan Am. He smiled.

"They like what you are saying," he said.

Tears came to my eyes. I walked out from behind the table; I wanted the elders to feel my emotions. "It's up to you all," I said. "I just want you to know your lawyers are behind you. In a week this will be all over and then a court of law will show you the America of today is not the America of Louis Beam, but an America where the color of your skin or the country you came from doesn't make a difference."

I moved back behind the table.

Colonel Nam nodded. "Please wait with the priests while we talk," he said. I was pacing restlessly in the priests' office when the colonel returned from the meeting room. "We'll continue the lawsuit," he said. . . .

After Phuoc Dang testified, Judge McDonald gave us a short recess. Margaret Anderwall was in the witness room with her priest. We had ten minutes to persuade her to help us.

I could tell by looking at her that she was good woman. She reminded me of Grandmother Dees, an honest soul with a strong religious background—white-haired with glasses, stout, perhaps sixty years old. She spoke in short bursts, quickly growing breathless.

"Mrs. Anderwall," I said. "I read your statement. Could you kind of tell me what happened over the last year?"

She told me about the threats to her family, the visit from the Klan, and how, despite the fact that she and her husband liked Khang so much, they had asked him to move his boat because they didn't want their house burned.

When she finished, I knelt down on the floor and took her hand, speaking softly. "Mrs. Anderwall, you need to get up on the stand, because I'm trying to get the federal court to stop the Klan from doing this."

Her reluctance was understandable. This lawsuit wasn't hers. Some people think that witnesses just naturally want to come forward and tell everything they know, but think for a moment: A lot of folks don't want to get involved in what they really see as other people's business.

"Mrs. Anderwall, you just told me of how hardworking and good Khang and the other Vietnamese people are. You know, they're new Americans just like our founding fathers were when they came to this country."

Mrs. Anderwall still looked uncertain.

"Ma'am," I continued, "if you would just get up and tell the judge what you know, it won't be as bad as you think. We're shining the bright light of day on the Klan, and everyone is looking—the press, the FBI. They'd arrest them in a minute if they bothered a witness from the federal court."

Mrs. Anderwall looked at me sadly. "Mr. Dees, I don't think I can do it. I just can't do it. My heart won't stand it. They're such nice people. They rented a house near us and I was in it and it was spotless. They are really fine people. But I don't think my heart can stand it."

I looked over to her priest. He nodded that she could testify. I held her hand a little tighter. "Mrs. Anderwall, I'm going to go out there and call you as the next witness. I think you'll feel proud of yourself if you go out and do your Christian duty."

"I don't think I can, Mr. Dees."

I walked past the priest and tugged on his sleeve, as if to say "Please help."

The court convened a moment later. I called Margaret Anderwall, turning to the back of the courtroom. In she came, slowly, tentatively. I walked back to her. She was trembling. I escorted her all the way to the witness stand. "This will be all right," I whispered.

When she was sworn in and settled down, I asked her the standard opening questions. What was her name? She told me. Where did she live? She told me. Did she have a pier behind her house? "Yes," she said hesitantly. Did she know a man named Khang? That simple query opened the floodgates. Margaret Anderwall told her story without waiting for any more questions. How Khang was such a nice man; how a caller had told her he would burn Khang's boat if she and her husband didn't move it; how someone threatened to burn their house if they didn't move Khang's boat; how they had received threatening phone calls from individuals claiming to be in the Klan; how the phone calls told them they would die; how they had received Klan calling cards in their mailbox.

"We didn't want trouble from anyone, and these threats made us afraid and upset," Mrs. Anderwall said. "We didn't want to make Khang move, but we had no choice. We didn't want to hurt his feelings. We said he had to move his boat so we could prepare for our daughter's wedding. His boat had been parked here for two years, and he'd never given us any trouble. But no one wants to have their house burned down or receive threats against their life. We've been ostracized by our neighbors. We just didn't want any more trouble."

As Mrs. Anderwall spoke, she turned to the judge. It must

have seemed natural to tell what she knew to the robed authority figure. Judge McDonald nodded. Our witness was moving her. Margaret Anderwall's honesty was obvious; she admitted that she was scared and didn't want to testify. The judge and the gallery and the lawyers and young Truc Dang were all spellbound by her presence—an ordinary American speaking up, telling the truth about the Ku Klux Klan. She stepped down from the witness stand confidently, striding past Beam, her chin held high. . . .

Judge McDonald agreed. On May 14, the eve of the new fishing season, she ruled. Finding violations of the civil rights statutes, the Sherman Antitrust Act, and Texas's common law tort of interference with contractual relationships, she entered a preliminary injunction barring the defendants from engaging in unlawful acts of violence or intimidation against the Vietnamese. This included putting armed persons on boats within view of the refugees, burning crosses in the area where the plaintiffs lived and worked, having gatherings of two or more robed members of the Knights of the Ku Klux Klan or affiliated organizations within view of the plaintiffs, and engaging or inciting others to engage in boat burning, armed boat patrols, assault and battery, or threats of such conduct.

Louis Beam's hands had been slapped and then tied. Colonel Nam and his countrymen could go safely onto the waters when the new shrimping season began in less than twenty-four hours. . . .

V. A Memorable Day   *February 1987*
                                             Mobile, Alabama

The Imperial Wizard slid his wire-rimmed glasses up his nose as I handed him plaintiff's exhibit seventeen, a 1979 copy of the *Fiery Cross.*

"Mr. Shelton, I ask you to look at this document here. . . . What is this a picture of?"

He looked the paper over and gave me an angry look. "It's a picture of an individual looking out. Apparently it's a white man," he said impatiently.

"Okay. And what does it say?" He lowered his eyes to the page. "It says, 'It's terrible the way blacks are being treated. All whites should work to give the blacks what they deserve.' Then it says, 'Turn page.' "

"What do you see on the other page?"

Several jurors were straining to see the document Shelton held in his hand. "And it is a black with a rope on it. . . ."

As plaintiff's exhibit seventeen made its way around the jury box, I could see the jurors were no longer bored. One by one they looked at the top page, then turned it over to see the lynched black man. Several shook their heads in disbelief. Life had imitated art two years later when Unit 900 gave Michael Donald what they thought he deserved. . . . I returned to the counsel's table, taking my seat next to Beulah Mae Donald. Nodding, she patted my pale white hand with her weathered brown one. She looked considerably older than sixty-four: diabetes, high blood pressure, and Michael's death had taken their toll. She moved slowly but proudly, a daughter or niece always at her side, the matriarch of a close-knit family. Beulah Mae Donald had reared seven children from two marriages almost single-handedly, working as a hotel maid, living in public housing. Michael, her youngest and pride and joy, was still living at home when Henry Hays and Tiger Knowles assaulted him.

Now Knowles sat no more than thirty feet from the woman whose son he lynched. . . .

This was clearly the most important case of my life . . . this case was not about a present or future danger. It was about history, about accountability for past sins, murderous sins.

Some individuals had been punished for those sins—although not nearly enough—but the Ku Klux Klan itself had never been held accountable. And of all the Klan groups, the most powerful, the one that had symbolized hatred and violence most during the civil rights movement, was Bobby Shelton's United Klans of America. The assault on the Freedom Riders, the bombing of the Sixteenth Street Baptist Church, the murder of Viola Liuzzo—the most famous, most vicious attacks of the era could be traced to the lead pipes, matches, and bullets of the UKA. Justice delayed is better than justice denied. . . .

I called Tiger Knowles to the stand. Knowles had undergone a major transformation over the last three years: He had shed a good twenty pounds, cut his sideburns, and styled his hair, losing the young punk image he had swaggered to the witness stand with at Henry Hays's murder trial. If it is possible to feel sympathy for someone who has done something so brutal, I did. At the Hays trial I had been shocked by the coolness with which Tiger Knowles recounted the murder, but at his deposition and in subsequent conversations, I found he truly regretted what he had done. A teenager, younger than his nineteen-year-old victim, he realized he had also destroyed his own life with this one senseless act. There was no going back, he told me, but he hoped he could go forward.

I wanted three things from Knowles at this trial: a logical explanation of the Klan structure and hierarchy to strengthen our agency theory, testimony that this was a Klan killing, and a detailed account of the murder itself that would horrify the jury, leave it gasping, move it to tears, and convince it that someone had to pay.

How did the Klan operate structure-wise?
On a military basis. . . . Each person carried out the orders

that was given to him from his commanding officer.

Was Mr. Robert Shelton the Klan official directly above you that you took orders from, or was it Mr. Hays?

Mr. Hays is who I took orders from.

Okay. And then Mr. Hays took orders from whom?

Mr. Shelton.

We could now focus on the murder, beginning with the plan. Knowles explained that the racial makeup of the Anderson jury had triggered his discussion with Bennie and Henry Hays about hanging a black man. What was the reason for killing a black person?

"Because he was—black people shouldn't be on our juries . . . it was strictly white supremacy," said Knowles.

From the back of the gallery, I heard the testifying that goes on in some southern black churches, an emotional commentary in response to Tiger Knowles's testimony.

Why had the murderers decided to hang the body out on the street?

"To get the message out to, not just the state of Alabama, but the whole United States that the Klan didn't want black people on juries," Knowles answered. They had wanted to emphasize the Klan connection, he said—thus they burned the cross on the courthouse lawn.

Knowles described Michael Donald's abduction. Donald had asked what they were going to do to him, Knowles remembered, and then, "Henry said, 'You know all those little nigger kids that's been getting killed up in Atlanta? Well a lot of people think the Klan is behind it. But we are not. You know the same thing could happen to you.' " Tiger Knowles paused for a moment. "And then he started pleading for his life. He said, 'Please don't kill me. You know you can do whatever you want to, beat me or anything else. But just don't kill me.' " It was impossible not to feel Michael Donald's terror.

I looked back at Mrs. Donald. Sitting silent, she squeezed the hand of Michael Figures, our co-counsel, her tearless eyes holding Knowles's.

How had hatred based on skin color been so thoroughly ingrained in these two young men that they could carry this out. *They didn't even know Michael.*

"And finally Donald just fell," Knowles told the silent courtroom. "And then Henry rushed over to the other end of the rope and grabbed the rope and started pulling it and it was like he was enjoying this. And then he was pulling it and then I finally said, 'Well he's dead.' And so we got him and we put him in the trunk of Henry's car. And then Henry took a razor knife and cut his throat and I asked him what for. He said: 'To make sure he was dead.' "

Somebody from the Donald family said, "Dear Lord." Mrs. Donald, tears in her eyes now, rocked back and forth in her chair, fighting to maintain her composure. The jury sat frozen in horror. . . .

When we reached the courtroom, I put my briefcase on the counsel table and then went out in the hallway to find a quiet spot where I could be alone. Before facing a jury, I need this private time. I need to get in touch with my feelings about the case, need to remember why I have become involved. It was not difficult to remember why the Donald case meant so much to me. My personal history and the history of the South were inextricably woven into the rope with which Michael Donald had been hanged. It was time to put that rope to rest forever.

I don't review my argument during this quiet time. I think about the simpler times of my life. On this day, I remembered a small boy walking along Line Creek with Daddy to check the catfish lines, riding my horse into the late evening sun at Rolling Hills Ranch, holding my children in my arms when they were born.

47

I also thought about my very first public speech as a sixteen-year-old contestant in a Future Farmers of America oratory competition. I'd written every word, memorized and practiced it for weeks, and then fainted flat out in front of five hundred students when I lost my place—perhaps the most embarrassing moment in my life. Today the words I wanted the jury to feel were etched in the last twenty-five years of my life, not typed on paper.

I stood before the jury for a long time before beginning. I wanted the jurors' attention and anticipation. After summarizing the facts and making the points Ellie and Richard suggested, I slowed the pace and lowered my voice.

"We told you when we started this case that we would show you that a conspiracy existed. And I believe we've shown you that the defendants conspired to kill a human being to retaliate against a jury for returning a verdict that was contrary to what they believe in. And what they believe in is white supremacy. God-given white supremacy." . . .

I walked over to the Klan's table and continued.

"But I do not want you to come back with a verdict against the Klan because they have unpopular beliefs. In this country you have the right to have unpopular beliefs just as long as you don't turn those beliefs into violent action that interferes with somebody else's rights. . . . [I raised my voice and motioned directly toward Bennie Hays and Bobby Shelton.] But they put a rope around Michael Donald's neck and treated him to an awful death on a dirt road in Baldwin County so that they could get out their message."

I walked back to our table and stopped beside Beulah Mae Donald.

"You have an opportunity to send a different message. A message that will ring out from the top of this courthouse and be heard all over Alabama and all over the United States—that an all-white jury from the heart of the South will not tolerate racial violence in any way, shape, or form. . . .

"No amount of money can ever truly compensate Mrs. Donald for her son's death. But if you return a large verdict—a very large verdict—you will be telling Mrs. Donald and this nation that her son's life was as valuable and precious as anyone's."

I put my hands on Mrs. Donald's shoulders, then returned to the jury, tears trickling down my face. I felt Mrs. Donald's pain and the hurt and outrage of a civilized society for what these barbarians had done. I was not ashamed for the jury to know.

I paused, I cleared my throat, and looked each juror in the eye.

"No matter what you decide, Michael Donald will take his place in history along with others whose lives were lost in the struggle for human rights. And when the final roll is called in heaven—when they call Dr. Martin Luther King, and Medgar Evers, and Viola Liuzzo—they will also call Michael Donald. I hope the verdict you reach will also go down in history on the side of justice."

I returned to my chair. Still rocking slowly, Mrs. Donald nodded.

The defendants were about to begin their closing arguments when I got word that Tiger Knowles would like to see me. I hurried to the tiny cell where he was being held when court was not in session.

"Do you think I should say something, Mr. Dees?" he asked.

"That's up to you, Tiger," I said.

"I'd like to," he said.

"Then do it."

"What should I say?" he asked.

"I can't answer that, Tiger. Just say what you feel."

The young man who had murdered Michael Donald addressed the court: "Everything I said is true," Tiger Knowles began. "I was acting as a Klansman when I done this. I hope that people learn from my mistake. I've lost my family. I've got people after me."

Tears filled Knowles's eyes and I began to feel them again well up in mine.

Knowles pivoted and faced Beulah Mae Donald. "I can't bring your son back, but I'm sorry for what happened." He was sobbing now. Mrs. Donald rocked back and forth. "God knows if I could trade places with him, I would. I can't. Whatever it takes—I have nothing. But I will have to do it. And if it takes me the rest of my life to pay it, any comfort it may bring, I hope it will. I will."

Knowles paused to compose himself. I looked at the jury, Judge Howard, the Donald family. There were no dry eyes.

Knowles gave up trying to fight his own tears. "I want you to understand that it is true what happened and I'm just sorry it happened."

Beulah Mae Donald stopped rocking. "I forgive you," she said softly.

The jury retired early in the afternoon. It returned with a verdict four and a half hours later. Judge Howard instructed the clerk to read it. "We the jury find for the plaintiff and against defendant United Klans of America. . . . We the jury find for the plaintiff and against the defendant Bennie Hays." It was the same with respect to the remaining defendants— judgment for the plaintiff. After the final defendant's name was read, the clerk concluded: "We fix plaintiff's damages at seven million dollars."

There were gasps from both counsels' tables and both sides of the gallery. Mrs. Donald grabbed my hand and Michael Figures's hand. Richard quickly scribbled a note to me. "Thank you for letting me be part of this."

The verdict's size did not sink in immediately. I was more excited that the quest to get Shelton and the United Klans of America had succeeded. History would show that an all-white southern jury had held the Klan accountable after all these years. The healing could begin. Indeed, it already had when Tiger Knowles and Beulah Mae Donald had reached out to one another.

Shelton and Hays avoided my eyes. They rose and quickly left the courtroom. Richard Cohen, Michael Figures, Mrs. Donald, and I eventually made our way to the packed pressroom.

Mrs. Donald said, "I don't want no other mother to go through what I did."

I said I hoped the verdict would mean just that.

After leaving the press conference, I called Ellie. "We won, sweetheart," I said.

"I heard," she said. "I'm really proud of you. I understand why you do what you do, Daddy."

A wonderful ending to a memorable day.

Betty Friedan graduated from Smith College. She is the founder of the National Organization for Women (NOW) and organizer of the National Women's Political Caucus. She is the author of *The Feminine Mystique, It Changed My Life,* and *The Fountain of Age.* She has written articles for the *Atlantic Monthly, New York Times, Cosmopolitan,* and *Good Housekeeping,* among others.

The Way We Were—1949

Betty Friedan

Getting married and raising children conflicted with the idea of gender equality for Betty Friedan. Jobs that paid well were seldom available for women. In 1949, women were told in movies, magazines, and books that having a man around was more important than anything else. Less value was placed on intelligence than on the ability to get a guy to propose. After all, who needed college? Betty Friedan was raising her first child. Social and economic equality were illusions for Ms. Friedan. An excerpt from It Changed My Life *(1976).*

In 1949 I was concentrating on breast-feeding and wheeling Danny, my first baby, to the park, and reading Dr. Spock. I was beginning to wonder if I really wanted to go back to work, after all, when my maternity leave was up. I bought a pressure cooker and *The Joy of Cooking* and a book by George

---

"The Way We Were" is excerpted from *It Changed My Life*, by Betty Friedan, published in 1976 by Random House, Inc. Used by permission of Curtis Brown Ltd.

Nelson about *The Modern House.* One Saturday, though we had no money, we went out to Rockland County and looked at old barns that my husband might be able to convert into a house. And I wrote my mother that I wanted the sterling silver—which she had offered us as a wedding present and I had scorned as too bourgeois—after all.

That was the year it really hit, the feminine mystique, though at the time we didn't know what it was. It was just that our lives seemed to have shifted in dimension, in perspective. The last of our group, which had come to New York after Smith and Vassar and shared an apartment in the Village, was getting married. During the war, we'd had jobs like "research" or "editorial assistant," and met GIs at the Newspaper Guild Canteen, and written V-mail letters to lonesome boys we'd known at home, and had affairs with married men—hiding our diaphragms under the girdles in the dresser. And we had considered ourselves part of the vanguard of the working-class revolution, going to Marxist discussion groups and rallies at Madison Square Garden and feeling only contempt for dreary bourgeois capitalists like our fathers—though we still read *Vogue* under the hair dryer, and spent all our salaries on clothes at Bergdorf's and Bendel's, replacing our college Braemer sweaters with black cashmere and Gucci gloves, on sale.

And then the boys our age had come back from the war. I was bumped from my job on a small labor news service by a returning veteran, and it wasn't so easy to find another job I really liked. I filled out the applications for Time-Life researcher, which I'd always scorned before. All the girls I knew had jobs like that, but it was official policy that no matter how good, researchers, who were women, could never become writers or editors. They could write the whole article, but the men they were working with would always get the by-line as writer. I was certainly not a feminist then—none of

54

us were a bit interested in women's rights. But I could never bring myself to take that kind of job. And what else was there? The wartime government agencies where some of us had worked were being dissolved. The group on Waverly Place was breaking up—Maggie, Harriet, Madelon, everyone was getting married (and Abe Rosenthal was waiting greedily to move into that apartment so that *he* could get married).

It was very hard to find an apartment right after the war. I had left the group and found a funny apartment in the basement of a townhouse on West 86th. You had to go through the furnace room to get to it, there were pipes on the ceiling, and the cold water didn't work in the bathroom so you had to run the hot an hour ahead to take a bath. It didn't even have a kitchen, but since I had no interest in cooking, I didn't mind. It had a brick wall and lots of shelves, and a terrace door, and when Carl Friedan came back from running the Soldier Show Company in Europe to start a summer theater in New Jersey, his best friend, whom I worked with, said he knew a nice girl with an apartment. He brought me an apple and told me jokes which made me laugh, and he moved in. We got married in City Hall, but went through it again with a rabbi in Boston for Mother's sake. And while I was in the hospital having Danny, he painted the pipes on the ceiling and made a kitchen out of the closet and moved our bed into the living room so Danny could have a nursery.

After the war, I had been very political, very involved, consciously radical. Not about women, for heaven's sake! If you were a radical in 1949, you were concerned about the Negroes, and the working class, and World War III, and the Un-American Activities Committee and McCarthy and loyalty oaths, and Communist splits and schisms, Russia, China and the UN, but you certainly didn't think about being a woman, politically. It was only recently that we had begun to think of ourselves as women at all. But that wasn't political—

it was the opposite of politics. Eight months pregnant, I climbed up on a ladder on a street corner to give a speech for Henry Wallace. But in 1949 I was suddenly not that interested in political meetings.

Some of us had begun to go to Freudian analysts. Like the lady editor in Moss Hart's *Lady in the Dark,* we were supposedly discovering that what we really wanted was a man. Whatever the biological, psychosexual reality, a woman was hardly in a mood to argue with that message if *(a)* she was lonesome and tired of living alone or *(b)* she was about to lose her job or *(c)* had become disillusioned with it. In 1949, nobody really had to tell a woman that she wanted a man, but the message certainly began bombarding us from all sides: domestic bliss had suddenly become chic, sophisticated, and whatever made you want to be a lady editor, police reporter, or political activist could prevent or destroy that bliss—bourgeois security, no longer despised.

The magazines were full of articles like: "What's Wrong with American Women?"; "Let's Stop Blaming Mom"; "Shortage of Men?"; "Isn't a Woman's Place in the Home?"; "Women Aren't Men"; "What Women Can Learn from Mother Eve"; "Really a Man's World, Politics"; and "Nearly Half of the Women in *Who's Who* are Single."

The short stories in those women's magazines we still read under the hair dryer were all about miserable girls with supposedly glamorous jobs in New York, who suddenly saw the light and went home to marry Henry. In "Honey, Don't You Cry" (*McCall's,* January 1949), the heroine is reading a letter from her mother: "You should come home, daughter. You can't be happy living alone like that." In "The Applause of Thousands" (*Ladies' Home Journal,* March 1949), the young woman *pities* her poor mother who dreamed of being an actress; she is gong to get married before she can even be tempted by such dreams.

I remember in particular the searing effect on me, who once intended to be a psychologist, of a story in *McCall's* in December 1949 called "A Weekend with Daddy." A little girl who lives a lonely life with her mother, divorced, an intellectual know-it-all psychologist, goes to the country to spend a weekend with her father and his new wife, who is wholesome, happy, and a good cook and gardener. And there is love and laughter and growing flowers and hot clams and a gourmet cheese omelet and square dancing, and she doesn't want to go home. But, pitying her poor mother typing away all by herself in the lonesome apartment, she keeps her guilty secret that from now on she will be living for the moments when she can escape to that dream house in the country where they know "what life is all about."

I remember about that time running into a real psychologist, a woman slightly older than I was whom I had known in graduate school. She had been brilliant and ambitious. Unlike me, she had taken the fellowships and gotten her Ph.D. What was she doing now? "I am married," she said with great satisfaction, "and I am pregnant." When I asked, she said that she had picked her husband up on the subway. And I understood, because in 1949 I was also becoming infected by the mystique, that it almost didn't matter who the man was who became the instrument of your feminine fulfillment. I was awed by the strength and sincerity of her new psychological awareness, that she would even find him on the subway.

That year saw the last of the spirited, brave, adventurous heroines who had filled the magazines and movies of the 1930s and 1940s—the Claudette Colbert, Myrna Loy, Bette Davis, Rosalind Russell, and Katharine Hepburn types. These heroines, in the end, got their man, but they were usually working toward some goal or vision of their own, independent and determined and passionately involved with the world. They were less aggressive in pursuit of a man, less kittenish than the Doris Day little housewife that followed, and the men were drawn to them as much by their spirit as by their looks. "Career woman" in the 1950s became a pejorative, denoting a ball-busting man-eating harpy, a miserable neurotic witch from whom man and child should flee for very life.

In March 1949, the *Ladies' Home Journal* printed the prototype of the innumerable paeans to "Occupation: Housewife" that were to flood the women's magazines into the 1960s. It began with a woman complaining that when she has to write "housewife" on the census blank, she gets an inferiority complex. ("When I write it I realize that here I am, a middle-aged woman, with a university education, and I've never made anything out of my life. I'm just a housewife.") Then the author of the reply, who somehow never is a housewife (in this case Dorothy Thompson, newspaperwoman, foreign correspondent, famous columnist), roars with laughter. The trouble with you, she scolds, is that you don't realize that you are expert in a dozen careers, simultaneously. "You might write: business manager, cook, nurse, chauffeur, dressmaker, interior decorator, accountant, caterer, teacher, private secretary—or just put down philanthropist. . . . All your life you have been giving away your energies, your skills, your talents, your services, for love." But still, the housewife complains, I'm nearly fifty and I've never done what I had hoped to do with my youth—music. I've wasted my college education.

Ho-ho, laughs Miss Thompson, aren't your children musical because of you, and all those struggling years while your husband was finishing his great work, didn't you keep a charming house on $3,000 a year and paper the living room yourself, and watch the market like a hawk for bargains? And in time off, didn't you type and proofread your husband's manuscripts, play piano duets with the children to make practicing more fun, read their books in high school to follow their study? "But all this vicarious living-through others," the housewife sighs. "As vicarious as Napoleon Bonaparte,"

Miss Thompson scoffs, "or a queen. I simply refuse to share your self-pity. You are one of the most successful women I know."

That year the *Ladies' Home Journal* serialized Margaret Mead's *Male and Female,* with its deceptively tempting version of a South Sea world where a woman succeeds and is envied by men, just by "being" a woman.

> In Bali, little girls between two and three walk much of the time with purposely thrust-out little bellies, and the older women tap them playfully as they pass. "Pregnant!" they tease. So the little girl learns that . . . some day she will have a baby, and having a baby is, on the whole, one of the most exciting and conspicuous achievements that can be presented to the eyes of small children in these simple worlds, in some of which the largest buildings are only fifteen feet tall. . . . Furthermore, the little girl learns that she will have a baby not because she is strong or energetic or initiating, not because she works and struggles and tries, and in the end succeeds, but simply because she is a girl and not a boy, and girls turn into women, and in the end—if they protect their femininity—have babies. . . . In our Occidental view of life, women, fashioned from man's rib, can at the most strive unsuccessfully to imitate man's superior and higher vocations.

That it was slightly schizophrenic to try to live through your pregnant belly, as it were, in an increasingly complex world where the largest buildings were a lot taller than fifteen feet—well, we only woke up to that later. In 1949 we were suckers for that apple—we could cop out from the competition, the dull, hard work of "man's higher vocations," by simply "playing our role as women." No more need to rock the boat, risk failure or resentment from men.

That year, the *Ladies' Home Journal* also serialized *Cheaper by the Dozen,* the story of the lady engineer who applied her scientific know-how to raising that newly fashionable large family. Very good reporters were given the assignment of documenting in minute detail every detail of the daily life of the newly glamorous American housewife—cooking in her own kitchen, with all her new appliances. It was also reported in the fall of 1949 that "something new in birth rates has occurred in the U.S. Between 1940 and 1947, the reproductive rate of women college graduates increased 81% compared with an increase of only 29% among women who had completed only grade school."

It certainly did not occur to any of us then, even the most radical, that companies which made a big profit selling us all those washing machines, dryers, freezers and second cars were overselling us on the bliss of domesticity in order to sell us more things. Even the most radical of us, in our innocence, wanted those pressure cookers.

We were even more innocent in our sophistication as women. Though I was virtually a virgin myself when I came to New York after college, it was my lot to arrange abortions for our entire Smith group. Why me? Because I was the radical, also a psychologist and unshockable (I knew all the Freudian words). More practically, as a newspaperwoman, I was supposed to know my way around. The men I worked with during the war, necessarily over draft age, were *Front Page* types who taught me to write a jazzy lead after three martinis at lunch. They were avuncular to my innocence, with occasional lecherous lapses. The first time I said, "Trav, you have to help me. A friend of mine is pregnant," the whole office sprang into action. I was told, in serious, sinister secrecy, where to take my "friend." It would also cost $1,000, and they were concerned where my "friend" would get the money. Six months later, I had to come to them again. This time, the reaction was not so warm. It was years before I realized that they had assumed each "friend" needing an abortion was *me*.

I myself never had an abortion, though I personally accompanied several of these friends to scary, butchery back rooms, and shared their fear and distrust of the shifty, oily, illegal operators, and sat outside the room and heard the screams and wondered what I'd do if they died, and got them into the taxis afterward. Dear Virginias who read this now—when our efforts have gotten you legal abortion in New York, and a historic Supreme Court decision affirming your right to control your own body, and sexual privacy, and birth control and abortion—you can't imagine how humiliating, traumatic, horrible it was, to need an abortion in 1949. Nor can you whose parents buy you the pill understand the awkward indignity of getting a diaphragm in New York, in 1949, if you weren't married—and sometimes even if you were.

My last task, as the group broke up, was to find an Episcopal priest to marry Maggie and Roger in a fancy church acceptable to her mother. But in 1949 not even a young pacifist minister would perform the ceremony for a man who had been divorced. It was harder to find such a minister than an abortionist. Divorce was unthinkable, in our very buying of the feminine mystique. In fact, no woman I knew personally had been through divorce herself in 1949, and that was still true fifteen years later when the first threat of its personal possibility paralyzed me with terror in the security of my own suburban dream house.

"Security" was a big part of what began to happen in 1949. "Security," as in "risks," was in the headlines, as in atomic secrets, Communist espionage, the House Un-American Activities Committee, loyalty oaths, and the beginning of blacklists for writers. Was it unconscious political retreat that so many talked so bravely, and marched, suddenly detoured to the security of the private four walls of that house in suburbia—everything that was "bourgeois." Suddenly, we stopped using the word "bourgeois." We were like our parents, it seemed. Suddenly, we were very interested in houses and *things:* chairs, tables, silverware. We went to the Museum of Modern Art to study furniture and displays of modern architecture, and bought our first possessions—Eames chairs, a blond free-form sculptured Noguchi dining table, and a Herman Miller couch-daybed with a plain tweed-covered mattress and bolsters, so modern, so different from the over-stuffed, tufted davenport at home (whose comfort I have now gone back to).

Toward the end of the year I read a story in the *Times* about a new garden apartment community in Queens called Park-way Village, built for the UN with some vacancies for ex-GIs. It was almost like having your own home: the apartments had French doors opening on to a common lawn where the children could go out and play by themselves, instead of having to be taken to the park. And there was a cooperative nursery school. During my lunch hour I took the subway to the wilds of Queens, and so began the fifteen-year trek of my own particular nuclear family away from the city, to that garden apartment in Queens, to a rented barn in Sneden's Landing, to our own eleven-room Charles Addams Victorian house in Rockland County, where my children (in-creased to three) grew up, and I chauffeured, and did the PTA and buffet dinners, and hid, like secret drinking in the morning, the book I was writing when my suburban neigh-bors came for coffee, *The Feminine Mystique.*

I felt that I would never again, ever, be so happy as I was living in Queens. The floors were parquet, and the ceilings were molded white plaster, no pipes, and the plumbing worked. The rent was $118.50 a month, for four and one-half rooms, and we thought that was enormous. And now our friends were the other couples like us, with kids at the nur-sery school who squealed at each other from the baskets of the grocery carts we wheeled at the supermarkets. It was fun at first, shopping in those new supermarkets. And we bought barbecue grills, and made dips out of sour cream and dried onion soup to serve with potato chips, while our husbands made the martinis as dry as in the city and cooked hamburgers on the charcoal, and we sat in canvas chairs on our terrace and thought how beautiful our children looked, playing in the twilight, and how lucky we all were, and that it would last forever.

There were six families in our group, and if your child smashed his finger in the manhole cover and you weren't home, one of the others would take him to the doctor. We had Thanksgiving and Christmas and Passover Seders as a joint family, and in the summer rented houses together, on Lake George and Fire Island, that we couldn't afford separately. And the support we gave each other hid the cracks in our own marriages—or maybe kept them from getting serious. As it is, of the six families, three couples are now divorced, one broken by suicide.

Having babies, the Care and Feeding of Children according to Doctor Spock, began to structure our lives. It took the place of politics. But the mystique was something else—that college graduates should make a *Career* of motherhood, not just one or two babies, but four, five, six. Why even go to college?

I remember the zeal with which we took the classes at the Maternity Center. Our husbands were envious, but then with natural childbirth the husbands could take the classes too, and breathe along, and show off at dinner parties, doing the exercises on the floor. And then there was the moral, political seriousness of our breast-feeding. In the summer of 1949, I was frowned on for breast-feeding in public, on the front steps of my husband's summer theater. It wasn't fashionable then. But it's so *natural,* we gloried, feeling only scorn for our superficial selfish sisters who thought breast-feeding was animal and would spoil their figures. (Actually, I did not breast-feed in public—I'd retire to the back row of the darkened theater where they were rehearsing. But I did sit out on the front steps afterwards burping him in the sun.) And how proud I was, continuing the breast-feeding nearly all that year, even after the milk began to give out and I had to sterilize bottles anyway. And how furious I was when they called from the office and insisted I come back to work, one month before that year's maternity leave was over, because it was messing up vacation schedules.

So twenty-five years later when that grown-up boy is having trouble with his girl, and—knowing Freudian words by himself, if not yet Dr. Spock—says his insecurity in love is all my fault, I still feel the pains of the guilt caused by leaving my first baby with a nurse when I went back to work. Would all that guilt have been necessary if Dr. Spock hadn't said, in the section on "Should Mother Work?": "In most cases, the mother is the best one to give him this feeling of 'belonging,' safety and security. . . . If a mother realizes clearly how vital this kind of care is to a small child, it may make it easier for her to decide that the extra money she might earn, or the satisfaction she might receive from an outside job, is not so important after all."

To be honest, those years were not all products of the "mystique." I still remember the marvelous dark night in the spring of 1949 when we were wheeling Danny home in the baby carriage. I looked down as we passed under a streetlight, and he was smiling at me, and there was recognition in his eyes. A person was there, and he knew me.

Besides, the reality of the babies, the bottles, the cooking, the diapering, the burping, the carriage-wheeling, the pressure cooker, the barbecue, the playground, and doing-it-yourself was more comfortable, more safe, secure, and satisfying—that year and for a lot of years thereafter—than that supposedly glamorous "career" where you somehow didn't feel wanted, and where no matter what you did you knew you weren't going to get anywhere. There was a guilty feeling, too: it was somehow your fault, *pushy* of you, to want that good assignment for yourself, want the credit, the by-line, if the idea, even the writing, had been yours. *Pushy,* too, if you felt rejected when the men went out to lunch and talked shop in one of those bars where women were not allowed—even if one of those same men asked you out to lunch, alone, in the other kind of restaurant, and held your hand, or knee, under the tablecloth. It was uncomfortable, unreal in a way, working in that kind of office with "career" still driving you, but having no words to deal with, even *recognize,* that barrier that you could never somehow break through, that made you invisible as a person, that made them not take you seriously, that made you feel so basically unimportant, almost unnecessary, and—buried very deep—so angry.

At home, you *were* necessary, you were important, you were the boss, in fact—the mother—and the new mystique gave it the rationale of career.

The concrete, palpable actuality of the carpentry and cooking you could do yourself, and the surprising effectiveness of the changes you could make happen in school boards and zoning and community politics, were somehow more real and secure than the schizophrenic and even dangerous politics of the world revolution whose vanguard we used to fancy ourselves. The revolution was obviously not going to *happen* that way in American by 1949: the working class wanted those pressure cookers, too. It was disillusioning, to say the least, to see what was happening in the trade unions, and in Czechoslovakia and the Soviet Union, even the myth of the Communist menace was mostly an excuse for red-baiting. In 1949, McCarthyism, the danger of war against Russia and of fascism in America, and the reality of U.S. imperial, corporate wealth and power all made men and women who used to have large visions of making the whole world over uncomfortable with the Old Left rhetoric of revolution.

Suburbia, exurbia, with the children as an excuse—there was a comfortable small world you could really do something about, politically: the children's homework, even the new math, compared to the atomic bomb.

The feminine mystique made it easier for a woman to retreat smugly, without the pangs of conscience and self-contempt a man might feel while using all his wits to sell cigarettes that would cause cancer, or deodorants. We could be virtuous and pure of compromise, and even feel a smug contempt for the poor man who could not so easily escape the ulcerous necessity of really conforming and competing. For a long while, it looked as if women had gotten the better of that bargain. It was only later that some of us discovered that maybe we had walked as willing victims into a comfortable concentration camp.

Shortly after 1949, I was fired from my job because I was pregnant again. They weren't about to put up with the inconvenience of another year's maternity leave, even though I was *entitled* to it under my union contract. It was unfair, *wrong* somehow to fire me just because I was pregnant, and to hire a man instead. I even tried calling a meeting of the people in the union where I worked. It was the first personal stirring of my own feminism, I guess. But the other women were just embarrassed, and the men uncomprehending. It was my own fault, getting pregnant again, a *personal* matter, not something you should take to the union. There was no word in 1949 for "sex discrimination."

Besides, it was almost a relief; I had begun to feel so guilty working, and I really wasn't getting anywhere in that job. I was more than ready to embrace the feminine mystique. I took a cooking course and started studying the suburban real-estate ads. And the next time the census taker came around, I was living in that old Charles Addams house we were fixing up, on the Hudson River in Rockland County. And the children numbered three. When the census taker asked my occupation, I said self-consciously, virtuously, with only the faintest stirrings of protest from that part of me I'd turned my back on—"housewife." . . .

Howard Zinn taught history and political science at Spelman College in Atlanta and at Boston University where he is professor emeritus. He is the author of *A People's History of the United States, Disobedience and Democracy, Vietnam: The Logic of Withdrawal,* and *Declarations of Independence* and over sixty articles that have appeared in journals such as *Harper's, The Nation, New Republic, New York Times,* and the *Review.* His most recent book, *You Can't Be Neutral on a Moving Train,* was published in 1994.

———————

Going South

Howard Zinn

Teaching history at Spelman College in Atlanta in the late 1950s and early 1960s, housing, education and employment were "as rigidly segregated as Johannesburg, South Africa," Zinn writes. A college education was "a matter of life and death" to the black women that he taught. A stone wall and a barbed-wire fence separated these students from the world outside while keeping the "outsiders" ignorant about the young African-Americans studying so diligently inside. In this excerpt from You Can't Be Neutral on a Moving Train *(1994), Zinn describes a visit he took with his students to the Georgia legislature in 1957 and the legislators' reaction to their presence in the state capitol.*

It is too easy to mistake silence for acceptance. That may be the most important thing I learned teaching and living for seven years in the black community of Spelman College in Atlanta, Georgia, in the years of "The Movement."

No, I did not seek out a "Negro college" out of an urge to "do good." I was just looking for a job.

I had worked for three years loading trucks in a warehouse on the four-to-midnight shift, while going to New York University and Columbia. One day I hurt my back lifting one eighty-pound carton too many, and began to teach part-time (what a joke—I learned soon that "part-timers" work longer and get paid less than full-timers). I taught four courses, Monday-Wednesday-Friday, at Upsala College, a Swedish-Lutheran, absurdly up-tight college in New Jersey, and two courses, Tuesday-Thursday evenings, at absurdly chaotic Brooklyn College. So, from "the project" where we lived in lower Manhattan I traveled an hour west to New Jersey on some days, an hour east to Brooklyn other days, teaching six courses for a total of $3,000 a year.

Close to finishing my Ph.D. work in history at Columbia University, I was contacted by the Placement Bureau of Columbia for an interview with the president of Spelman College, who was visiting New York. (The idea of a "Negro college" hadn't occurred to me. Spelman College at that time was virtually unknown to anyone outside the black community.) He offered me the chairmanship of his history and social sciences department, and $4,000 a year. I summoned up my courage: "I have a wife and two kids. Could you make it $4,500?" I would still be poor, but prestigious.

Chairman of the department! True, it was a tiny department, and scoffers might say it was like being headwaiter in a two-waiter restaurant. But in my situation, it was very welcome.

And so, that August of 1956, my wife and I trundled our two kids and our belongings into our ten-year-old Chevy and drove south, arriving in Atlanta on a hot and rainy night. Roz and the children (Myla was nine, Jeff almost seven) awoke to watch the shimmering wet lights on Ponce de Leon Avenue. We were in a different world, a thousand miles from home, a whole universe removed from the sidewalks of New York. Here was a city thick with foliage, fragrant with magnolias and honeysuckle. The air was sweeter and heavier. The people were blacker and whiter; through the raindrops on the windows they appeared as ghosts gliding through the night.

The campus of Spelman College was not far from the center of town, an oval garden of dogwood and magnolia trees, ringed with red brick buildings. Our family was given temporary quarters in one of those buildings until we could find a place to live in town. That wasn't easy. Landlords wanted to know where I worked. When I told them I was teaching at Spelman, the atmosphere changed; apartments were no longer available. This was our first personal encounter with the depth of the malignancy that had for so long infected all of America, but was more visible in the southern states.

What for us was an inconvenience was for blacks a daily and never-ending humiliation, and behind that the threat of violence to the point of murder. Just ten years earlier, a sheriff in Baker County, Georgia ("Bad Baker," as it was known), taking a black man to jail, smashed his head repeatedly with a blackjack, in view of witnesses. The man died. The sheriff, Claude Screws, was acquitted by a local jury, found guilty by a federal jury under an old civil rights statute, and was sentenced to six months in prison. This was overturned by the Supreme Court on a technicality. One day I looked down the list of members of the Georgia legislature and saw the name of Claude Screws.

The city of Atlanta at that time was as rigidly segregated as Johannesburg, South Africa. Peachtree Street, downtown, was white. Auburn Avenue, ("sweet Auburn," as it was known in the Negro community) was a five-minute ride away from downtown, and was black. If black people were downtown, it was because they were working for whites, or shopping at Rich's Department Store, where both races could come to buy, but where its cafeteria was for whites only. If a white person and a black person walked down the street together, as if they were equals, with no clear indication that the black was a servant of some kind, the atmosphere on the street suddenly became tense, threatening.

I began my classes. There were no white students at Spelman. My students, in a rich variety of colors, were shy and lovely. They had wonderful names, like Geneva, Herschelle, Marnesba, Aramintha. They were from all over the country, but mostly from the South, and they had never had a white teacher. This was the reason, mostly, for their shyness, which disappeared after we came to know one another. Some were the daughters of the black middle class—teachers, ministers, social workers, small business people, skilled workers. Others were the daughters of maids, porters, laborers, tenant farmers.

A college education for these young women was a matter of life and death. One of my students told me one day, sitting in my office: "My mother says I've got to do well because I've already got two strikes against me. I'm black and I'm a woman. One more strike and I'm out." Be careful, was her mother's advice.

And so they accepted—or seemed to accept—the tightly controlled atmosphere of Spelman College, where they were expected to dress a certain way, walk a certain way, pour tea a certain way. There was compulsory chapel six times a week. They had to sign in and out of their dormitories, and be in by 10:00 P.M. Their contacts with men were carefully monitored; the college authorities were determined to counter the stories of the sexually free black woman, and worse, the pregnant unmarried black girl. Freshmen were not permitted to go across the street to the library at Atlanta University, where they might encounter the young men of Morehouse College. Trips into the city of Atlanta were closely supervised.

It was as if there was an unwritten, unspoken agreement between the white power structure of Atlanta and the administrations of the black colleges: "We, the white people of Atlanta, will let you, the colored folk, have your nice little college. You can educate your colored girls to service the Negro community, to become teachers and social workers, maybe even a doctor or lawyer. We won't bother you. You can even have a few white faculty. At Christmas some of our white citizens may come to the Spelman campus to hear the famous Spelman choir. And in return, you will not interfere with our way of life, with racial segregation in Atlanta. *You will leave us alone.*"

This pact was symbolized by a twelve-foot-high stone wall around the campus. At certain points, a barbed-wire fence. After our family moved into an apartment on campus, near that fence, Jeff, our seven-year-old son, who seemed to be an expert on such matters (he spent his spare hours with the black buildings-and-grounds workers on campus) pointed out to us that the barbed wire was slanted not so as to keep intruders out, but to keep the Spelman students in.

One day, the students would leap over that wall, climb over that barbed-wire fence; the city of Atlanta would never be the same, and the "Spelman girls" would never be the same.

But in the fall of 1956, there was no sign of that. One year before, the bus boycott in Montgomery had ended in victory. The year before that, 1954, the Supreme Court had finally come around to deciding that the Fourteenth Amendment—"the equal protection of the laws"—prohibited racial segregation in the public schools. Very little was done to enforce that decision; the Supreme Court order was "all deliberate speed," and the key word was not "speed" but "deliberate." Still, expectations rose in the black community, and fear spread among many whites.

I soon learned that beneath my students' politeness and decorum, there was a lifetime of suppressed indignation. At one time I asked my students to write down their first memory of race prejudice, and the feelings tumbled out.

One told how, as a teenager, she sat down in the front of

the bus next to a white woman. "This woman immediately stormed out of her seat, trampling over my legs and feet, and cursing under her breath. Other white passengers began to curse under their breaths. Never had I seen people staring at me as if they hated me. Never had I really experienced being directly rejected as though I were some poisonous, venomous creature."

A student from Forsyth, Georgia: "I guess if you are from a small Georgia town, as I am, you can say that your first encounter with prejudice was the day you were born. . . . My parents never got to see their infant twins alive because the only incubator in the hospital was on the 'white' side."

Every one, without exception, had some early experience. I thought of Countee Cullen's poem, "Incident":

> Once riding in Old Baltimore,
> Heart-filled, head-filled with glee,
> I saw a Baltimorean
> Keep looking straight at me.

> Now I was eight and very small,
> And he was no whit bigger,
> And so I smiled, but he poked out
> His tongue, and called me, "Nigger."

> I saw the whole of Baltimore
> From May until December;
> Of all the things that happened there
> That's all that I remember.

I had been at Spelman six months when, in January of 1957, my students and I had a small encounter with the Georgia state legislature. We had decided to visit one of its sessions. Our intent was simply to watch the legislature go about its business. But when we arrived we saw (of course we should have known) that the gallery had a small section on the side marked "Colored." The students quickly conferred and decided to ignore the signs, to sit in the main section, which was quite empty.)

As our group of about thirty filed into the seats, panic followed. The fishing bill was forgotten. The speaker of the House seemed to have an apoplectic fit. He rushed to the microphone and shouted into it: "You nigras get over where you belong! We got segregation in the state of Georgia."

The members of the legislature were now standing in their seats and shouting up at us, their shouts echoing strangely in the huge domed chamber. The regular business was forgotten. Police appeared quickly and moved threateningly toward our group.

We conferred again, while the tension in the chamber thickened. Students were not ready, in those years before the South rose up en masse, to be arrested. We decided to move out into the hall and then to come back into the "colored" section, me included.

What then followed was one of those strange scenes that the paradoxes of the racist, courteous South often produced. A guard came up to me, staring very closely, apparently not able to decide if I was "white" or "colored," then asked me where this group of visitors was from. I told him. A moment later, the speaker of the House, the same one who had shouted at us, came up to the microphone, again interrupting a legislator, and intoned, "The members of the Georgia State Legislature would like to extend a warm welcome to the visiting delegation from Spelman College."

A few male students from Morehouse College were with us on that trip. One of them was Julian Bond, son of the distinguished educator and former president of Lincoln University, Horace Mann Bond. Julian was an occasional visitor at our house on the Spelman campus, introducing us to the records of Ray Charles, bringing poems he had written.

(A decade later, Julian, now a well-known civil rights

75

leader, would be elected to the Georgia state legislature, and, in an odd reprise of our experience, would be expelled by his fellow legislators because of his outspoken opposition to the war in Vietnam. A Supreme Court decision, upholding his right to free speech, restored him to his seat.)

Some years after our trip to the legislature, in 1963, my students and I had the satisfaction of sitting in the main section of the gallery and watching the induction to the Georgia Senate of Leroy Johnson, the first black to be elected to that body since Reconstruction days. It was the habit of the new senators to place their hands one atop the other on the Bible to take their oath of office. The touch of Leroy Johnson's dark hand was not enough to deter the three new white senators from taking the oath.

Sometime in early 1959, I suggested to the Spelman Social Science Club, to which I was faculty adviser, that it might be interesting to undertake some real project involving social change. The discussion became very lively. Someone said: "Why don't we try to do something about the segregation of the public libraries?" And so, two years before the sit-ins swept the South and "The Movement" excited the nation, a few young women at Spelman College decided to launch an attack on the racial policy of the main library in Atlanta, the Carnegie Library.

It was a nonviolent assault. Black students would enter the Carnegie Library, to the stares of everyone around, and ask for John Locke's *An Essay on Human Understanding* or John Stuart Mill's *On Liberty* or Tom Paine's *Common Sense*. Turned away with evasive answers ("We'll send a copy to your Negro branch"), they kept coming back, asking for the Declaration of Independence, the Constitution of the United States, and other books designed to make sensitive librarians uneasy.

The pressure on the libraries was stepped up. We let it be known that a lawsuit was next. One of the plaintiffs would be a professor of French at Spelman, Dr. Irene Dobbs Jackson. She came from a distinguished Atlanta family. Her sister was Mattiwilda Dobbs, the first black woman to sing at the Metropolitan Opera. Her father was John Wesley Dobbs, a great orator in the old southern tradition. Once, sitting in the Wheat Street Baptist Church, I heard John Wesley Dobbs keep a crowd of a thousand in an uproar: "My Mattiwilda was asked to sing here in Atlanta," he thundered. "But she said, 'No sir. Not while my daddy has to sit in the balcony!' "

Years later, Irene Jackson's son, Maynard Jackson, would be elected the first black mayor of Atlanta. That seemed far off, in that time when we were pressing for something so absurd as the right of black people to go to the library.

In the midst of our campaign, I was sitting in the office of Whitney Young, dean of the School of Social Work of Atlanta University, who was working with us. We were talking about what our next moves should be, when the phone rang. It was a member of the Library Board. Whitney listened, said "Thank you," and hung up. He smiled. The board had decided to end the policy of racial segregation in the Atlanta library system.

A few days after that, four of us rode downtown to the Carnegie Library: Dr. Irene Jackson, Earl Sanders, a young black professor of music at Spelman, Pat West, the white Alabama-born wife of Henry West, who taught philosophy in my department at Spelman, and myself. As the youngish librarian handed a new library membership card to Irene Jackson, she spoke calmly, but her hand trembled slightly. She understood that a bit of history was being made.

Pat and Henry West, both white southerners who scandalized their families by coming to live in a black community, had a three-year-old boy who was the first and only white child in the Spelman College nursery school. At Christmas time, it was traditional for schoolchildren to be taken to

Rich's Department Store downtown to meet Santa Claus, where the children would take turns sitting on Santa's lap and whispering what they wanted for Christmas. Santa was a white man in need of a job, and he had no qualms about holding little black kids on his lap. When little Henry West climbed onto his lap, Santa Claus stared at him, looked at the other children, back at Henry, and whispered in his ear: "Boy, you white or colored?" The nursery school teacher stood by, listening. Little Henry answered: "I want a bicycle."

I have told about the modest campaign to desegregate Atlanta's libraries because the history of social movements often confines itself to the large events, the pivotal moments. Typically, a survey of the history of the civil rights movement will deal with the Supreme Court decision in the *Brown* case, the Montgomery bus boycott, the sit-ins, the Freedom Rides, the Birmingham demonstrations, the March on Washington, the Civil Rights Act of 1964, the March from Selma to Montgomery, the Voting Rights Act of 1965.

Missing from such histories are the countless small actions of unknown people that led up to those great moments. And only by understanding that can we see the importance of the tiniest acts of protest in which we engage, which may become the invisible roots of tumultuous social change.

Sitting in our living room on the Spelman campus one evening, Dr. Otis Smith, a physician, told of his recent departure from Fort Valley, Georgia, an agricultural town of 12,000 people where he was the only black doctor. "Run out of town," he smiled. "It sounds like something out of an old Western movie."

Dr. Smith had been a star athlete for Morehouse College, then a student at Meharry Medical School in Nashville, when he accepted an offer from the Georgia Board of Regents to help pay for his last year in medical school, in return for a promise to spend fifteen months in a rural area of Georgia.

Fort Valley, in Peach County, seemed a likely place. The last black doctor in town had died several years before, leaving blacks there (60 percent of the population) at the mercy of those humiliations that often accompanied white doctor–colored patient relations in the Deep South: entrance through the side door, a special "colored" waiting room, and sometimes the question "Do you have the money?" before a sick call was made to the house.

Otis Smith made a down payment on a home, hung out his shingle, and in no time at all his office was full. But when he showed up at the Fort Valley hospital, for his first obstetrical stint in the town, the two white nurses stared at him and left the room, with a black woman in labor on the table. He delivered the baby with the aid of a black attendant.

One evening, while he was talking on the telephone to a patient who needed his help, a white woman cut in on the party line, and demanded that he get off so she could speak. He told her he was a doctor talking to a patient. She replied: "Get off the phone, nigger." Perhaps an old-style Negro doctor would have responded differently, but the young Dr. Smith said: "Get off the phone yourself, you bitch."

He was arrested the next day, brought into court before his attorney even knew that the trial was going to take place, and sentenced to eight months on the chain gang for using obscene language to a white woman. In prison, facing the chain gang, he was offered his release if he would leave town immediately. Dr. Otis Smith decided to leave, and the next day, the black people of Fort Valley were without their doctor.

In Atlanta, as all over the South, in the "quiet years" before the eruption of the sit-ins, there were individual acts, obscure, unrecorded, which kept the spirit of defiance alive. They were often bitter experiences, but they nurtured the anger that would one day become a great force and change the South forever.

Julian Bond graduated from Morehouse College. He was one of the founders of the Student Nonviolent Coordinating Committee (SNCC). He was elected to the Georgia legislature in 1965 where he served until 1987. He narrated both parts of the "Eyes on the Prize" documentary on the civil rights movement. He recently coedited *Gonna Sit at the Welcome Table* and is the author of numerous articles on civil rights. He is currently a lecturer in the Department of History at the University of Virginia.

A Participant's Commentary—The Voting Rights Act of 1965

Julian Bond

Julian Bond discusses the impact of his early life in generating a strong interest in issues affecting African-Americans (or "the race," as he puts it). He describes how he became involved in sit-ins and became one of the leaders of the Student Nonviolent Coordinating Committee (SNCC) in the early 1960s.

Bond was personally involved in voting rights litigation as the Georgia legislature expelled him twice from the seat to which he had been duly elected. In 1981, Bond took legal action to help create a majority Black voting district in Georgia.

The Voting Rights Act of 1965 (the Act) is generally agreed to be the "most effective civil rights legislation ever passed." It protects the "crown jewel" of our democracy, the right to vote.

Before the Act became law, Blacks in the southern states were helpless victims of a century-old system of legally sanctioned white supremacy, enforced by private and state terror. In all but a few isolated instances, Blacks were excluded from voting and had no influence in the conduct of public affairs.

The years since 1965 have seen a dramatic if slow reversal of this exclusion. Within the first two years following passage of the Act, the percentage of Blacks registered to vote in my home state of Georgia almost doubled, from 27.4 percent to 52.6 percent. Today, twenty-five years after the Act's passage, Blacks have begun to participate in electoral politics at levels nearly equal to those of whites.

What follows is an account of the author's experiences with voting rights litigation and the Voting Rights Act, as beneficiary of the Act's provisions and as intervenor and plaintiff—one of many who have used the Act to advance civil rights for all.

Like many southern Black youth of my generation, I came to the civil rights movement from college. I grew up on Black college campuses—from my birth in 1940 while my father, the late Dr. Horace Mann Bond, was president of Fort Valley State College for Negroes in Georgia, from 1945 until 1957 on the campus of Lincoln University in Lincoln, Pennsylvania, where he served as the first Black president, and in Atlanta from 1957 forward in university housing owned by Atlanta University where my father ended his career as dean of the School of Education.

While local and state racial politics often froze the Black college, its faculty and administrators and students, into political inactivity and grudging acceptance of the status quo, the best schools served to keep alive the rich tradition of protest and rebellion that existed throughout the Black communities since slavery.

That was my experience at Fort Valley, Lincoln, and in Atlanta. At three, I posed with my sister Jane, my father, and noted scholars E. Franklin Frazier and W.E.B. Du Bois, while the elders pledged us to a life of scholarship. At seven, I sat at

Paul Robeson's knee while he sang of the "Four Insurgent Generals." NAACP Executive Secretary Walter White visited the Lincoln campus, escorted by an impressive phalanx of black-booted Pennsylvania state troopers whose shiny motor- cycles were surely designed to attract the attention of small boys and impress them with the importance of the white- looking Black man whom they protected. When my father came to Atlanta University, I entered Morehouse College, the alma mater of Martin Luther King, Jr. and Sr., and both Kings and a long list of race men and women dedicated to the uplift of their people were paraded before us in daily, required sessions of morning chapel.

But school alone did not fuel my civil rights fires; my father's house and my mother's table served daily helpings of current events, involving the world and the race, and the race's problems and achievement were part of everyday dis- cussion.

When fourteen-year-old Emmet Till was kidnapped, beaten, castrated, and murdered in Mississippi, it terrified fifteen-year-old me. I asked myself, "If they will do that to him, what won't they do to me?"

When, in early February 1960, a schoolmate approached me in a café and invited me to join him in organizing Atlanta's first sit-in demonstrations, I—like so many oth- ers—was ready.

He showed me a story in that day's *Atlanta Daily World;* it said something like "Greensboro Students Sit-in for Third Day."

"Have you read this?" he asked.

I answered a quick "Yes," initially believing the question was a test of whether or not I read a newspaper. But it was the story he was interested in.

"What do you think about it?" he asked, pointing to the Greensboro story.

I had read it. It told how four students from Greensboro's

North Carolina A&T University had entered a Woolworth's Department Store on February 1. After making purchases elsewhere in the store, they took seats at the segregated lunch counter, but were refused service. They sat there until the store closed for the day, returned the next day with reinforcements, and now were occupying every seat at the counter.

"I think it's great," I enthused.

"Don't you think it ought to happen here?" he countered.

"It will happen here," I said. "Someone will make it happen here."

"Why don't we make it happen?" he countered. "You take this side of the café and I'll take the other," he said, and we did, gathering recruits as we went from booth to booth.

In a few days we had gathered students from each of the schools making up the Atlanta University Center—Clark, Morehouse, Spelman, and Morris Brown colleges, Atlanta University, and the Interdenominational Theological Center.

Word of what we were planning reached the ear of Atlanta University President Rufus Clement; he called us in and told us that much was expected of Atlanta students. He urged us to present a statement of purpose to the Atlanta community before we committed any action. Another student and I wrote "An Appeal for Human Rights," borrowing liberally from a pamphlet, *A Second Look at Atlanta,* published by a group of young Black businessmen and intellectuals. Dr. Clement arranged to have our version printed in Atlanta's three daily newspapers. It created a sensation.

Georgia's governor, S. Ernest Vandiver, said it read "as if it had been written in Moscow, if not Peking." It gave the student group that launched Atlanta's sit-in demonstrations a name, "The Committee on Appeal for Human Rights."

In early May, we received a letter from Martin Luther King and the acting executive director of his organization, the Southern Christian Leadership Conference, inviting us to a "student-centered" meeting over Easter Weekend in Raleigh, North Carolina.

We went to Raleigh, found three hundred other like-minded young Black people there, and founded the Student Nonviolent Coordinating Committee.

From 1960 until the fall of 1965, I worked for the Student Nonviolent Coordinating Committee (SNCC), the organization that played an important and often overlooked role in pre-Selma southern voter registration organizing and in increasing public consciousness of the South's blatant denial of the right to vote and the terror used to enforce white supremacy at the ballot box.

SNCC sent field secretaries to Selma in 1963, two years before Martin Luther King Jr. arrived. With the National Association for the Advancement of Colored People (NAACP) outlawed in Alabama and the late Medgar Evers the only full-time civil rights worker in Mississippi, SNCC field secretaries were often the only professional organizers seen in many rural southern communities between 1961 and 1964.

In Selma, as elsewhere, SNCC workers helped to bolster indigenous leadership and local organizations, like Selma's Dallas County Voters League. By 1965, SNCC's organizers had conducted dangerous voter drives in parts of the Black Belt in Mississippi, Alabama, Arkansas, and Georgia; had forced a reluctant Department of Justice to take its first tentative steps toward protecting voter registration workers; and slowly had laid the groundwork for the political revolution that would sweep the South.

After SNCC worker John Hardy was pistol whipped by the Walthall County Mississippi, registrar John Q. Wood and arrested for disorderly conduct, the Justice Department sought and won a temporary restraining order to block Hardy's prosecution. On January 1, 1963, SNCC field secretaries Robert Moses, Sam Block, and Hollis Watkins filed suit in Washington against FBI Director J. Edgar Hoover and Attorney General Robert F. Kennedy seeking an injunction ordering enforcement of the Federal Code which made it a crime to harass or intimidate those seeking to vote. On April 3, 1963, Assistant Attorney General John Doar sought an injunction ordering officials of Greenwood, Mississippi, to vacate the sentences of eight SNCC workers as illegal interference with the right to vote. At best, the federal government was an unwilling bystander passively observing the growing southern voting rights movement, becoming a reluctant participant only when violence seemed imminent or actually occurred.

The origin of the southern voting rights movement can probably be traced to slavery. No recounting of the modern movement can afford to ignore the heroic and often unheralded work of the South's Black citizens and the organizers who assisted them.

The year following the passage of the Voting Rights Act, I was a plaintiff in a case that reached the U.S. Supreme Court that strongly reinforced the right to vote.

The case, *Bond* v. *Floyd,* grew from my first election in 1965 to the Georgia House of Representatives. Federal lawsuits had reapportioned the Georgia General Assembly, overturning a legislature where cows and horses were better represented than human beings.

The Court ordered new, equal districts created in urban Fulton County and ordered elections for a one-year term. As a successful candidate for one of those new seats, I was to take the oath of office on January 10, 1966.

On January 3, 1966, Samuel Younge Jr., a Tuskegee Institute student and SNCC worker, was shot and killed while trying to use the segregated bathroom at a Tuskegee service station. Spurred by his murder, on January 6, 1966, SNCC became the first civil rights organization to link the prosecution of the Vietnam War with the persecution of Blacks at home.

SNCC issued a statement that accused the United States of deception "in its claims of concern for the freedom of colored peoples in such countries as the Dominican Republic, the Congo, South Africa, Rhodesia, and in the United States itself."

"The United States itself is no respecter of person or laws," the statement said, "when such persons or laws run counter to its needs and desires."

The statement created a sensation. In the civil rights community, it marked a break in the relationship between the more militant civil rights organizations and the administration of President Lyndon B. Johnson and further widened the gap between SNCC and the civil rights mainstream.

The reaction in the white South was even more severe, including harsh criticism from southern white liberals, such as Ralph McGill and Lillian Smith, whose anticommunism competed with their commitment to equal rights for Blacks.

I was SNCC's communications director, and when I appeared to take the oath of office on January 10, 1966, hostility from white legislators was nearly absolute. They prevented me from taking the oath, declared my seat vacant, and ordered another election to fill the vacancy.

I won that election and was expelled again; by the time I approached a third election, this time for a two-year term, I had filed suit in federal court.

Judge Griffin Bell wrote the majority decision for the three-judge court that refused to overturn the Georgia legislature's decision to deny me the seat I had already won twice.

His decision was in turn overruled by a unanimous U.S. Supreme Court, and a year after my first attempt, I became a member of the Georgia House of Representatives.

Before the three-judge court, I was represented by Charles Morgan Jr. of the southern regional office of the American

Civil Liberties Union (ACLU) and Howard Moore. For the appeal to the Supreme Court I secured the services of Victor Rabinowitz and Leonard Boudin.

I had never been to the Supreme Court; as I sat and listened to Georgia's Attorney General Arthur Bolton argue that Georgia had a right to refuse to seat me, I found myself nodding in agreement. Rabinowitz elbowed me and whispered, "Stop that!" Following Bolton's argument, the justice asked a few questions. When Justice Byron White asked, "Is that all you have? You've come all this way, and that's all you have?" I knew we had won.

Chief Justice Earl Warren's decision in *Bond* v. *Floyd* was more than a victory for the First Amendment; it was a reaffirmation of my constituents' right to free choice in casting their votes.

I ran afoul of Judge Bell again in 1971. Once more the unfettered right to vote was at issue; once again, Judge Bell ruled against me.

In *Bond* v. *Fortson,* Andrew Young and I challenged Georgia's general election majority vote provisions for members of Congress. Judge Bell granted summary judgment to the defendants on the ground that the issue was not ripe for review, since neither Young nor I knew if we would ever run for Congress.

Finally, I was party to a suit in 1981 in which the Voting Rights Act's protections were invoked to help create a majority Black congressional district in Georgia.

Busbee v. *Smith* stands as an important landmark in voting rights litigation. In *Busbee,* a federal court found impermissible racial intent in a voting rights case, requiring creation of a majority Black district for the first time. *Busbee* grew from my unsuccessful legislative attempts to create a majority Black congressional district in Georgia. . . .

In a special 1981 session of the Georgia General Assembly,

called to consider reapportionment of legislative and congressional districts, I made several attempts to introduce and pass a reapportionment plan that would have created a majority Black congressional district.

My white colleagues in the Senate and House also introduced a variety of plans—in each one, the Fifth, or Atlanta, Congressional District was drawn in basically the same fashion. In almost all of the plans submitted by white legislators, the Fifth followed the lines drawn in 1971; it stretched from north to south, with part of East Fulton County lying in the Fourth Congressional District. In three plans, Fulton County was divided between Congressional Districts Five and Six. In each plan submitted by white legislators the Black population percentage in the Fifth District remained between 51 and 52 percent.

On August 12, 1981, the State House Reapportionment Committee adopted a plan that gave the Fifth District a Black population of 51.73 percent.

Five days later, I introduced in the Senate Reapportionment Committee a plan that would have created a 73.38 percent Black congressional district encompassing the Black communities of Fulton and DeKalb counties. I had waited until disputes involving eight of Georgia's ten congressional districts were resolved. The eight districts, One through Three and Six through Ten, surrounded Fulton and DeKalb counties, creating a predominantly white doughnut around two heavily Black counties. The hole in the doughnut would be my playground and battlefield.

The Bond Plan's rationale, I told my colleagues, was

> to put together a large, harmonious, homogenous Black community living in southern Fulton and DeKalb counties who share a common income generally. The value of their housing stock is generally the same. Their education level is generally

the same. And most important, their race is almost absolutely the same.

My plan did not affect the eight districts in the (predominantly white) "doughnut" surrounding Fulton and DeKalb counties and covering the rest of the state.

After the Bond Plan was introduced, the chairman of the Senate Reapportionment Committee adjourned the meeting without seeking a vote. On the next day, the committee adopted a Congressional Reapportionment Plan that included the Bond Plan. The chairman cast the sole vote against the plan, in violation of Senate rules, which permitted his vote only to break a tie.

On the Senate floor, the chairman of the Reapportionment Committee—at the urging of the lieutenant governor, Zell Miller—introduced an amendment to the committee plan. The chairman's amendment accomplished two tasks: it split prosperous Gwinnett County between two districts so the county would not overshadow the Ninth, or mountain, districts, where the lieutenant governor lived, and it drew a Fifth District with a 55.74 percent Black population.

I moved to amend the chairman's plan. . . . After failing to adopt five conference committee reports, the General Assembly agreed to a plan with a 57.28 percent Black population Fifth District.

I knew a 57 percent Black population majority meant a 46 percent Black voting minority; because Blacks are, on the whole, younger than whites, equal numbers of Blacks and whites will not produce equal numbers in both races old enough to vote.

I knew too—and subsequently proved in court—that voting in Atlanta had become more racially polarized in the years since Andrew Young had been elected to Congress. The election of a Black mayor in Atlanta in 1972 had decreased the possibility that white voters would cross the color line. Atlanta's first taste of Black power had reinforced the tribal tendencies of white voters, solidifying their bloc vote.

With the assistance of Georgia Republican Senator Mack Mattingly, I sought a meeting with William Bradford Reynolds, the assistant attorney general for civil rights.

When Senator Mattingly was unable to arrange such a meeting, I turned to Senator Paul Coverdell (R.-Fulton), the minority leader of the state Senate. He secured a meeting with Reynolds and he and I flew to Washington.

Reynolds received us graciously, heard our arguments, and imposed a section 5 objection against the Georgia plan. Georgia sought a declaratory judgment against his decision in the Federal District Court in Washington.

With a number of other legislators, I intervened, and *Busbee v. Smith* was joined.

During the legislative debate and the court fight that followed, the proponents of a majority Black Fifth District were abused and scorned.

An *Atlanta Constitution* editorial accused me of creating "a ghetto district" whose representative would be "ineffective." Senator Paul Coverdell was shown in an editorial cartoon in a graveyard, unearthing the coffin of segregation.

Coverdell and legislative Republicans were accused in the media of trying to move Blacks from the Fourth District to the Fifth, solidifying the already Democratic strength of the Fifth while increasing Republican hopes in the Fourth.

Republicans were willing to help Black legislators—all Democrats—create a Blacker, more Democratic Fifth; Blacks were eager to accept whatever assistance was offered, and little was forthcoming from members of our own party.

After trial, the district court concluded that "the Fifth Congressional District was drawn to suppress black voting strength in Georgia."

The arguments against my plan in the Georgia legislature and the trial testimony in *Busbee* are richly illustrative of the congressional arguments that would rage over amending section 2 of the Act a year later in 1982. The *Busbee* arguments are predictive as well of arguments used today to discredit the Act and to limit its effectiveness in enfranchising and empowering minority voters. [In 1993, the Supreme Court rejected so-called racial gerrymandering in a case that originated in North Carolina. In deriding the "bizarre" shape of a district Justice Sandra Day O'Connor concluded that the Constitution did not permit states to construct "odd-looking" districts " 'solely' " for racial purposes."—Ed.]

Those arguments lost in *Busbee;* they deserve to lose today. Racial prejudice and racial prejudice alone motivated the defenders of the final legislative plan. The court found that

- Lieutenant Governor Zell Miller believed keeping white, rural mountain voters in a cohesive district was crucial; keeping Black, urban voters in a cohesive district was not.
- Legislative leadership abandoned its standards for proper reapportionment when considering districts other than the Fifth; the goals of maintaining historical borders, preserving county and city lines, avoiding a Republican Fourth District were all pretexts for discrimination. These goals were ignored when drawing Districts One, Three, Six, Seven, Eight, Nine, and Ten.
- House Reapportionment Chairman Joe Mack Wilson was "a racist" and opposed drawing what he called "a nigger district." Wilson said, "I'm not for drawing a nigger district."
- Lieutenant Governor Miller's stated opposition to the Bond plan for allegedly creating a Republican Fourth District was "suspect." Neither Miller nor any other sen-

ator expressed any fear of Republican domination of the Fourth District; Miller, in fact, approved a reapportionment plan that preserved the Sixth District, represented by Representative Newt Gingrich (R.-Ga.), and supported placing a portion of heavily Republican Gwinnett County in the Fourth District.

Because the evidence of racially discriminatory intent was overwhelming, the court denied Georgia the preclearance it sought.

Intent is difficult to prove; public officials seldom announce that their actions are undertaken for a racial purpose. Such actions may frequently be disguised as having a nondiscriminatory function; judges are reluctant to label white officials as racists to grant relief to Blacks. In 1980, the Supreme Court, in *Mobile* v. *Bolden*, reinterpreted the Fourteenth Amendment standard to require proof of discriminatory intent. Requiring such proof effectively gutted enforcement of the Act.

In 1982, Congress amended section 2 of the Act to prohibit any voting law or practice that results in discrimination, regardless of intent.

Proving intent and result was no problem in *Busbee* in 1981. Both the legislative record, accounts offered in deposition by sympathetic white and Black legislators and legislative aides, the testimony of white opponents of a majority Black district, and newspaper accounts were proof positive of the racial motive of the plaintiffs in *Busbee.*

Today, the Act faces attacks similar to those raised in *Busbee* nine years ago.

Today's neosegregationists argue that majority Black districts set impermissible quotas for minority officeholders and guarantee proportional representation, despite a prohibition against quotas in the amended Act.

93

They argue that majority Black districts "resegregate," creating racial polarization in the electorate, a criticism majority white districts have never engendered.

They argue, laughably, that race has vanished as a consideration in American politics, despite all the evidence to the contrary. These neo-Bourbons say they are color-blind. They are blind, but only to the consequences of color consciousness in American life.

The Voting Rights Act of 1965 has begun to level the playing field for America's racial minorities in politics. It would be foolish to imagine that the passage of twenty-five years has erased the heavy hand of white supremacy from any aspect of American life.

The blatant use of racist appeals in the 1988 presidential campaign and in election contests in Alabama, California, and North Carolina in 1990 demonstrates that race remains a potent factor in our national political life.

Georgia subsequently passed a reapportionment plan the Justice Department found met preclearance standards. In an election in the Fourth and Fifth districts held a month later than the general election elsewhere in Georgia, Representative Elliot Levitas was reelected from the new Fourth and Wyche Fowler was reelected to the U.S. House of Representatives from the new Fifth.

Levitas would later lose his seat to Republican Patrick Swindall. Embroiled in scandal, Representative Swindall lost in 1988 to Representative Ben Jones.

Fowler was elected to the U.S. Senate in 1986, defeating incumbent Mack Mattingly. I became the first candidate in 1986 to announce for the Fifth District seat but lost in a runoff to Atlanta City Council member John Lewis.

Judge Bell became attorney general in the Carter administration. Maynard Jackson, who saw the 1970 Georgia legislature set the Fifth District line one block past his house, served as mayor of Atlanta from 1972 to 1980; in November 1989, he was elected mayor again. He succeeded Andrew Young, who served from 1981 until 1990, and who was a candidate for governor in Georgia's Democratic primary. One of his opponents was Lieutenant Governor Zell Miller, who won in the general election on November 6.

Senator Paul Coverdell was named director of the Peace Corps in 1990. In 1992 he defeated Wyche Fowler and became a U.S. Senator.

There are lessons to be drawn from *Busbee.* They are that racists—whether wool-hat boys from below Georgia's gnat line or sophisticated at college campuses in service to a conservative agenda—will employ any argument to oppose racial progress.

They may be as crude as Joe Mack Wilson in his opposition to "nigger districts" or as clever as an academic in manipulation of fact and misquotation of the record; their racist intent and racist result are the same.

Black Americans fought and died to force their way into the political process and to erect an effective federal apparatus to protect their continued participation in that process.

No American—Black, Brown, or White—can afford to have that right destroyed or its protections relaxed because of the shallow protestations of present-day apologists for yesterday's status quo.

Donna Lopiano is executive director of the Women's Sports Foundation. She received her doctorate from the University of Southern California. Dr. Lopiano has previously served as the University of Texas director of women's athletics and has been a college coach of men's and women's volleyball, and women's basketball, field hockey, and softball. As an athlete, she participated in twenty-six national championships in four sports.

Growing Up with Gender Discrimination in Sport

Donna A. Lopiano

Donna Lopiano was excluded from Little League Baseball at the age of ten, even though she was more talented than the boys she was competing with. Encouraged by parents who did not accept traditional sex-role stereotypes, education and sports became central components of her life.

Dr. Lopiano became director of women's athletics at the University of Texas where she stayed for seventeen years. Now, as director of the Women's Sports Foundation, she has committed her life to gender equity in all aspects of sport.

I never really wanted to be the executive director of the Women's Sports Foundation, or the director of women's athletics at the University of Texas at Austin, or a coach or a teacher. From the age of five, I dreamed of the day that I would pitch for the New York Yankees. And I didn't just dream. I practiced and prepared myself for that career. Every day after school I would throw five hundred pitches against the side of my parents' garage. By the time I was ten, I had developed a rising fast ball, an impressive curve that would drop off the table, and was hard at work on a Bob Turley drop. There was no doubt that I was more than prepared to take the first step in the rites of passage to becoming a major league ballplayer—Little League.

I can remember the Saturday morning when I and a bunch of the "guys" on my street went to tryouts. We were nervous, but I knew that I was good. I remember my intensity—the serious way I threw the ball and swung the bat. I remember how good it felt trying to make my glove "pop" every time I caught the ball. I was drafted number one and was not surprised. I was bigger, faster, more coordinated, and simply better than all of the boys.

Imagine my excitement when we were assigned to a team and lined up for uniforms! My team colors were navy blue and white—Yankee colors! And we were getting real hats, wool baseball caps for which you had to know your head size—not those caps with plastic backs. Everyone knows how important uniforms are to little kids. Well, I was literally trembling with excitement. The moment ranked high as one of the best feelings of my life.

I was standing there, punching my hand into my glove, grinning, when a very tall father came to stand beside me. He held a rulebook that was open to page 14. On the right-hand side of the page were four words that would change my life forever: "No girls are allowed." For the first time in my life, I was told that I couldn't play with my friends. I was devastated. More disappointed than angry. I cried for three months and couldn't even bring myself to go to the park after school to watch my friends play the game I was supposed to be playing.

I didn't really get angry about this terrible occurrence until I was much older. You see, I had secretly rationalized that even if I were allowed to play baseball, I was too small to make it in the major leagues. I rationalized being satisfied with my status as an internationally recognized softball player. That is, until Ron Guidry enjoyed his years of stardom as an all-star pitcher with the New York Yankees. Ron Guidry, 5 foot 10 inches and 170 pounds soaking wet. I have exceeded both those parameters for most of my life. It was hard to take.

My second surge of anger came when I saw the film, *A League of Their Own* and discovered the All American Girls Professional Baseball League. My second rationalization was revealed. I convinced myself that it was okay not to have played for the Yankees because, after all, no woman had ever played baseball. It would be different if some women had a chance to play. And they had.

My anger is not the volatile kind. It's the long-lasting kind that will stew under the surface for a long time. And it's not really about not being able to play for the New York Yankees. It is all about someone telling me that I could not pursue my dream, my most passionate belief about how good I could be and what I wanted to do in life. I am angered about the prospect of any child being told that he or she could not chase a dream—could not even try. I do what I do today because I do not want any little girl to feel the way I felt or to go through life wondering if she could have realized her dream.

Despite the early devastating experience with gender discrimination, I was more fortunate than most girls. At least I wasn't programmed by my parents to limit my dreams to gender-appropriate roles. I grew up with parents who did not know the meaning of sex-role stereotypes. Not because they were not taught these stereotypes, but because their aspirations for their children in terms of educational opportunity and success superseded any notion of traditional male or female roles.

The children of Italian immigrants, both of my parents experienced the subtle and not so subtle pains of ethnic and socioeconomic level discrimination. The Depression of the 1930s prevented both of them from finishing high school and taught them what it was like to be without money and food. They had to go to work to support themselves and to help support their families. They viewed with envy those who had the resources to go to college. They both became obsessed with the importance and power of education rather than money.

Their view of the good life was not material wealth. It was clear that education was the way to gain the respect of your peers. Being a good person and being respected by your peers was the wealth they pursued.

Their lack of educational opportunity created a sensitivity about the importance of education. Their number-one goal in life was to acquire the financial resources necessary to guarantee that their children had every educational opportunity. My father communicated this worry and concern about the importance and necessity of education. My younger brother and sister and I heard about it every day. "You can have everything you want, as long as you go to college and get a good education." This obsession with education overshadowed any need to conform to a sex-role stereotype.

While my father's enduring influence was a focus on my learning, my mother brought an equal gift to the table, a confident, "You can do anything" attitude.

World War II created a situation where my mother was part of the first wave of women employees taking the place of men in factories, earning good wages and proving themselves the equals of men. My mom had "attitude"—the confidence of someone who knew she was good at what she did and could be self-sufficient rather than dependent on any other person. Although she probably didn't think about it at the time, she entered marriage and family life as a choice rather than a preordained expectation or necessity. She transferred that confidence and independence to me simply by her example. I saw, heard, and felt her "attitude" every moment I was with her. To my mom, no task was too hard or goal too high that it couldn't be attempted and conquered. It was okay for me to aspire to be whoever I wanted to be. It was no accident that my first career aspiration was to be the first woman on the moon.

Both of my parents learned from working hard and watching others. After the war, they started a family with my mom staying home to take care of me. My dad worked from early morning to late at night as a waiter and kitchen help for low wages. He and my mom figured it out right away that if they both worked at their own business there would be a bigger payoff than working for someone else. So they started a restaurant.

They understood from experience that financial success meant freedom from all sorts of discrimination. They saw that in a capitalist society, financial success resulted in people respecting you for your achievement even if you didn't have an education. Achieving educational degrees in a capitalist society resulted in the same respect. Being educated increased one's prospects of financial success.

This understanding of the relationship between achievement, financial success, education, and respect was the root of their work ethic. When you were respected for your achievements, people didn't notice your ethnicity as much as they did when you had no visible demonstration of achievement.

To my parents, the educational success of their children depended on reading books. My mother read to me all the time. I did crossword and word puzzles with my mother. So my life was filled with the adventure and joy of books. The oldest of three children born five years apart, I possessed both the junior and senior editions of the *Encyclopedia Britannica* by the time I was seven. I had hundreds of books and was a regular bookworm. I can remember reading three and four books a day and loving every minute of it.

Reading was education. Good grades were education. All of these things were to be rewarded. Dollars for A's. Compliments for finishing books. Applause for education. I learned to love learning because it was so rewarding. My educational achievements made my parents happy, so I wanted to do well in school.

All achievements made my parents happy—even sports achievements. My dad and mom loved sports. My mom played basketball in seventh and eighth grade and she reflected on how good she was simply because she was tall. I grew up proud of being tall and the advantages of size. My dad took me to Yankee games. I grew up on a street with fifteen boys and only one other girl. Sports were an integral part of my life.

Although I could not pursue my dream of playing major league baseball, I was luckier than most girls. My parents found a softball team on which I could play. And it wasn't just any team. This team, the Raybestos Brakettes, was the most famous and well-supported women's softball team in the United States. At the age of sixteen I played in the first world softball championships in Australia and completed a trip around the world. I saw Hawaii, New Zealand, Australia, Manila, Hong Kong, Taiwan, India, Teheran, Italy, France, Holland, Germany, and London. Few girls or women have had such opportunity. I played with that team from 1963 through 1973, through high school and into college. I went to college close to the town where I played softball.

I decided to be a physical educator and coach and eventually an administrator because I loved sports. I wanted to stay close to what I loved to do. I certainly loved teaching sports and physical education and, eventually, administering those same sports programs. I never seriously considered another profession because of this passion for sports.

I went to a state teachers' college to pursue my dream of being a college coach well before athletic scholarships for women were offered—a good decade before. As a national-caliber athlete in basketball and softball and a pretty decent field hockey and volleyball player, all of my national tournament competition occurred outside of school sports. My corporate-sponsored softball team played open amateur softball, and we stayed together to play open amateur basketball and volleyball, too. My finest hockey experiences were as a member of the United States Field Hockey Association club hockey teams.

I was able to take advantage of these unusual opportunities for women of my era because my parents were successful business people. I had my own car. I could afford to buy my own sports equipment and travel to practices that were often far away from my school. I was a member of the "advantaged" class. My parents were right. If you had the money, you could access your dreams. But I was also fortunate enough to be involved with one of the few teams in the country that received extraordinary financial support from a large corporation. In all the teams I played on outside amateur sport, from the age of sixteen through twenty-six, I never played on the same team with an African-American woman, although I did play against a few.

Through the age of twenty-six, sport was my life. School came easy. I did school because I had to. I did sport during every waking moment because I loved to. What I learned in school was what I was told to learn. None of it was meaningful in the sense that I could identify with an experience I had in reality. I did my student teaching as an undergraduate physical education major in the mid-1960s—well before I read my first feminist book, well before I intellectually understood the meaning of sex role stereotyping. I can remember conducting a softball game between my fifth and sixth graders and not giving it a thought that the girls wanted to be cheerleaders. I let them. I did not ask whether any of them had dreams of being a softball player. I acted like all who came before me. I didn't question or push the envelope.

Apart from playing for the Brakettes, gender discrimination in sport lurked around every corner of my life. I wasn't allowed to play for my high school softball team unless I gave up playing for my outside softball team. Every job I held in educational sports, as a coach or administrator, paid me less than my male counterparts. I knew, since entering the field in the early 1970s, that my chances of getting to be the boss were slim to none. At Brooklyn College from 1970 to 1975, as an assistant professor of physical education, I started my career in athletic administration by volunteering for assistant athletic director duties. Eventually I received release time for the assignment. I did this job in addition to coaching three teams and teaching two undergraduate and one graduate theory course.

I was fortunate in that I became a "boss," an athletic director, during a curious one-time window of opportunity for female administrators that occurred during the mid-1970s. The regulations promulgating Title IX, a federal law prohibiting gender discrimination in educational programs, including athletics, had just been issued. High schools and colleges across the country were faced with the requirement of offering varsity sports opportunities for girls and women. Many university athletics programs were headed by football coaches who doubled as athletics directors. They didn't want to have anything to do with women's sports. They didn't value sports opportunities for women and they didn't want to be saddled with the responsibility for developing or paying for them. They simply didn't need the extra work or burden of financial responsibility. At big-time football schools where the football coach/athletics director received whatever he wanted, this meant that the women's athletics programs would be established as a separately administered entity from men's programs and another athletic director hired to run them. The University of Texas at Austin was one such program.

I was only twenty-nine years old; the university hired me on the strength of my educational credentials (an earned Ph.D. in athletic administration), experience as an assistant athletic director (which few women had), and athletic achievements, despite severe reservations that I was a very aggressive "Yankee." I can remember going to my first football game and having an alumnus and major donor stand up and put his hands on my shoulders, saying, "Howdy, you must be Donna Lopinino [sic], our new director of ladies athletics!" Texans really didn't have much practice with Italian names. I responded that I was this person. He smiled and said, "My friend Lorene tells me that you are going to be a very reasonable woman." Lorene was Dr. Lorene Rogers, then president of the University of Texas.

Less than three weeks after being hired, I managed to get into a political maelstrom—although I wasn't aware that my job was endangered until almost six years after the fact. It was a great lesson in the power of knowledge.

It was a difficult time for women's sports, despite the existence of Title IX. Darrell Royal, the head football coach/athletic director at Texas, was the president of the American Football Coach's Association. He had just returned from Washington, D.C., where he met with another football crony who lived on Pennsylvania Avenue, then President of the United States Gerald Ford. The headlines across the country read *Title IX and Women's Sports to Be the Death of College Football.* Fear was rampant that the money required to develop women's sports programs would be taken away from football. John Tower, a Texas senator, had recently offered an amendment to Title IX, that would exempt football and men's basketball from being included in the regulations. The effect of the Tower Amendment, were it to pass, would have been to gut Title IX, since close to 80 percent of all athletic funds were being expended on these two sports.

One morning I received a call from an attorney from Washington, D.C., who was putting together a panel of experts on women's sports to testify before the Senate subcommittee conducting hearings on the Tower Amendment. This lawyer was trying to get ammunition to prove that exempting men's football and basketball moneys from Title IX calculations would virtually render opportunities for two hundred men to play sports uncountable. She was also trying to prove that women's athletics were given next to nothing to exist while male athletes were treated like kings. She was frantic because no college or university would give her their budgets for men's and women's sports. She informed me of her plight and I told her not to worry. I knew Darrell Royal, he had just given me some great football tickets, and I was sure that he would give me a copy of his budget if I asked. I told her that I would call her back.

I trekked across campus to Darrell's plush offices (my office was in the old women's gym built in the 1930s) and asked if I could have a copy of his budget. He said: "Sure, just ask my secretary." And it was a cinch. I went back to my office and called the attorney to assure her that I would send both Darrell's and my budgets. Darrell's budget was a multimillion dollar affair that was thirty pages thick. My budget was one page. I believe the total budget was $70,000, of which $20,000 was my salary and $10,000 was our total expenditures on athletic scholarships. The D.C. attorney was speechless. There was a moment of silence before she asked, "How about coming to Washington to testify before Congress on how your budget compares to your men's budget?" I responded, "I would be honored." All I could think of was calling my mom and dad to let them know and thinking how proud they would be that their twenty-nine-year-old daughter would be testifying before Congress!

I did go to testify, and I didn't lose my job. Fortunately,

Dr. Rogers (the Texas University president) called me the morning I was to leave and told me to do two things that, as I found out, enabled her to defend my actions. First, she said, you must make a courtesy visit to John Tower to explain to him that you are testifying as an expert in athletic administration and are not representing the University of Texas at Austin. Second, she said, in your written and oral testimony, be sure to make the same disclaimer that you are an expert rather than representing the university. I did both things and she was therefore able to defend my actions on the basis of free speech and the fact that I held a university lecturer appointment. University professors were always testifying before Congress as experts in various subjects, she was able to say.

Close call. As I look back on the occurrence, I recognize how important my education was. I had the Ph.D. I was qualified for a university faculty appointment as well as my contract agreement as director of women's athletics. Being a faculty member afforded me considerable protection and was due to the respect in which my degree, my education, was held. On that occasion, the power of my education allowed me to do something that many others, older, wiser and more politically adept, would have never attempted to do. Thank God for the ingredient of naiveté, too.

Finally, what I learned in theory was kicking in because these concepts were finally becoming applicable to my experiences in reality. I had learned in the classroom that power was usually derived from three sources: knowledge, position, and authority. Knowledge is simple. You know more than anyone else about what you are trying to do. Position is simple, too. Am I the "boss" or in a position to dictate or effect change because it is my area of responsibility? Authority is a little more subtle, but not really. Do I have the power of money or influence? A good example is a football booster who gives $4 million to the university. Would the president listen to what he has to say about women's sports? I didn't need to be a rocket scientist to realize that the key to changing the world of sport and to treat women equally would always be a matter of knowing more than those who didn't want women to be treated fairly. Getting into a decent position of power, even if it wasn't the top position, and getting the respect and support of people who are in positions of power and who have money and influence was the next important step.

My seventeen years at the University of Texas as director of women's athletics really allowed me to *practice* in this campus level world of power. My current position as executive director of the Women's Sports Foundation lets me use those skills in a much larger and more powerful context.

On the college campus the authority power group is relatively small—influential alumni, major donors, former trustees (current trustees carry influence by virtue of their current positions). Those in positions of power at the level of vice-president, president, and trustees are also few in number. In the national arena in which I am now playing, the big players are more numerous and both easier and harder to touch. Easier in that you aren't as easily blocked from influencing them with knowledge. Nationally, people get to be successful people because they are master students, eager to learn, listeners—as opposed to local parochial power brokers who use their positions to prevent distribution of knowledge—sheer muscle to prevent getting to anyone's brain. Looking back at my campus days, getting to the right people was a task in and of itself. At the national level, powerful people are easier to get to but harder to deliver knowledge to because they have to deal with so much information that you need the right time, place, and message and person to deliver it. So, campus access to power is an issue of physical accessibility. National access to power is an issue of method of delivery—a much more subtle game—the difference between checkers and chess.

The higher you go in power structures, the more important it is to see the big picture. You need to see where you are going and be able to anticipate all the problems you will encounter along the way to get there. You also need to deal on multiple fronts with ever-changing parameters. One of the most valuable exercises I ever experienced in my professional life was being involved in the development of "Twenty Challenges for the Next Twenty Years," a Women's Sports Foundation blueprint on how those committed to gender equality must act to give back to those following in our footsteps and to ensure that no girl or woman will face unfair barriers to sports participation.

The twenty challenges are based on four simple hopes: (1) that our society will accomplish a basic cultural change toward full acceptance, support and encouragement of girls and women who participate in sports and fitness so that there is no longer a contradiction between being a woman and being an athlete; (2) that we will value men's and women's sports and sports participants equally; (3) that all benefits and opportunities in sports and fitness will be equally available to men and women; and (4) that women will have learned how to use sports and fitness to enhance their health and well-being and that the contributions of participation in sports and fitness activities to their health will be better understood and recognized by all women. In order to translate these hopes into reality, all of us must work on the following challenges:

1. *Role Model Responsibilities.* We must give back to girls following in our footsteps by accepting our responsibilities as role models, conducting girls' sports clinics and speaking to girls on the importance of sports participation and how much fun they can have playing sports. Young athletes will imitate us whether we want them to or not. We must know that our

109

words and behaviors will be repeated by those who admire our achievements. Girls in particular are in need of female athlete, coach, and athletic career role models because the print and electronic media do not regularly transmit these images. We must do more to encourage their participation in sport and sports-related careers.

2. *Parental Education, Support, and Example.* We must encourage all parents to introduce their daughters to sports and fitness participation at an early age, to understand the importance of participation by example and to support the efforts of all girls and women in sports. All parents must be educated about the benefits of sports participation for girls and those factors that encourage girls to start and continue their sports participation. Parents must also know that their children will mimic their sports and fitness participation.

3. *Media Coverage and Images.* We must work to increase media coverage of women's sports, encourage more balanced coverage of men's and women's sports and discourage sexist images and descriptions of female sports participants and the use of unrealistically thin ideal female images for promotional purposes. When girls do not see images of women achieving in sports, they do not envision themselves as sportswomen or believe that society values their sports participation. It is inappropriate for women athletes to be portrayed as sex objects in athletic settings or to be described in a manner that devalues their skill or participation vis-à-vis their male counterparts. Unrealistically thin women in advertisements create unfair pressures on females to be thin. Eating disorders are a serious problem in the general female population and especially in sports where there is an aesthetic value attached to thinness.

4. *Support the Sports Programs of Youth-Serving Agencies.* We must work to ensure that community-based youth-serving agencies receive adequate financial support and make a spe-

cial effort to increase girls' participation in their sports programs. Many children do not have the financial means to participate in sports or play in settings where sports participation is possible. If our children are not provided with the opportunity to play on sports teams or participate in similarly positive youth activities, they will be more susceptible to involvement in gangs or other negative pursuits.

5. *Early Encouragement.* We must encourage others to give books about female sports heroes and sports equipment and apparel to girls at an early age and take boys and girls to watch women's sports contests. Children form values at an early age. Girls must know that sports participation is valued, especially when female athlete images are omitted from traditional media (i.e., girl sports heroes in books, on television and in newspapers). When girls see that only boys receive sports gifts and sports heroes are always men, they assume that sports participation is not as acceptable for girls as it is for boys and there are no female sports heroes.

6. *Girls Playing with Boys.* We must encourage boys and girls to play with and against each other in fairly matched contests and competitive formats in order to encourage respect for each other's abilities. Although boys and girls should have separate and equal opportunities to participate in sports at the highest skill levels because there are real physical differences between genders, there must also be opportunities for males and females to play with each other.

7. *Homophobia.* We must oppose the use of homophobia to discourage girls from participating in sports. The negative use of the lesbian female athlete stereotype discourages girls from participating in sports and is offensive to both heterosexual and homosexual female athletes.

8. *Salary Discrimination.* We must support the principle of equal pay for equal work in the context of purses for professional sports events as well as salaries in sports-related careers

and work to encourage corporate support of female athletes and women's sports. Women athletes and women in sports-related careers are still underpaid in comparison with their male counterparts doing the same jobs.

9. *Professional Teams Sports Opportunities.* We must encourage the establishment of professional sports opportunities for women in the United States. There are limited opportunities for talented female athletes in team and individual sports to continue playing at the elite level without traveling to Europe to participate on professional teams or to compete in individual sports. Professional athletes represent the dreams of young people who love sport. There must be women in these dreams.

10. *Amateur Sports Act.* We must encourage the USOC and our national governing bodies to achieve gender diversity and equity in governance and participation opportunities. Few of our country's national governing bodies are currently in compliance with the 1978 Amateur Sports Act. This law requires nondiscriminatory sport opportunities for girls and women at the grassroots and elite level as athletes, coaches, officials, and administrators. The act also prohibits discrimination in the conduct of programs and contains a specific charge to meet the needs of women and physically challenged athletes through support and financial assistance and adequate representation on the United States Olympic Committee and national sport governance structures.

11. *Title IX.* We must work to ensure that schools and colleges provide female athletes with equal sports participation opportunities, equal educational opportunities funded by scholarships, and the same benefits as male athletes. Few if any schools and colleges are currently in compliance with Title IX of the 1972 Education Amendments Act, which requires that women be provided equal opportunities to participate and receive the benefits of athletic participation in

secondary and postsecondary educational institutions that receive federal funds.

12. *Concerns of Women of Diverse Races.* We must support the issues and concerns of women athletes of diverse races. Sport and sport-related career participation by women of color is significantly lower than women in general.

13. *Concerns of Disabled Women Athletes.* We must support the issues and concerns of disabled women athletes. Sport and sport-related career participation by physically challenged women is significantly lower than women in general.

14. *Employment Discrimination.* We must encourage women interested in sports to pursue sport-related careers and employers to hire more women in these positions. Women in sport-related careers experience employment and salary discrimination at every level and are significantly underrepresented in all sport-related careers. These women represent the future career dreams of many women who love sports.

15. *Right to Participate in All Sports.* We must support the rights of girls and women to participate in every sport, including those in which women have not traditionally participated (i.e., football, wrestling) and those which discriminate on the basis of age. The interest to play traditionally labeled "boys" sports is evident at the high school level. There is also evidence of the interest of mature women to stay involved in sports. All sports should consider the establishment of competitive divisions by age.

16. *Gender Testing.* We must oppose gender testing in sports if it is not done for both genders and if tests are invalid or inappropriate with regard to assessment of physical advantage. Society has traditionally imposed a double standard on girls participating in sports and questioned the gender of women who have excelled in sports. We must not continue to impose this unfair burden on female athletes when their male counterparts remain unquestioned.

17. *Embrace a Healthy Model of Sports.* We must embrace and promote a sports model based on positive values in which all athletes and officials are treated with respect, achieving one's best effort is placed above the value of winning, athletes do not attempt to harm one another physically, and all players, spectators and sports leaders demonstrate the highest standards of sportsmanship and ethical conduct. A significant decline in sportsmanlike conduct at all levels of sports and the valuing of winning over all other benefits of sports participation is well documented.

18. *Promote Research.* We must promote systematic research on the relationships between athletic and fitness activity and the prevention of mental illness among women. Less than 3 percent of all research is done on women. Even less is done on the effects of exercise on the health of women, despite clear indications from limited research that benefits are significant.

19. *Sexual Harassment/Unethical Relationships.* We must empower female athletes to be intolerant of sexual harassment and unethical relationships between sport leaders (i.e., coaches, administrators) and athletes over whom they have an authority relationship. Athletes, coaches, and other athletic leaders receive little or no training in the area of ethical conduct. Typically, incidences of inappropriate relationships between coaches and athletes are seldom reported and, when discovered, perpetrators go unpunished. Given the close relationship between athletes and coaches and the athlete's dependence on the coach for technical knowledge and emotional support, athletes are often confused about inappropriate relationships and too accepting of physical and emotional abuse.

20. *Nonuse of Performance Enhancing Substances.* We must oppose taking any illegal or banned substance which alters the normal functioning of the mind or body for the purpose of

114

enhancing athletic performance. Taking such substances is a decision to cheat, endanger one's health, and encourages others to cheat.

I've grown up with gender discrimination in sports and have chosen to stay in an organization, the Women's Sports Foundation, that keeps me in the middle of trying to get rid of it. These twenty challenges will undoubtedly keep me busy. What has always kept me from being overwhelmed with the magnitude of the task of eliminating unfairnesses to girls and women who want to play sports is the realization that big change is really an accumulation of a lot of many small individual acts over time.

I keep going back to the answers my mother used to give to my seemingly incessant questions and statements: "Mom, it's not fair." "Mom, could you do this?" "Mom, why can't I be an altar boy?" "Mom, why can't I play for the New York Yankees?"

She would always throw the responsibility back on me while offering her assistance. "What can we do?" "How about you doing it?" "If it's not fair, what could you do about it?"

Michael Lerner is editor and publisher of *Tikkun Magazine, A Bimonthly Jewish Critique of Politics, Culture and Society.* He completed his Ph.D. in philosophy at the University of California and subsequently received a second doctorate in clinical psychology at the Wright Institute. He founded the Institute for Labor and Mental Health in the 1970s. His most recent books include *Jewish Renewal: A Path to Healing and Transformation, The Politics of Meaning,* and *Jews and Blacks: Let the Healing Begin.*

Equality Requires a Fight for Recognition and Meaning

Michael Lerner

How does being Jewish affect one's perception of equality? For Michael Lerner, the Nazi destruction of his people raised the issue to a central place in his life. Judaism taught Lerner that each person is "fundamentally valuable and deserving of equal treatment." As a graduate student at Berkeley, Lerner became a civil rights activist. As he grew older, his faith in education as a means of bringing about an end to discriminatory treatment—social inequality—waned. He sought answers in psychology. Lerner now believes that inequalities so prevalent in the treatment of our fellow human beings are rooted in a profound absence of a sense of meaning and recognition in our lives.

I was ten years old when I first began to struggle with what became a central question in my life: "If human beings are equal and deserving of equality of treatment, how come so many people are unable to see that?" For me, that question arose in trying to grapple with the Nazi destruction of my people. A large part of my family in Europe was wiped out by the Nazis, and throughout my childhood I kept asking myself, "How could that have happened? How could people look each other in the eyes and not see that each was fundamentally valuable and deserving of equality of treatment?"

The question was intensified for me by what I was learning in Hebrew school. At ten, we began to study the Book of Genesis accompanied by insights from the stories and commentaries that are called Midrash. I was struck by Midrashic stories related to the creation of what we in those days called "man." The Midrash relates that God formed Adam by taking earth from all corners of the world so as to ensure that no one would say that their land was more valuable than anyone else's, and that God created a single human being so that no one could say that their ancestors were more favored by God than anyone else's. Written close to two thousand years ago, the Midrash was already deeply involved in the struggle for equality.

No wonder, Judaism emerged in the world as the revolutionary religion par excellence—and as a challenge to every existing system of oppression. Every existing religion had as part of its task to justify extant levels of inequality, or at least to convince people that existing inequalities could not be changed. But Judaism told a very different story, a story of the way that inequality had in fact been overcome: the slaves had become free. And we, the Jewish people, were those former slaves, and our task was to tell this story about the possibility of overcoming inequality.

Such a religion flew in the face of the elites of the ancient world, and quite understandably they were angry at the Jews and sought to stir up antagonism toward the Jews among their own population lest the people listen to this Jewish message and begin to question the necessity of their own subordination and inequality.

I quickly learned that the task of the Jew was to challenge the world to live up to this potential for equality and to critique and struggle against all systems of inequality.

It didn't take much for a Jewish child in the 1950s to realize that the world had not yet gotten the message. On the one hand, there was the emerging civil rights movement with its insistence that America's delusion that it was a country based on equality could only be maintained by ignoring the actual plight of African-Americans. On the other hand, there was the growing awareness of the Holocaust and the monumental failure of people to recognize that Jews too were deserving of equal treatment.

What blocked this recognition and what could be done to unblock it?

In the liberal Jewish culture of the 1950s and 1960s the answer that surrounded me and which I quickly bought went something like this: "People have been miseducated to seeing others as unequal. This prejudice is based on ignorance. If people would only encounter each other in some more immediate way, for example in the world of work or in schools or neighborhoods, they'd recognize each other for who they really are, namely, human beings of equal worth, and that would undermine inequality in society."

It was a nice story, and I bought it. For years I identified with the growing civil rights movement, eventually becoming part of pickets, sit-ins, and demonstrations aimed at disrupting the practice of segregation. If segregation could be eliminated and people were able to encounter each other, things would be okay. So I became part of the civil rights movement in the North and cheered on and supported those who fought in the South.

Yet there was a part of me that held back. I went to demonstrations, but I wasn't sure I would want to risk my own physical safety or security, so I held back from getting arrested or being on the front lines. That began to change for me, however, during the Free Speech Movement in Berkeley in 1964. I had arrived on the campus as a graduate student that fall and was determined to get my career going as a professional philosopher. So I was only peripherally interested in "student politics," though I certainly read about and was annoyed by the attempts of the university administration to prevent students who were engaged in the civil rights movement to organize for off-campus activities on the campus. But then a dramatic event happened that would change me, tapping into my earliest issues about equality and the Nazis.

In defiance of campus rules, a Jewish student named Jack Weinberg had set up a card table on campus to distribute information about the Congress of Racial Equality (CORE) and its efforts to organize pickets against local stores that refused to hire Black employees. The administration had sent a police car onto the campus to arrest Weinberg, but when he was placed in the car several hundred students sat down around the car and prevented it from being driven off to take Weinberg to jail. For the next fifteen hours, students used the car as a podium and began a nonstop teach-in on inequality in America and the way the campus administration was supporting it through its ban on campus organizing. I stood at the periphery of the demonstration, listening to speeches, convinced of the students' cause but seeing it still as "their" cause, since I had no desire to get personally involved. But around ten in the evening a group of what seemed to be several hundred fraternity boys arrived and began yelling to "give us our car" and throwing beer bottles and insults at the demonstrators, who responded with nonviolent singing of civil rights songs. The inability of the fraternity boys to understand the justice of the demonstrators' cause, combined with their vulgarity and violence, suddenly made things seem clear to me. Looking at the faces of these fraternity boys, mostly blue-eyed and yellow-haired WASPs, and the faces of those demonstrators, mostly Jews from the East Coast or Los Angeles, made it obvious what I had to do. The Nazis were surrounding the Jews, and I belonged with the Jews. I could no longer stand, because to stand was to be seen as part of the hostile crowd from the standpoint of the demonstrators. So I sat down and became part.

In the next eight years it was relatively easy to sustain this imagery. The Vietnam War brought incredible brutalization to the Vietnamese population as the world's most powerful military machine sought to uproot an ideology by making war against a peasant population in South Vietnam. However much I detested communist totalitarianism (and I unequivocally supported demonstrations against the communist invasion of Czechoslovakia and identified with those in the movement who insisted that we were radical democrats), it was difficult to watch American conduct in the war without feeling that we were the bullies and the Vietnamese people were the victims. More immediately, I was experiencing that directly when police rioted against student demonstrators, over and over again provoking violence, which was then blamed on demonstrators by a media subservient to establishment interests.

Faith in the strategy of education began to decrease, however. On the domestic front, the achievement of integration didn't seem to have the consequences of increasing mutual understanding. In fact, as focus switched from the South to the North, it became increasingly obvious that we in the civil rights movement had been ignoring the obvious reality that as Blacks and other groups mingled in the North, shared jobs and education, there had *not* been a growing sympathy and mutual recognition, but a growing antipathy and anger. Similarly, the willingness of the media to portray the horrors of Vietnam on television had not been sufficient to bring a majority of Americans to sympathize with the plight their government was causing the Vietnamese peasantry.

How could this happen? Why was it that people couldn't recognize others as fundamentally equal to them, as being

121

created in the image of God, and hence as worthy of fundamental respect of treatment?

There was growing support among movement activists for an answer to that question that I found difficult to accept. Many movement activists were beginning to see their fellow Americans as distorted by their growing material success. As America provided opportunities for its various ethnic groups from European stock to achieve material success, more and more of them began to identify with the existing capitalist/imperialist system of oppression. Though there was a ruling elite that benefited disproportionately from the system of oppression, the old class struggle had largely disappeared inside America because the elites had been able to extract enough wealth from the Third World to "buy off" white working people in the United States. As a result, white Americans had developed a major stake in the system. They had acquired "white-skin privilege," the privilege of sharing in the wealth brought home from the Third World by virtue of America's success as the world's leading imperialist power.

Indeed, the white-skin privilege worked to explain why whites in the North turned their backs on Blacks rather than acknowledge them as equal human beings deserving of equal treatment. Ruling elites in the United States had never been willing to grant full employment, recognizing that if they did that working people would be empowered to struggle for a higher portion of the pie and for more power to control their working conditions. But these elites had also become aware of the danger of working-class militancy, brought home to them by the powerful worker struggles of the 1930s and 1940s. They did not want worker power that would accrue to full employment, but they did not want worker solidarity that would accrue with high levels of unemployment. The solution was racism: foster class divisions by ensuring that the worst impact of unemployment would fall disproportionately on Blacks. Whites, then, would benefit from their white-skin privilege by being protected from the business cycle and the worst aspects of the irrationality built into the system. But they would also be unable to achieve full solidarity because they could only sustain the system by turning their backs on Blacks, failing to recognize them as equals deserving of equal treatment. Thus, white-skin privilege gave whites a stake in the system, but it was a stake that could only be maintained by failing to recognize the victims of imperialism around the world and the victims of domestic racism as equals.

In this case, of course, the enemy switched from being ruling elites to the entire American population. And to me and many other Jewish activists, there was something very familiar in thinking about the world in these terms. We the activists were the Jews facing a hostile anti-Semitic world— exactly the picture that many of us had held as children growing up into a community that often taught us that the whole world had abandoned the Jews, that no one had been there for us when the Nazis came, and that wherever we turned we might reasonably expect anti-Semitism to reappear. The anger that many of us felt against the German people for betraying us could now shift to the American population that had, through its white-skin privilege, become insensitive and unwilling to risk its white-skin privilege by opening its eyes and seeing "the Other" as actually human.

Our task in the movement on this theory was to confront people until they were forced to open their eyes—to make it impossible for them to avert their attention. If you could confront them deeply enough, they would see what they were doing. And when that didn't work, movement activists moved to a more resigned and anti-the-people feeling, in which we conceptualized ourselves as unable to win mass support, but nevertheless having the task of remaining true to our understanding by becoming a group committed to what Herbert Marcuse had called "the grand refusal" to participate in an oppressive society. If people were so deeply locked into their white-skin privilege that they could not see that a Jew was a human being in Germany, we reasoned, what we would have wanted of those who could see it was that they would take individual acts of resistance even if they had no hope that those actions would ever change anything. Better to stand true to one's beliefs in the fundamental equality of every human being and die for it than to accommodate to a system based on the denial of equality. So, too, we in America must commit our lives to testifying to that truth even if we could never reach anyone in the process.

Looking back on this position from the standpoint of the 1990s, it still seems to me that there was a fundamental goodness and decency in the impulse that led so many of us to this stance. There was an idealism and caring about others that all too rarely manifests itself in mass movements in the 1990s.

Yet there was also a fundamental flaw that I encountered as I began to talk to those who were supposedly in the throes of their white-skin privilege. My task in the movement was to speak to audiences of "middle Americans" who were not liberals. So, in the late 1960s and early 1970s I began to encounter and talk to many people who were supposedly bought off by the many ways they benefited from imperialism and racism. I went to churches and community centers and city councils and civic organizations. And when I listened to people talking, I found it difficult to square who they seemed to be with our theories. I had expected to find people who were happy, self-satisfied, and smug. There were certainly a share of these. But I also found many people who were deeply dissatisfied with their lives, and it seemed obvious to me that some of their reactionary or racist views were connected to what seemed to me to be an obvious pain in their lives.

I turned to the writings of Wilhelm Reich and his classic

study, *The Mass Psychology of Fascism.* Reich sought to understand what drove people into the hands of the Nazis in Germany, and his analysis was powerful and provocative. Reich discovered a great frustration in the lives of most Germans that was based on the systematic frustration of their sexual needs, and it was the ability of the Nazis to at once speak to those needs and simultaneously channel them into nationalistic celebration and fantasy that provided the fascists with their emotional power. What moved me most was not his answers, but the way he formulated questions. What Reich taught me was that instead of assuming that people were moving to the Right or in support of destructive positions simply because they were evil or selfish human beings, to instead ask, "What legitimate needs might people have which are being frustrated, and do the fascists seem to address those needs in ways more effectively than the Left?"

Whatever the applicability of Reich's analysis of what those frustrated needs might be in regards to the 1920s and 1930s, it was clear to me that repressed sexuality was not the key to understanding America. As Marcuse had already pointed out in his work, American society, far from repressing sexuality, made it liberally available and incorporated it into its attempts to sell its products and accommodate people to the existing social reality.

Although by this point, in the early 1970s, I had completed my Ph.D. in philosophy and was now teaching at a prestigious liberal arts college, I realized that change in America would not be accomplished simply by propagating a smart analysis of the situation. If the key to understanding how people could sustain inequality had something to do with the way their needs were not being met, I had to understand those needs much better. So I returned to graduate school and received a second Ph.D., this time in social/clinical psychology, and then proceeded to join with a group of psychiatrists, psychologists, social workers, family counselors, and union activists to create the Institute for Labor and Mental Health, whose aim was to discover what it was that pushed people to the Right and how that might be countered.

For the next ten years my colleagues and I created groups of working people in which they discussed their lives and the stresses that they faced at work and in family life. Many of these people lived in middle-income suburbs that were giving their votes to Ronald Reagan and to a newly reinvigorated California Republican Party. We went to extraordinary lengths to ensure that we were recruiting people who were quite representative of the population as a whole. We worked though the labor movement, through churches, and through civic groups. People who needed mental health counseling were referred to those services, but our "occupational stress groups" and "family support groups" were explicitly marketed as groups for those who were *not* in trouble but who wished to learn some basic stress reduction skills or family communication skills.

As we listened to these people, we found a tremendous amount of pain in their lives. But the pain was not about not having enough material goods or wanting to protect their "success." Rather, most of these people felt badly about themselves and their lives. At work, they reported the frustrations attendant not only in not having power to control one's circumstances but in having to spend their lives engaged in activities that served no higher goals than to maximize the profits of the owners. People felt they were wasting their lives, and though they compensated for this by demanding higher wages and more material benefits, they also felt that the wages and what they could buy for them were never quite compensated.

The stress and sense of meaninglessness in their work was built into the way work was organized and controlled. Yet most of these people did not blame the job, but blamed themselves for having this kind of work in the first place. They had bought the dominant ideology of meritocracy and had come to believe that anyone who had frustrating work deserved it. We came to see that virtually everyone in America nurtures a self-blaming story that explains to themselves why they deserve the frustrations in their lives, and what they have done or who they are that caused their current failures.

Because they nurture this self-blaming story, few people took their anger into political directions. Rather, they sought to escape from the world of work into personal life, hoping to find compensation for their wasted lives at work. Coming home from work, most working people find it immediately necessary to drown out or repress the terrible feelings that they have been having about themselves and their work all day long. They engage in a variety of narcotizing activities, including alcohol, drugs, or television, or other activities that are perfectly fine in and of themselves, like politics, religion, sports, or aerobics, but that they engage in a frenetic way to drown out the pain they have been having as a result not only of the stress caused by relative powerlessness and the frustration of their abilities to use their intelligence and creativity at work but also as a result of the powerful self-blaming in which they have been engaged.

People who are involved in drowning their feelings about themselves are poor candidates for love and intimacy, and so even though many people do succeed in blotting out all memory of work once they are in family life, they do so only by cutting themselves off from emotional reality. For some, this produces a gradually deepening depression that gives them less and less energy over the years to give to their families or relationships. For others, the repression is only partially successful, and so they find themselves with a tinge of anger or outburst of anger against their spouse that seems irrational and destructive. Not understanding the relationship between the problems in their families and the psychological dynamics that they have been going through all day, people often interpret the tensions they have in their family life as reflecting a deep personal failure in themselves, and this only further convinces them that they are the kind of human being who deserves not to have the fulfillment they want.

These ideas, in turn, play into a childhood dynamic in which they learned as children that in order to be recognized by their parents they would have to suspend who they really are and try to accommodate to their parents' needs for who they should be. Unfulfilled parents frequently seek from their children the compensation from a life that otherwise feels pointless or meaningless. Their children will be the kinds of people that we wanted to be but couldn't. Rather than acknowledge the children for who they really are, the parents desperately need to find within children the being who will make things okay for the lives of parents that feel empty or deeply disappointing. Children find that they must conform to these roles in order to get any recognition whatsoever, but then feel deeply misrecognized since the love they get is too often tied to their ability to present themselves as being someone whom the parents need them to be rather than as their own authentic selves. When such children grow up, they are not surprised to find themselves in work situations that are unfulfilling or with relationships that are in trouble. At some deep level, they had come to expect that they were not the kinds of people who were entitled to genuine recognition and fulfillment.

And yet, most of these people deeply hunger for something more, for a way to find real recognition, for a life that has some transcendent meaning. We discovered an intense hunger for some kind of meaning and purpose that would transcend the selfishness and me-firstism of the competitive market and allow these middle-income working people to connect to a community that had some higher ethical or spiritual purpose. They could not find this in the Left, the Democratic Party, the social change organizations, or the labor movement that assumed their interests were material or that they had become narrowly focused on the needs of those who had been left out of the material successes of the 1960s and 1970s. In fact, what they heard from the Left was that they had "made it" and now the only appropriate thing to do was to focus their energies on bringing in others to have equal opportunities.

But most of the people we were talking to, though they were succeeding economically, didn't feel as if they had made it at all. On the contrary, they felt that they had never been fully recognized for who they were, and they weren't being recognized now either. The Left was telling them they had made it, but their actual life experience was quite different.

The Right spoke to these people by acknowledging that there was a real crisis in families and in human relationships in the society. Using code words like "pro-family" and "ethical and spiritual crisis," the Right was able to signal to them that it recognized that most people were *not* happy with the quality of their lives, that things felt bad, alienating, and insecure. When people listened to the Left, they seemed to be hearing a message that they had already made it and that if they weren't feeling good about their lives they had nobody to blame but themselves and they should seek personal therapy or some private solution. Politics for the Left was about bringing into the society those who had been left out, and if these middle-income working people wouldn't put their energies into that, they had to be seen as racists or xenophobic nationalists. After all, they had their white-skin privilege, and so the only reason they weren't willing to share it had to be because of their disgusting selfishness.

Most of the people I worked with understood this message from the Left and heard it as a form of elitism and condescension. They felt misunderstood and their pain unacknowledged.

On the other hand, when the Right came to power in the 1980s, the actual pain in their life did *not* decrease. Why? The Right had a ready answer: the problems in this society are based on the fact that some groups were seeking special advantages for themselves at the expense of everyone else. These groups were selfish, self-centered, and willing to destroy the fabric of society for their own gain. Whether through participation in crime or only through using the mechanisms of politics and the assumptions of contemporary liberalism, these selfishness-oriented groups had managed to take advantage of everyone else and undermine the good community that the Right might otherwise deliver.

The strategy of blaming a demeaned "Other" had a long history in right-wing movements, and was the center of the anti-Semitism that dominated European history for much of the past eighteen hundred years. In America, the demeaned Other of choice had long been African Americans, and the liberal support for affirmative action and other compensations for the long history of slavery and oppression was now being used by conservatives as proof that this group was getting "too much" and was only out for itself. In addition, the Right turned on gays and lesbians, on uppity feminist women, and on liberals in general as the Other to be blamed.

I don't deny that there may be a significant percentage of hardcore haters in this society whose racism or fear of others has different routes than those I am exploring. I was interested in the sector of the society that was not racist at its core, that had at times been part of the Democratic Party coalition and had supported the initial civil rights agenda, but now had switched to the Right. And what I found was

130

that most people who had taken this move did not take it because of a deeply ingrained racism but because they wished to identify with communities of meaning and purpose that spoke to their pain, and that most of the available meaning-oriented communities tied themselves to the Other-blaming ideologies that people bought as part of the cost of being part of those communities.

The task, I concluded, was to separate out the legitimate meaning-oriented needs from the illegitimate racist forms in which they found expression. What we needed, in short, was a progressive politics of meaning that could speak to the hunger people had for a life that transcended the individualism, materialism, and selfishness of the competitive market and that linked them to a higher ethical and spiritual vision. Such a progressive politics of meaning would provide a way to delink this hunger for meaning from the racist, homophobic, and xenophobic forms in which it had found expression.

Unfortunately, I found little openness to these ways of thinking on the Left. All too often I found liberals and leftists were stuck in a worldview that assumed that anyone who was not with them was not with them for irrational or evil reasons. They found it impossible to imagine that there could be legitimate needs that would lead people into a different kind of politics. Quite the contrary, these Leftists assumed that the agenda of a meaning-oriented politics was to subvert the progressive causes and to lead people to the Right, whether we intended to do so or not. There was a fierce resistance to ethical and spiritual categories, which far too many liberals dismissed as empty shells that were mere glossings on the underlying self-interests that "really" motivated people. Deeply attached to a worldview that assumed that people could only be motivated by material self-interest or by the desire to increase their own individual freedom to get what they wanted for themselves, these liberals felt that meaning needs were either an overt cover for racism and homophobia or a self-deceiving illusion.

Suddenly I discovered myself a nonperson in many liberal circles, since I seemed to be challenging their most sacred beliefs.

I began to realize that the liberal world was into Other-demeaning in a deeper way than I had expected. Just as so many Jews had been so traumatized by our history of oppression that it became extremely difficult to trust that others would ever be sane and morally decent human beings, so many liberals had come to assume that those who were not on their side were fundamentally flawed beings whose needs were fundamentally bad or distorted. Any theory that validated this assumption that the others were evil others, had some credibility, whereas a theory like that on which the politics of meaning was based, precisely because of its fundamental optimism about the nature of those who disagreed with us, was discarded as either naive or dangerous. To be on the liberal side was to be constantly vigilant against the majority who were to be seen as fundamentally selfish. Conversely, the task of liberalism was to appeal to their self-interest.

Of course, in a way I agreed with liberals that the task was to speak to self-interest, but to qualify that by understanding that this self-interest included the need for genuine recognition and for the fulfillment of our need for meaning and purpose in our lives. Yet in another sense, a politics of meaning seemed at variance with the gut instinct of many liberals to demean the other, to assume that people "really" were little proto Nazis who would go in that direction if not restrained.

The irony here, of course, is that I had begun to discover that liberals themselves were unable to maintain a view of equality about people with whom they disagreed. They, too, were seeing others as fundamentally less valuable, as people who were so distorted that they did not deserve equality of respect. Of course, the more sensitive liberals would respond by saying that it was not the people but their views that they didn't respect. And yet, in my actual experience I was encountering something much deeper—a deep pessimism among liberals about the American majority, a pessimism that strangely replicated the pessimism so many Jews adopted after the Holocaust.

Although I have never sided with this pessimism in the case of the Jews, I have a great deal of compassion for Jews who hold that position. The level of oppression and the continuing experiences of betrayal by the Left (documented in my book *The Socialism of Fools: Anti-Semitism on the Left*) had left many Jews bitter and angry at non-Jews that it hardly seemed reasonable to be judgmental about those who had drawn these (in my view) mistaken conclusions. And I am reasonably certain that if I knew enough about the personal history of many on the Left and in the liberal world, I could eventually find a compassionate story that would explain why they too had reached such a deep pessimism about others.

Yet even though I could have compassion and understanding of their conclusions, in their essence they put many people on the Left in a somewhat analogous place to people on the Right—sharing an inability to see others as equally valuable and equally deserving of respect. I know that many people on the Left would insist that their ultimate worldview would lead them to feel that all people are equal and their only quarrel is with the behavior of Rightists, not with their souls or some ontological aspect of their being. But I've heard the same argument being made by people on the Right who maintain that they are only against the behavior of African Americans, homosexuals, or feminists, not against their fundamental being. In my experience, these distinctions don't amount to much. In my actual experience in both worlds, I find people having a great deal of difficulty maintaining their ability to see the Other as fundamentally human and fundamentally valuable.

All this has led me back to the need to understand and address the deep hunger for authentic recognition and for a more meaningful life in this society, and to a politics that seeks to address these needs. I have concluded that the struggle for equality cannot be won on its own terms. No matter how convincing is the demand that all people be treated equally, that demand cannot be won as long as people need to demean others as a way to cope with their own pain. All the powerful education in the world will not undermine this dynamic, nor will legislation or social programs. Rather, we need to deal with the hurts and pains of the American majority, recognizing that as long as they remain in pain they will be easy targets for demagogues who seek to manipulate that pain and direct it against some demeaned Other. I started *Tikkun* magazine and I have sought to popularize a politics of meaning precisely in order to deal with this question, and this has become the center of my current intellectual activities.

I now firmly believe that when we formulate the struggle for equality in terms of increasing people's "rights," we end up getting nowhere. Instead, we need to see equality as the by-product of a society in which each person gets the authentic recognition she or he needs, each person gets the opportunity for meaningful work, and each person gets the opportunity to participate in a society based on loving and caring relationships. Until we focus on the kinds of societal changes that are necessary to achieve these goals, we will never be able to achieve a society that grants substantial equality of respect to all. For over three decades we tested the hypothesis that if we imposed various forms of equality by law, we would eventually see a decline in the demeaning of others that leads to inequality of treatment. But this strategy has failed. Though we have a substantial increase in formal equality, we have not seen a substantial increase in economic equality or equality of treatment in the society as a whole. That outcome cannot be imposed by law, nor will it come about through "education" or good television shows that attempt to "humanize the Other."

Inequality is rooted in a deeper set of societal problems. Unless liberals are able to address this deeper pain that most people are in, they will be unable to get the support they need to create a society based on a recognition of genuine equality. The reason is that equality requires us to see the fundamental worth of others. But that is extremely difficult to do for people who have not been able to see their own fundamental worth.

Yet the treatment necessary is not individual therapy. People's inability to see their own worth is not merely a psychological question but also a social one, based in part on the way society and the economy are organized. A politics of meaning, then, is not a strategy to get people into therapy, but a strategy to struggle for the kinds of societal changes that could produce a society that generates genuine recognition and fosters caring and ethically sensitive human beings.

The task facing me and others who follow this reasoning is to build a movement capable of fighting for such a society. Until we do that, the struggle for equality will never be won. Ultimately, then, we need a movement that can see that every person is created in the image of God, and that includes ourselves as well. But to take this ancient wisdom seriously, and to build a movement that really believes in this principle, may be as hard for many of us as it has been for the society as a whole.

Gayle Pemberton is the William R. Kenan Professor of the Humanities and chair of African American Studies at Wesleyan University. She is the author of *The Hottest Water in Chicago: Notes of a Native Daughter*, as well as *And the Colored Girls Go . . . Black Women and the American Cinema* (forthcoming). She received her Ph.D. in English from Harvard University.

Another "Theme for English B"

Gayle Pemberton

Gayle Pemberton learned about imagination from her father as a little girl and from the poetry of Langston Hughes as an adult. She learned something powerful about what had taken her father out of a small Iowa town: "He had imagined himself someone other than a poor, rural colored boy in an apartheid America." Pemberton believes that one of the basic equalities between black and white today is that we have lost our ability to imagine—to see ourselves in the hopes and lives of others.

Montage of a Dream Deferred is Langston Hughes's multi-voiced, fragmented poem about Harlem at midcentury. Published in 1951, it contains some of Hughes's finest poetry—a terse, poetic version of be-bop filled with complex rhythms, improvisations, and shifts in mood that echoes the intricate timbre of life in Harlem, the black capital of the United States. Some of Hughes's most famous lines are from *Montage*—including the gnomic "Harlem" and its question "What happens to a dream deferred?" Part of *Montage* is a quiet musical interlude, where a Columbia University student writes his "Theme for English B" (Rampersad 1994, 409–10). There are probably some autobiographical dimensions to the poem, as Hughes had been one of very few black students at Columbia in 1921. But his own autobiography is unimportant to this poem; his stay at Columbia was brief as he left in 1922 for Harlem, Europe, Lincoln University, the world, and a career that lasted until 1967. More important, the narrator is every black student asked to imagine the self and write about it.

"Theme for English B"

The instructor said,

Go home and write
a page tonight.
And let that page come out of you—
Then, it will be true.

I wonder if it's that simple?
I am twenty-two, colored, born in Winston-Salem.
I went to school there, then Durham, then here
to this college on the hill above Harlem.
I am the only colored student in my class.
The steps from the hill lead down into Harlem,
through a park, then I cross St. Nicholas,
Eighth Avenue, Seventh, and I come to the Y,
the Harlem Branch Y, where I take the elevator
up to my room, sit down and write this page:

It's not easy to know what is true for you or me
at twenty-two, my age. But I guess I'm what
I feel and see and hear, Harlem, I hear you:
hear you, hear me—we two—you, me, talk on this page.
(I hear New York, too.) Me—who?
Well, I like to eat, sleep, drink, and be in love.
I like to work, read, learn, and understand life.
I like a pipe for a Christmas present,
or records—Bessie, bop, or Bach.
I guess being colored doesn't make me *not* like
the same things other folks like who are other races.
So will my page be colored that I write?
Being me, it will not be white.
But it will be
a part of you, instructor.
You are white—
yet a part of me, as I am part of you.
That's American.
Sometimes perhaps you don't want to be a part of me.
But we are, that's true!
As I learn from you,
I guess you learn from me—
although you're older—and white—
and somewhat more free.

This is my page for English B.

The narrator—a representative of the historic African American odyssey from South to North—encounters the academic ivory tower looming over a black world, and he attempts to straddle the divide. The distance is more than a footpath through Morningside Park or streets off of the A train leading to the Harlem YMCA. It is a territory defined by boundaries of time, history, habit, and the peculiar notion called *race,* which attempts to locate and define interiority through a systematic and crude measure of the exterior.

Our society has measured equality by utilizing those external categories that are available to us—employment, income, housing, education, crime, and health. Statistics can be culled, comparisons made, patterns discerned, futures predicted. In 1942, it was Gunnar Myrdal's two-volume tome, *An American Dilemma,* that classified the boundaries of "the Negro problem." In 1992, fifty years later, Derrick Bell's *Faces at the Bottom of the Well: The Permanence of Racism* and Andrew Hacker's *Two Nations* illustrate that no matter how the statistics are read, inequality and racism are ingrained in society in a complex pattern that is not adequately understood or likely ever to be undone.

Langston Hughes's young narrator cautiously dares to "dream a world" (Rampersad 1994, 311), to imagine himself part of a mutuality called American. Like W.E.B. Du Bois, who confidently invoked Shakespeare, Balzac, Dumas, Aristotle and Aurelius, all of whom joined him "graciously with no scorn nor condescension" (Du Bois 1986, 438), Hughes's narrator finds Bessie, bop and Bach. He knows that black identity is a cultural amalgam. And his theme reminds his teacher that white identity is, too. In the face of the inequality that is signified by his walk from a segregated Upper West Side Columbia to the black Harlem YMCA, the narrator nonetheless assigns himself an equal share of the possibilities of imagination. "That's American," he says.

The last year has seen an enormous amount of videotape, film, print, and thought devoted to retrospectives on 1954 and the Supreme Court *Brown* v. *Board of Education* ruling. Hindsight has not clarified the debate among and between blacks and whites of the utility of school integration then or now. Neither have schools, or neighborhoods—or our society—really become integrated. Regardless of statistics that prove and disprove, sometimes simultaneously, black advancement in the past forty years, there are those who believe that the current state of black America more closely resembles the 1890s of *Plessy* v. *Ferguson* —the ruling *Brown* overturned—than a stage on the road to equality. Still others argue that the proverbial playing field is now level and that race-blind economic, education, and employment practices are all that is needed to save the union. The reality is doubtless somewhere in between these extremes.

It might well be that the world of cautious hopefulness characterized in "Theme for English B" is much, much farther away from us today than time or any statistical measurements can reveal. The Harlem of *Montage of a Dream Deferred* may have been in decline when Hughes wrote the poem, but the 1950s set the stage for the last half century's debate on race. There was black optimism following World War II that led to rejoicing over the potential of *Brown* and emerged in full force in the 1950s and 1960s civil rights movement. Technological wonders and the presence in the White House of a five-star general helped create a sense of hopefulness and progress for white Americans—the Cold War and Joseph McCarthy notwithstanding. The 1950s as a "golden age" for white Americans is attested to by the decade's current popularity among political conservatives and pundits.

But what about the *imagination* today? Coloring, with hope, the pages of our themes and dreaming of a better world was fundamental to the survival of black Americans during slavery and through this bloody twentieth century. Despite the statistical reality of outward inequality we could believe we were equal in imagination—perhaps even superior. This is cold comfort and filled with Pyrrhic victories. But for many black generations the inventions of the mind that ranged from political theory to fiction and jazz, to speech, style, and religion, all suggested a vitality of spirit and imagination equal to any group on earth.

When my sister and I were small and too curious about circumstances decidedly none of our business, our parents would encourage us "to use our imaginations." Our interests were piqued by our parents' cryptic remarks about friends, relatives, or finances. This lent an air of mystery to the commonplace for my sister and me, and we amused ourselves by following their orders, becoming detectives poring over minutiae—with magnifying glasses. Our play satisfied our parents because if we ever came close to discovering the real truth, they never let us know. The game was all, and we were spared information—usually about sickness, divorce, or death—that would have unfairly moved the focus of our parents' concern from the victims and the problem to two unsettled children. Mrs. Jones might have cancer, but my sister and I separately had created fantasies and *films noir* with castles, real and fake toads, and an occasional cigarette-smoking babe hanging on to a duplicitous private eye. It was fun.

Other circumstances calling for the use of our imaginations were more taxing. On Memorial Day—Decoration Day as we called it—my family would drive to my father's birthplace of Clarinda, Iowa, and place flowers on and otherwise attend the graves of his family members. Clarinda is a "don't blink, you'll miss it" American town that in the nineteenth century had things to do with livestock, rivers, and railroads. Glenn Miller was born there in 1904. My father was born four years later. Daddy loved jazz and occasionally had good words for white swing bands, but he never mentioned Miller as someone he knew. This, I assume, meant that the Millers moved before Glenn went to school, or that even in a tiny town four years is much too great an age chasm for there to be acquaintanceships, particularly across racial lines.

I loved car trips, even if it meant the destination would be Clarinda—where the only family left there would remain for eternity. We drove from Kansas City, Missouri, on B roads, through hamlets and towns, crossing into Iowa and then, Clarinda, less than an inch away from Missouri on the map and the seat of Page County. Like clockwork, as we passed through Maryville, Missouri, on the way to Clarinda, my father would tell us of lynchings there and a subsequent black exodus out of town. I would break into goose bumps looking out the window and silently pray that we, too, would make it out of town safely. The cemetary would be waiting for us and the many others—mostly white—who trekked there on Decoration Day. My father would pick up flowers from the florist and vases at the cemetery office. Then we would drive past Clarinda's dead population—guaranteed to be larger than the living one—trying to remember the site of the family plot.

I have no recollection of participating in any of the tending of the graves. I believe my father did everything himself, from clearing the grass and dirt, to washing the headstones, to pumping water for the flowers and placing them on the graves. I spent most of the time looking at birth and death dates, calculating ages in this modest cemetery.

We never began our journey home until we drove through the town. My sister and I slumped in the back seat of the car, feigning invisibility, as my father slowly drove up and down the streets, staring at houses and people on porches staring at us. He never stopped. He pointed out houses and said the so-and-sos had lived there. But who they were was a mystery to my mother, my sister, and me. How could we care, and if it mattered, why didn't Daddy stop? The driving was part of the ritual: the black son, complete with family and tail-finned car, returned to pay homage to his forebears.

I became claustrophobic in an automobile going five miles an hour through dead streets, and I would entreat my father to go faster—and away. But he persisted, carrying out his own plan. I could not abide the sensation of being watched as my father searched porches for faces he had left before World War I began. And I did not want to participate as a spectator, either, looking at mostly white people sitting still on rattan rockers and wooden swings as if posing for midwestern versions of Dorothea Lange and Walker Evans 1930s photographs.

I think about our Decoration Days that were so full of symbolism and ritual. The trip meant that we were literally leaving a city I disliked and longed to escape, even if the journey was backward in time toward memories and faces known only to my father. Our flowers were not reserved for dead military men; no miniature flags fluttered in the late spring wind—except for Uncle Pearce, who had served in World War I. Rather, flowers brightened the headstones of warriors of the other, more enduring war—the one in black and white. Advancing at five miles an hour in our Buick, looking out and being looked at, reinforced the abysmal distance between blacks and whites that peppered my father's memory and that dominates the racial scene today.

I now realize why my father took us to Clarinda. He had broken all the rules and expectations of what he was supposed to have become. He had *imagined* himself someone other than a poor, rural colored boy in an apartheid America. He had become neither rich, Glenn Miller, nor president of the United States, but he had worked himself through the University of Minnesota and became a race man. He was celebrating—and rightly so—the imagination.

The rest of us were spectators, not witnesses, to each other on those Decoration Days of the past. Such spectatorship defines what used to be called euphemistically *race relations*. It is so easy to look upon each other and see only strangeness when we reek with familiarity. Now, in this country, the imaginations of both blacks and whites are equally incapable of taking us to such a shock of recognition. Media fascination with the "pathological" black family, man, woman, neighborhood, athlete, and entertainer; the ongoing celebration of the First Amendment in defense of racial hatred; and the periodic pseudo-scientific proofs of black inferiority, like *The Bell Curve*, written by an Iowan—all in the face of presumed white "normality"—suggest that we all are, like my family on its journey to Clarinda, moving backward. But unlike those journeys, it is unclear what our present regression seeks to celebrate, to remember or recover.

In Clarinda, my father bathed in flowers the graves of the women who had raised him: his grandmother, Carrie, and his mother, Phalbia. There were other graves to decorate, too: of bachelor uncles who, like Faulkner's McCaslins, taught my father to whittle and fish. His father, long dead and buried in some unknown place, had been a victim of racism, his talents and intelligence finding no home within the restrictions of this culture. It was his mother—alone and in retreat from her abusive husband—who worked jobs far beneath her own talents in order to send my father and aunt to college.

Whenever I think the nineteenth century was a long time ago, I am reminded that my father was in elementary school less than fifty years after the end of the Civil War—roughly equivalent to a contemporary second grader's distance from World War II. Fifty years is ancient history to the second grader, and I'm sure my father spent little time as a child thinking about the Civil War. But the passions of war do not disappear so quickly. They reverberate in our own times and hover around how we write history, celebrate anniversaries of victory, make trade policy, or decide what brand of automobile to buy. The short fifty years between the Civil War and my father's second-grade life was made apparent one Saturday afternoon when my sister and I were adolescents. My father had said something about Denmark Vesey—who had led an important slave revolt in the early nineteenth century. My sister asked who Denmark Vesey was. Daddy was surprised and outraged, wondering in turns what was wrong with her school, what was wrong with her, what was wrong with him. How could she not know about Denmark Vesey, Nat Turner, Harriet Tubman, Sojourner Truth, and the whole pantheon of enslaved and free black men and women who fought for freedom?

He feared that the history of these people and their deeds would disappear from the face of the earth. Most galling, perhaps, was the certainty that their imagination—which had engendered a host of logical and creative answers to oppression and self-delusion—would die, too, unless preserved in our memories. But then my father was five years old when Harriet Tubman died. He wasn't learning black history in school; he was gathering current events.

As I write this, a six-year-old white friend is visiting my household. She picked up a *Jet* magazine—the small format, black news and photo weekly—and looking at the photographs of black men and women throughout announced that "it's all Martin Luther King." I believe my father would have understood the semiotics of the revelation and doubtless his distress would have recalled the Denmark Vesey moment some forty years earlier. My sister had no knowledge or image of a particular black heroic figure; for this six-year-old, one particular black heroic figure delineated the whole race. Both events bespeak our country's willful lack of imagination in dealing with race.

One late fall day not long ago, I had a craving for grease and salt—not the kind one can find at home—but the ultimate cholesterol rush of a fast-food chicken joint. It was about five o'clock and only three other patrons were in the shop. I ordered my two-piece dark meat with biscuit, and as I waited I overheard the conversation behind me. A black man in work clothes, somewhere between twenty-five and thirty-five, was sitting with two children—a girl about ten and a slightly younger boy. I assumed they were his, but I don't know. He was helping them do their homework, and as I left he said to the small boy, "See, that wasn't as hard as you thought."

For a brief second, I wanted to interrupt them—to say something about how wonderful it was to see him doing that. I did not, however. And I chided myself for even thinking about it—for being sentimental, for conforming to popular imagery in deciding that some great and significant and *public* uplifting activity was occurring. He may have been the children's father; he may or may not have lived with them. This may or may not have been a divorced father's ritualistic Tuesday night treat. The scenarios are infinite. What mattered was that he was helping the children—with patience and kindness—and that a teacher in some elementary school had the nerve to give homework in the first place. No "film at eleven" with newscasters giving a condescending "aww" in unison: this was a sliver of three black lives lived. The only spotlight on them came from my headlights as I backed away from the chicken joint.

I thought about the scene all the way home and through the night, long after the chicken was gone. It was another scene involving imagination. I had lost mine; the man was trying to instill it in the children. If I had followed my first urge to commend the man for his attention to the children, he might well have wondered what was wrong with me? Was this a strange "come on" or simple rudeness? My intrusion, as a stranger, would have been one problem. But more serious was the implication that he should be congratulated for *not*

147

being a stereotype. As passing encounters between black and white go, few are more offensive than this. As passing encounters between black and black go, few are more unjustifiable.

My impulse to speak to the man also arose from a desire to bear witness, in the largest spiritual sense, to the good work he was doing—a witnessing divorced from the stock images that fuel the country's notion of what black people do, and who we are. Epiphanic moments can occur in chicken joints. They can also arise from lines like, "See, that wasn't as hard as you thought."

Explaining all this with my intended compliment to the man would have trespassed upon the time the three had together. I might have become an object lesson about crazy strangers in chicken joints. Such information is always educational and useful, but it was probably not a part of the children's assignment that night. Finally, I reasoned that it was wise to appreciate the scene and to say nothing to the participants because they were not performing for *me*. But late that night, my imagination took off, dreaming of millions of men, women, and children in chicken joints across the nation, on "Tuesday homework night" celebrating with wing, leg, breast, and thigh the reality that it isn't as hard as we think.

Equality may exist between black and white concerning the imagination: we have all lost it. Elementary and secondary school teachers report that their charges are increasingly unable to make up a story or draw something from their imaginations. Worse still, fewer and fewer children read often or well, while the rest rely on visual imagery to conceptualize almost everything. Television advertising and programming, computer games and sports take the place of tales and incorporeal thoughts. The phenomenon isn't new; how else could I have imagined the cigarette-smoking babe and private eye?

But television and movies were theater, not reality for me, when I was a child.

Black and white children, privileged, discarded, and abused children respond accordingly to this cultural drift, coloring their pages in the one or two colors offered by media, government, school, and their own families. What they imagine themselves to be and to become is defined by material space: they are what they occupy and have. Hence, it should surprise no one that while privileged children are involved in ongoing computer fantasy games, their inner-city counterparts are engaged in a real-life urban game of *Lord of the Flies*. The common denominator of both is violence; the dead of the former remain quick, those of the latter do not.

Adults in black and white display the same tendencies. Bumper stickers read, "The one with the most toys at the end wins." A husband and wife, having redesigned and redecorated their kitchen as a showplace of high-tech beauty and efficiency, announce that they can't wait to redo it again. Children kill each other over expensive sneakers, and imaginations are for sale at the CD-ROM and video game counters. Multimillionaire athletes pout.

The Christmas gift request of Hughes's black college student was modest: "a pipe . . . or records—Bessie, bop, or Bach." It is easy to say and see how a fixation with the material has left us bereft of the imaginative. How else can we explain the current anger and fury of a culture so overflowing with material wealth and so economically unequal? What prompts the viciousness of our driving etiquette, our impatience when standing in lines, our scapegoating of have-nots for the unarticulated and inarticulate wishes of the haves? Under such circumstances the guarded hope of mutual discovery, imagination, and life—of the mind, soul, and heart—found in Hughes's "Theme for English B" is an indecipherable hieroglyph from a long lost age.

149

Bibliography

Du Bois, W.E.B. 1986. *The Souls of Black Folk.* In *Du Bois: Writings.* New York: Library of America, Literary Classics of the United States.
Rampersad, Arnold, and David Roessel. 1994. *The Collected Poems of Langston Hughes.* New York: Knopf.

Part II

From the Beginning

Henry Gonzalez (D.-Tex.) was elected to the House of Representatives in 1961. He recently served as chairman of the House Committee on Banking, Finance and Urban Affairs. In reference to the savings and loan scandal of the 1980s, the *Almanac of American Politics* calls Gonzalez "utterly independent of the savings and loan lobby ... the big banks, the securities industry, the investment bankers." He has been particularly interested in housing discrimination issues during his long and distinguished public career.

From Participation to Equality

Henry Gonzalez

Congressman Henry Gonzalez grew up in Texas during a time when the Ku Klux Klan was very powerful in state politics. His first experience in local government was working on juvenile crime. He then focused much of his energy on housing discrimination in San Antonio. Gonzalez was first elected to office in 1953 and became a member of the House of Representatives in 1961.

In this essay Representative Gonzalez emphasizes housing issues and economic policymaking. His discussion of decision making at "the Fed" demonstrates how equal opportunity to participate in the political processes that affect basic economic policy is denied.

Local Government: "The Equal Right to Participate"

American educator and author Henry Van Dyke once said, "Democracy declares that men unequal in their endowments shall be equal in their right to develop these endowments." Equality demands opportunity and the right to participate in all aspects of education, work, and society—equality flows from participation. When one is denied participation in education, in the marketplace, in free travel, and most importantly in jobs and economic opportunity, through explicit or implicit discrimination on the basis of a fact of one's birth, whether it be race, ethnicity, gender, religion, sexual preference, or alienage, there can be no equality. There is no discrimination more vile than that which denies a man or woman the opportunity to participate in the most basic institutions and pursuits of life.

Equality, however, does not equate with privilege. Equal opportunity must be the standard, not special consideration. For if special consideration is given on the basis of a fact of one's birth, then we have only justified the discrimination that has been exercised throughout the history of our country. But even to participate in life's pursuits, there are those who need assistance. It's not enough to open the door to education if some children cannot reach even the first step, and yet that is what so many people who come from poverty and segregation face. While those who have enough school supplies, who have had an adequate breakfast, and who have shoes to wear might be able to walk up to and through the open door of education, others are lacking in the basic necessities needed to take even this first step. For there to be true equal opportunity, everyone must be allowed to begin at the same starting point. Throughout our history, however, many people have been denied permission even to walk up to the starting line. My experience over the years, both in public and private life, is the basis for my beliefs, and I have always tried to do all that I could to equalize the rights of everyone to pursue life's endowments.

In 1946 I became the chief juvenile probation officer in Bexar County after having served two years as a juvenile probation officer. I was successful in decreasing juvenile crime in the county by over 36 percent during my tenure with the Juvenile Probation Office, and I also was the first officer to refuse to carry a gun. My philosophy was simple—I believed that families should be involved even more than the police or juvenile authorities. I had initiated the caseworker method and had insisted that before a youth was taken before a court, a caseworker first had to visit the youth's home. When I started as chief, only 20 percent of the juveniles referred to our office were referred directly from families who felt we could assist them in keeping their young people on the straight and narrow; when I left office one year later, this figure had risen to 80 percent.

I tried to hire Olive Daniel, an African American woman who had a degree in social casework (which, by the way, none of the rest of us in the office had). Ms. Daniel had been volunteering her time in the office, and she was extremely caring and effective. There was no juvenile facility then for African Americans girls who had been in trouble (and the "trouble" I'm speaking of was along the lines of truancy, not what we have today)—they were being sent to a facility in another part of the state that removed them from their families and all their support systems. I felt this was wrong, and wanted to do something about it. So I tried to hire Ms. Daniel, but the county judge refused. He said it would be all right if Ms. Daniel worked out of a field office, but it would not be right for her to work out of our office in the courthouse because Anglo employees would object.

I knew that this just was not right, not only because it was wrong to treat a human being this way but also because Ms. Daniel was the most qualified person for the job and we really needed her. So I resigned—over this, and over a budget battle I was waging with those who wanted me to increase the number of young people who were incarcerated in order to justify my office's budget. (I felt strongly that, if at all possible, the young people should remain at home and under the supervision of their parents, allowing all concerned to maintain their dignity. I had learned from experience that this was the most effective way to handle the problems.) I don't know what became of Ms. Daniel, but I hope she knows what an impact she had on my life and on the lives of the many young girls she helped while she did volunteer work for the office.

It was indeed ironic that while some advocated reducing juvenile crime, which was concentrated in the poorer Hispanic and African American areas of town, they nevertheless practiced racial discrimination and prevented the most effective worker from performing a service in the neediest areas of the community. And yet, at that time and perhaps still today, not only did discrimination exist against African Americans by Anglos, but it existed against African Americans by Hispanics.

After I had resigned as chief juvenile probation officer, and perhaps influenced by the Hispanic children I met who were in need of positive role models and the kind of influence Hispanic businessmen could offer, I organized and established the Pan American Progressive Association (PAPA). It was the only organization of its kind, and it responded to my belief that we in the Hispanic community needed to quit complaining about how bad things were and instead do something to help ourselves. At that time in San Antonio there were a number of Hispanic-owned businesses, but the Hispanic community as a whole continued to suffer great economic deprivation. We bemoaned the condition of our Hispanic community, but took few positive steps to help ourselves. Thus I created PAPA, and soon business leaders joined in order to coordinate and dedicate their energies to a social consciousness and purpose. I raised $25,000 from membership fees as we worked toward helping the Hispanic community. In the end, our greatest accomplishment proved to be our last accomplishment—one that led to PAPA's ultimate demise.

Soon after PAPA had been formed, I learned that Hispanics were being discriminated against in housing. In one particular case, the discrimination was caused by a restrictive covenant in a master deed which provided that if a particular piece of property, through any means, ended up in the possession of a "Negro or Mexican," the title would revert to the original grantor. The original grantor was Thurman Barrett Sr., and the property was located in the "Earl B. Mayfield" subdivision of San Antonio. Both Barrett and Mayfield had belonged to the Ku Klux Klan, and Mayfield was in fact a predecessor of mine, having been elected on the KKK ticket to Congress from San Antonio around 1920. The purchaser of the property in this case was a young man, a Hispanic World War II veteran, who was about to lose the house he had bought because of the restrictive covenant.

I had learned in law school (I had completed my legal studies several years earlier but had never practiced law) that restrictions on the free alienation of land were repugnant to the law. I wanted PAPA to challenge the legality of restrictive covenants to help out this young Hispanic veteran and all the others affected by this discrimination. I remembered reading that African Americans in St. Louis were challenging restrictive covenants in a case pending before the U.S. Supreme Court, and I thought it would help bolster the challenge to join that lawsuit on behalf of Hispanics. I used money from PAPA to pay the expenses of San Antonio attorney (later Texas Fourth Court of Appeals Judge) Carlos Cadena in order to join in that Supreme Court lawsuit in 1947 and to handle the local restrictive covenant case that had come to my attention.

Ironically, some members of PAPA objected to being

brought into a case that associated them with African American issues, even though the issue also affected Hispanics, and they did not want PAPA involved with the St. Louis restrictive covenants case. Thus they objected to my use of PAPA funds to pursue this cause. At that time in history, many Hispanics wanted to be labeled "Caucasian" and did not want to be associated with African Americans. I attended a PAPA board meeting called to discuss the issue, and I promptly resigned from the organization over this matter.

But the lawsuit proceeded anyway. On May 3, 1948, the U.S. Supreme Court ruled in the St. Louis case (with which PAPA was still officially associated) that restrictive covenants based on race, color, or creed were unconstitutional. The next day, the local San Antonio case that had prompted my interest in this issue was thrown out of court. It was appealed by Thurmond Barrett all the way to the Texas Supreme Court, but the restrictive covenants were consistently ruled unconstitutional. Thus, not only were restrictive covenants concerning African Americans found to be unconstitutional, but restrictive covenants concerning Hispanics were found to be unconstitutional as well. Further, it was established in Texas common law, based on the federal ruling in the St. Louis case, that such restrictive covenants were unconstitutional under the Texas constitution as well as under the U.S. Constitution. Had I not insisted that PAPA join the St. Louis case, the application of the U.S. Supreme Court ruling to Hispanics and to the Texas constitution would not have been established.

The outcome was historic for all minorities who had been, or ever would have been, the subject of restrictive covenants. The prejudice against Ms. Olive Daniel was not only a great disservice to Ms. Daniel, it was a great disservice to the Juvenile Office's goals and objectives of helping young people who were in trouble. Similarly, the refusal of the PAPA membership to associate with African Americans in the restrictive covenants case tore apart the PAPA organization, thereby diminishing the influence of this organization as a positive force in the San Antonio community.

After leaving PAPA, I held a series of jobs until 1950. One involved working for the International Ladies Garment Workers Union as a part-time educational director, teaching English and citizenship to seamstresses and organizing picnics, baseball games, and the like. Perhaps times are better now than they were in the late 1940s, relatively speaking. Yet we must be ever mindful of the harsh lessons learned from the early struggles for equality, particularly the struggles of the unions, lest we forget the stern basic practices and disciplines that brought progress and improvement to the lives of American laborers. All I know is that had it not been for the unions, American workers today—union and non-union alike—would be much worse off. Unions, after all, helped equalize power between workers and employers.

I recall, for example, my mother, my aunt, and my female neighbors rising at four in the morning, and then beginning at five in the morning hemstitching the infant dresses they would obtain from a business just down the street from our homes. On Thursday, I would accompany my aunt to return the sewn dresses to the business, and the owner would accept some and reject some, leaving my aunt with fifty to seventy-five cents total (five cents per garment accepted). This sounds absurd by today's standards, but at that time there was no union protecting the rights of workers or federal law protecting home workers. Ironically, home workshops are coming back in vogue today, and there is much pressure to eliminate protection for these workers—protection that was enacted precisely because of the abuses I observed as a child.

I remember when the International Ladies Garment Workers Union came to San Antonio. Its members threw up a picket line and advocated putting an end to this horrible and humiliating "homework." There was great dismay and distress among my relatives, as they thought the union wanted to take away the little money they were making. But I did not share that view and wondered why these women would get up at four, start at five, take time to clean the house and prepare the noon lunch, and then keep on going until eleven at night, day after day. I realized that something was terribly wrong and that these women were victims of an insidious practice of prejudice that perpetuated their unequal treatment in the workplace.

As the union became active, there were more and more reports of the Bexar County sheriff arresting union pickets, all of whom were women, throwing them in a truck, and taking them out to the edge of the city. He would just dump them there, forcing them to walk back home. He was the same man who, a few years earlier, when chief of police in San Antonio, violently put down the striking pecan shellers. A high school classmate of mine, Emma Tenayuca, had led the cause of the pecan shellers, who revolted because they were getting paid only a penny-and-a-half or, at the most, two cents per pound for the pecans they shelled.

There is no doubt that the unions growing out of situations such as these helped both the workers and business—the conditions of workers improved greatly, worker morale improved, and the production grew. Sadly, the trend has been reversed in recent decades, and the wages of working people have been declining. According to a most informative article written by John Judis in the February 14, 1994, *New Republic,* Americans' real wages have been falling at an increasing rate—1.6 percent from 1973 to 1978, and 9.6 percent from 1979 to 1993. Judis cites a number of causes for this decline, but primary among them is the deterioration of "the relationship between business and labor after the loss of American industrial supremacy." It is clear that on the strength of unions in the United States, workers achieved a level of equality in the workplace, and a large middle class was built and sustained. With the decline of union strength, the economic gap between rich and poor has widened, pulling apart the middle class and leaving workers with a sense of their own inequality in the workplace.

Judis states that the amicable business-labor relationship was sustained during a time when U.S. industry dominated the world market, but in the 1970s this all began to fall apart. American business began to lose its worldwide superiority, and executives began to compete, rather than cooperate, with workers. Business executives formed their own lobbying organization, the Business Roundtable, and during the past twenty years have increasingly fought against labor unions. As a result, workers' real wages declined. Certainly, not all American workers were union members prior to 1970, but because of the strength of unions up to that time, even the nonunion workers benefited. It is obvious that diminishing the strength of the unions and the power of workers in the workplace has served neither American laborers nor business.

Many American companies have now moved their manufacturing plants overseas to so-called developing countries whose citizens are desperate for work at any wage and under any conditions. The impact on American labor is enormous and quite adverse, and the one great equalizer—the union—is less and less a source of strength for the American worker. Economic equality will be even more difficult to achieve in today's global market where American labor is pitted against, and must compete with, what amounts to slave labor.

Elected in Texas

After having devoted time to endeavors in the private sector and in the public sector in unelected office, I grew frustrated with the lack of responsiveness of government to the needs of large segments of the community. I believed that to make progress, minorities needed to be represented among the decision makers, particularly the elected decision makers. In the 1940s, disease plagued the Hispanic community, especially tuberculosis; Hispanic infant deaths accounted for two-thirds of the city's infant death rate; and all around me I saw poverty, sickness, and prejudice. Yet the response from the city's so-called civic leaders was that the Hispanic families should voluntarily return to the small towns and farms from which they came. They wanted to get rid of us.

In 1950 I ran for Texas state representative, but lost. In 1953, I ran for San Antonio City Council, and won. Much discrimination existed then that was overt—denial of the use of city recreational facilities by minorities, for instance—but much discrimination existed as well that was not overt—denial of city services based on a claim of insufficient city funding, for instance.

And through my efforts the city's recreational facility segregation ordinances were repealed. As a child, I had been ordered to leave one of the city's swimming pools because I was Hispanic, so this victory was particularly sweet. Gradually, minorities were beginning to receive equal treatment from their elected officials and from their government.

Although I had made some progress through my City Council work, I had to move on because of my inability to serve on the City Council and survive economically (for my family was growing, eventually eight children in all). In 1955 I was reelected as the first independent council member, with only $750 in funds and running citywide, and I did not want to quit outright in 1956. So I resigned from the council and announced for the Texas Senate, which was considered an impossibility. I never expected to win, nor did anybody else. Besides, the state Senate's emolument was no

better ($25 per day for 120 days every 2 years). To the aston-
ishment of all, I was declared the winner by 309 votes after
three recounts. It is important to note that not only was there
still a poll tax at this time that prevented a lot of poor and
minorities from voting, but I ran citywide for my City Council seat and countywide for my state Senate seat. So, I never
really was a "minority candidate" or elected official—the people who voted for me came from a broad cross-section of the
community I represented. Not even 10 percent of the qualified voters were minorities back in 1956.

Less than a year after I was successful in repealing the city's
segregation ordinances for recreational facilities, I found myself confronted with ten segregation bills that were introduced in the 1957 state legislature. I participated in the
longest filibuster in the history of Texas in association with
then State Senator Abraham Kazen Jr. of Laredo (who followed me to the U.S. House of Representatives after being
elected to Congress). Our filibuster was directed against these
ten "race" bills previously passed by the Texas House of Representatives. We held the floor alternately for a total of
thirty-six hours and two minutes. Eight of the bills were
defeated, and of the two that passed, one authorized local
option on school integration while the other made possible,
in practice, the assignment of pupils on a racial basis. The
bills were passed in May, and in October 1957 the local
option law was declared unconstitutional by a federal court.

In a special legislative session later in 1957, I again filibustered, this time alone and for twenty consecutive hours
against three additional "race" bills, all three of which passed
and were signed by Governor Price Daniel. Eventually every
one of the bills that had passed was declared unconstitutional. Some might think that my fight was spurred by my
own background, but it went much deeper than this. Again,
my childhood memories of the Klan (who in the dead of

163

night would ride their horses into my neighborhood and threaten African American residents), my quitting the Juvenile Probation Office because they would not allow me to appoint an African American to work out of the courthouse, and my experience with PAPA surely contributed to my convictions.

But there were other battles to be fought in the state Senate, battles that were against inequality caused not by overt discrimination laws such as the thirteen segregation laws I filibustered against, but against inequality caused by denying some individuals access to the decision-making process, to educational and employment opportunities that would allow them to gain a foothold in the economy, and to fairness in the laws that governed them and affected their finances. In this vein, I fought against a state sales tax because it would fall most heavily on the poor, and against increases in the tuition at state colleges and universities (preferring other means of raising revenue by the state). Sadly, Texas now has one of the highest sales tax rates in the country, and the tuition at state colleges and universities has escalated in recent years.

It was through my work for the Housing Authority that I met a man who was to have a tremendous effect on my life, Jack Kennedy. We met at a housing conference in Washington, D.C., during the early 1950s while I was working for the Housing Authority and Kennedy was a U.S. representative from Massachusetts. We became friends and maintained our friendship until his tragic death in 1963.

When I first met Jack Kennedy, I never would have thought he would become president as he did not even look like a representative. He was meek and shy, but I saw him dedicate himself at that housing conference—he listened, observed, and studied the issues. I've never seen a man, before or since, grow in maturity, knowledge, and leadership as Jack Kennedy did throughout the 1950s. I truly believed that he was committed to using government resources to bring all people into the mainstream of American life. Although he was from a privileged background, his religion and ethnicity had subjected him and his family to a degree of scorn and revilement that may have provided the basis for his ability to identify with the struggles of people throughout America and the world.

Kennedy consulted with me about his 1960 presidential campaign, an outgrowth being my organizing and co-chairing (with then Senator Dennis Chavez of New Mexico) the "Viva Kennedy" campaign. President Kennedy returned the favor of support when, in 1961, I ran for and won a U.S. House seat in a special election—the first federal election during the Kennedy administration and one that was viewed as a referendum on the Kennedy agenda. Through Kennedy's help, I was able to bring a medical school and a veterans hospital to San Antonio.

Chairman of the House Committee on Banking— The Fed: Denial of "Equal Opportunity"

When I was first elected to the U.S. House of Representatives, I was assigned to what is now called the House Committee on Banking, Finance and Urban Affairs, then chaired by the great Representative Wright Patman of Texas, who was a mentor to me. I studied hard, and when I became chairman of that same Banking Committee I found myself fighting some of the very battles that Chairman Patman fought. Chairman Patman was commonly labeled a populist, and he was very much a representative of the people. In that capacity, he tried to make changes in the Federal Reserve System to restore control of events in our country to the people through the democratic process, which is something I am working on even today.

It is interesting to see how many people view the work of the Banking Committee, as the terms "banking" and "finance" conjure up images of stuffy Anglo men in business suits who control the flow of money, the pace of the economy, and the financial resources of the country. I cannot really argue with this because in large part it is true. In fact, being chairman now and being an American of Mexican descent has presented me with many occasions to blast apart the stereotypes held by the old financial wizards of the Northeast and of Wall Street with regard to "minorities" and "Mexicans."

This prejudice against those who traditionally have been excluded from business and power in our society extends even into the local San Antonio media. It results in censorship of news about my work in Congress, and the resulting censorship denies San Antonians access to information about the business world. Work that is performed by the Banking Committee rarely gets reported—the local media apparently believe that it does not affect San Antonians or that San Antonians do not understand the work or that San Antonians do not care about the work. But I know this is wrong because the work of the committee and the issues that fall under its jurisdiction certainly do affect every San Antonian and, indeed, every American.

For instance, the Housing Subcommittee I also chaired is a subdivision of the full Banking Committee. This subcommittee's jurisdiction covers federally insured mortgages, minimum standards for housing construction, the prohibition against discrimination in mortgage lending and in the sale of housing, public housing complexes, and a number of other issues. Nearly everyone is affected by the work of this subcommittee. The ability to buy a house is not only an indication of a level of economic achievement, but homeownership provides economic stability to a family as well as to a community.

I have worked for many years to equalize federal housing policy. It has always seemed to me that we should apply comparable federal policy to the poor and the wealthy. For instance, until recently there has been no limit on the amount of tax deduction one may take for home mortgage interest—interest on a $5 million house was just as deductible as interest on a $25,000 house. I calculated the amount of loss this deduction represented to the U.S. Treasury and introduced legislation to provide the same level of assistance in housing programs for low-income individuals. Thus far, I have not been successful in equalizing federal housing policy in this manner.

I have also been battling for years to force mortgage companies to pay interest on the money they hold in escrow accounts for the payment of insurance and taxes. This is, again, an issue that is both an issue of fairness but also one of importance to lower-income people for whom the small amount of interest earned on an escrow account might really help. Thus far, I have not been successful in this endeavor either—but the work continues.

It is similar to the matter of credit reports. It is only fair that people be allowed access to their credit reports, and it is only fair that the information in the reports be absolutely accurate. But the industry has fought against reforms that would ensure both of these fair policies. It is of vital importance to those at a marginal economic level, as they need access to credit to purchase many items for which the wealthier of society can pay cash.

So many of the scandals that the Banking Committee has investigated have involved people who were deemed to be the pillars of society—the privileged, the powerful, and the rich. When I saw in the early 1980s that the government-backed deposit guarantee for savings and loans was going to be raised from $40,000 to $100,000 at the same time regulation was being relaxed and restrictions were being lifted, I knew that this amounted to an extension of free credit to these so-called pillars by the American taxpayer. I protested at the time, to no avail, and I spoke out loudly and often throughout the 1980s, but again no one listened. When the whole house of cards came tumbling down, I took no comfort in being able to say "I told you so."

What was missing from the debate over the changes made in the S&L industry in the early 1980s, and what is missing now in the debate over funding for housing, for reform of the mortgage escrow laws, and for reform of fair credit laws is not only a sense of fairness but of true representation of the greatest good for the greatest number of people. The S&L deposit guarantee limit was made behind closed doors, without opportunity for public debate or input. How could the interest of the greater number of people be represented if they were not given a chance to voice their opinions? Likewise, the dominating influence on the debate over housing, mortgage escrow accounts, and fair credit are not the voices of the millions of people who would benefit by changes in the laws but the voices of the millions of dollars that run industry and lobby Congress. I have brought a number of ordinary citizens before the committee to testify, but the committee votes by and large have not reflected the interest of these individuals.

Whenever the voice of the people has been removed from what should be a public debate, and whenever the people then have not been allowed to participate in the processes and procedures of their government, I have tried to disseminate information to help the people get involved. When my voice is censored by the media, as it so often is, especially on the local level, it makes this harder—but I still have the House floor on which I can speak openly and without censorship.

A democracy, which is a great equalizing force when based on "one person, one vote," depends on an informed public.

Representative government depends on an informed and active public. The chance for equality in representation depends not only on hearing but on being heard. When others make all the decisions, when they withhold information, and when they make decisions in secret, then we can never have equality in government, in society, or in the economy.

The greatest example of the abuse of openness in government is the Federal Reserve System (the "Fed"). This is one of those issues that the local media in San Antonio do not believe is of general interest and thus do not report on, and yet the actions of the Fed affect the lives of every American. Interest rates, the flow of money, the amount of money that is printed—all of these factor into economic stabilization and economic equalization.

I have studied the Fed in depth for a number of years, and in the past five years I have had the assistance of Banking Committee staff. We have found, not surprisingly, that not only is the Fed's Board of Governors made up almost entirely of Anglo males, but the Fed's staff members (particularly the higher-level and higher-paid staff) have a similar composition. Consequently, the average American is not represented by the people serving on the Fed's Board of Governors and on the Fed's staff, and this is even more true with regard to the average low-income American whose interests are not represented when unemployment is increased by virtue of the Fed's actions.

I believe that the Fed's structure must be changed, just as the old San Antonio City Water Board's structure was changed, to make it more responsive to the needs of all the people. Under current law, the Fed's decisions and bookkeeping are not subject to review by Congress, by the General Accounting Office, or by any other outside entity. If the Fed justifies a decision it makes on the basis of its accounting, none of us in Congress or in the public has a right to look at the Fed's books to see whether we would reach the same conclusion. There is no other body in the United States with this kind of autonomy and this kind of power, nor should there be. The power to control the purse is the power to control the nation, and yet the average man and woman in this country have no right even to get transcripts of the meetings of the Fed. With arguments before the Supreme Court, deliberations and hearings in Congress, and administrative hearings and other official activities of the executive branch, the public not only has a right to attend these meetings but to have access to the written decisions and background materials.

The work of the Fed is just as important as the work of the three major branches of government, but we know next to nothing about how the Fed sets monetary policy. That is why it is critical that we hold the Fed's decision making branch, called the Federal Open Market Committee, accountable for the decisions it makes that affect our employment, inflation, and the value of our currency. Sadly, the officials of the Fed have been lying and covering up the truth, but my and my staff's work is finally uncovering the truth. It cannot be emphasized enough how important this is in terms of equality in the nation, for if the control of money is held by a few select people on a self-perpetuating board, there is no ability of the people to control—or even have a say in—their own economic destiny. The wealthy always complain when a government policy asks them to sacrifice according to their ability and thus make a greater sacrifice than those of more modest means, and yet the Fed has done just the opposite for over eighty years in making certain that money is transferred from lower-income people to higher-income people through manipulation of interest rates and other facets of monetary policy.

The Fed has clearly shown disdain for disclosure of their policies, minutes of their meetings, and their financial records. But not even the Fed's officials agree on whether they are a governmental agency or strictly a private agency. Regardless of the answer, which really is that the Fed is a federally chartered private agency, the reality is that the Fed consists of banks, and only bankers are selected to participate in the Fed's governing. And that reality is in conflict with democracy and the democratic principles that governing should represent the greatest interest of the greatest number of people.

Does the president sit in on the deliberations of the board? Of course not. Does the Congress have anything to do with the deliberations, or is it privy to the deliberations? Of course not. Does Congress or the president or the executive branch own stock in the Federal Reserve Board? Of course not. The commercial banks own it. The founders of our nation fought against control by bankers, and this was an observation that was made in the beginning of our nationhood when the First Continental Congress was formed. Back then, the need for a bank was apparent, and the decision was made to charter the Bank of the United States in Philadelphia. Thomas Jefferson inveighed against the bankers because, although they would provide the necessary banking services, Congress would have to pay a prohibitive usurious interest rate, and it was only because of men like Jefferson that this wasn't done.

Thomas Jefferson would similarly inveigh against the Fed, which was created in 1913, long after Jefferson had died. The Federal Reserve is run by the bankers. The twelve Federal Reserve Banks are organized as private corporations in which private banks that are members of the Federal Reserve are the stockholders. These stockholders elect six of the nine directors in each of the twelve Federal Reserve Banks, and thus have a controlling interest. The presidents of each Federal Reserve Bank are elected by these stockholders subject to the approval of the Board of Governors. There is no doubt that private bankers, not the general public, are the Federal Reserve president's preferred constituency.

What makes this even worse is the fact that although no

entity has the power to supervise or oversee the Fed, the Fed has the responsibility and authority to regulate bank holding companies. Bank holding companies are companies owning one or more commercial banks, and they represent 93 percent of the assets in the private banking system. Yet, as I stated before, the Fed is controlled by bankers; thus, bankers are overseeing themselves. There is no independence, no checks and balances, no separation of powers to ensure accountability, fairness, and sound decision making.

The poor, most minorities, and most women thus have no say in monetary decisions that affect interest rates, employment, the value of the dollar internationally (against foreign currency), and so on. Is this equality? Certainly not! The denial of representation in the major decisions affecting the economy is the denial of equality to most Americans. Thus this is an extremely important issue and one that some of us on the House Banking Committee are attempting to address.

As can be seen from all these examples of actions I have taken in my life, work that I have performed on the City Council, in the state Senate, and in the U.S. House of Representatives, there is much to be done until all Americans are truly guaranteed equality under the law, in the economy, and generally in their lives. Given that the power to influence decisions that affect our lives is concentrated in the established systems of our government, I felt that I could contribute by participating in the process. There is a place for those who remain outside these processes, but I felt that I could contribute by influencing policy from the inside. Yet even on the inside I have largely remained an outsider because of my refusal to surrender my independence.

I always knew that economic parity brought with it power, and power brought change. But to gain economic parity, equal participation had to be allowed and equal opportunity guaranteed—in jobs, housing, public accommodations, and

172

education. Education, not violence, is what makes the difference in whether people gain economic parity. You don't gain equality by making others unequal—by bringing them down, how have you elevated yourself? Fratricide is one sure way to make certain no one achieves equality.

Many of the battles have been to bring everyone to the same starting line, and many of my battles have been over the issues that have, or would have, removed power from the people. The right to participate, and through participation achieve some semblance of equality, can be greatly influenced by the legislative process. A legislative advocate such as myself can make some changes so that equity is ensured in our laws and policies, but the legislative process is a deliberative process and it moves at a deliberative pace. Achievement of true equality, true economic parity, and truly full participation and representation in the decisions that affect our lives— these all take time. As long as we remain vigilant in our pursuit, equality can be achieved for everyone.

Michael Parenti received his Ph.D. from Yale University. He has taught political science at a number of colleges including Howard University, the University of Canterbury in New Zealand, and California State University, Northridge. He is the author of *Democracy for the Few, Power and the Powerless, The Sword and the Dollar, Inventing Reality, Make-Believe Media,* and *Land of Idols, Political Mythology in America.* He lectures frequently on college campuses.

La Famiglia, La Famiglia

Michael Parenti

Michael Parenti grew up in an Italian family in East Harlem where one could hear "the cries of vendors" while "women sat at windowsills . . . catching the activity below" with few expectations for a better life. The men worked hard for low wages and dreamed of Italy, the "old country."

The role of the family was important in Parenti's youth, although its effect was a "mixed blessing" of loyalties and fights. He grew up in an environment where a high school education was "considered an unusual accomplishment."

Decades ago, in the northeast corner of Manhattan, in what is still known as East Harlem, there existed a congestion of dingy tenements and brownstones wherein resided the largest Italian working-class population in the world outside of Italy. The backyards were a forest of clotheslines, poles, and fences. The cellars, with their rickety, wooden steps and iron ban-

---

Originally published in *Central Park* (Fall 1988): 65–75. Used by permission of the author and *Central Park*.

isters, opened directly onto the sidewalks. On warm days the streets were a focus of lively activity, with people coming and going or lounging on stoops and chatting. Small groups of men shouted numbers at each other in Italian *morra* contests or engaged in animated discussions, while children played ball in the streets or raced about wildly. On certain days horse-drawn carts offered a lush variety of fruits and vegetables trucked in from New Jersey and Long Island farms. The cries of the vendors were of a southern Italian cadence unspoiled by almost a half-century in the new land. Women sat at windowsills with elbows planted in pillows, catching the activity below, occasionally calling down to friends and relatives or yelling at the children. There was always something of interest going on in the streets but rarely anything of special importance except life itself. Several hundred thousand Italian American working-class people lived crowded into this neighborhood, most of them poor but few miserably so.

It was in East Harlem of 1933 that I made a fitful entrance into the world. My birth was a caesarean because, as my mother explained years later: "You don't want to come out. You were stubborn even then." Since Mama suffered from a congenital disease called "enlarged heart," there was some question as to whether both of us would survive the blessed event. At the last minute the hospital asked my father to grant written permission to have my life sacrificed were it to prove necessary to save his wife. In those days, during a dangerous birth, a doctor might crush the baby's head in order to remove it from the womb and avoid fatal injury to the mother, a procedure the Catholic church strenuously opposed. The church's position was to let nature take its course and make no deliberate sacrifice of life. This sometimes meant that the baby came out alive but the mother died, or sometimes both perished. Obeying heart instead of the church,

Papa agreed to give the doctors a free hand. As it turned out, they decided on a caesarean, a risky operation in 1933 for a woman with a heart condition. Happily, both Mama and I came through.

To talk about my family I would have to begin with my grandparents, who came from the impoverished lands of southern Italy (as did 80 percent of the Italians in America), bringing with them all the strengths and limitations of their people. They were frugal, hardworking, biologically fertile—and distrustful of anyone who lived more than a few doors away.

One grandmother had thirteen children, of whom only seven survived, and the other had fourteen, also with only seven survivals. This was the traditional pattern of high fertility and high mortality, carried over from the old country. (Given the burdens of childbirth, small wonder that both my grandmothers died years ahead of my grandfathers.) Their children, however, adopted the American style of small families. The image of the large Italian family is an anachronism that hardened into a stereotype. By the 1930s and 1940s, Italian Americans—like everyone else—were rarely having more than two or three children.

My father's mother, Marietta, shared the common lot of Italian peasant women: endless cooking, cleaning, and tending to the family, constant pregnancy, pain, and a fatalistic submergence of self. *"Che pu' fare?"* ("What can you do?") was the common expression of the elderly Italian women. Given their domestic confinement, these women learned but a few words of English even after decades of living in New York. They accepted suffering as a daily experience, rather than as something extraordinary. They suffered while mending and washing clothes in their kitchens, or standing over hot stoves; they suffered while climbing tenement stairs or yelling at children, or fighting with relatives or sitting alone at the windows; and they suffered while praying to their saints, lighting candles in church, and burying their dead. Most of them went through life dressed in black in an uninterrupted state of mourning for one or another kin. They believed that a woman was born to obey, marry, bear children, and endure the pains and indignities of her station—although not necessarily uncomplainingly.

Grandma Marietta was a living portrait of her generation; a short, squat woman who toiled endlessly in the home, muttering supplications to Saint Anthony, looking up beseechingly at the light fixture on the ceiling—the closest representation of heaven her eyes could locate from her kitchen station. Grandma lived in fear of *u mal'occhio,* the evil eye. If any of the younger members of the family were sick, it was because someone had given them *u mal'occhio.* Like a high priestess, she would sit by my sickbed and drive away the evil eye, making signs of the cross on my forehead, mixing oil and water in a small dish, and uttering incantations that were a combination of witchcraft and Catholicism. Witchcraft was once the people's religion, having been in southern Italy centuries before Catholicism and having never quite left. The incantations seemed to work, for sooner or later I always recovered.

Some of the first-generation Italians were extreme in their preoccupation with *u mal'occhio.* I remember as late as the 1960s, a few of the postwar immigrants would put an open pair of scissors (with one blade broken) on top of the television set so that no one appearing on the screen could send *u mal'occhio* into their living rooms. In this way the magic of the seventeenth century protected them from the technological evils of the twentieth. Although, as we know, the contaminations of television are not warded off that easily.

My mother's mother, Grandma Concetta, was something of an exception to the picture of the Italian woman drawn above. Endowed with a strong personality and a vital intelligence, she turned to the only respectable profession open to rural Italian women in the late nineteenth century: she became a midwife, a skill she learned in Italy and brought with her to New York before the turn of the century. Midwives did more than deliver babies. They advised families on the care of children, diagnosed, and treated illnesses with herbs, dietary prescriptions, heat applications, and other natural remedies that were said to work with far less destruction and sometimes more efficacy than the expensive chemical remedies pushed by the medical and drug industries of today. Concetta was treated with much respect by men and women alike. My father spoke of her with a reverence he seldom expressed toward his own parents. She died at the age of fifty-nine, a few years before I was born. I knew her only from the testimony of others and from a few faded photographs of a woman who gazed into the camera with a friendliness and gentle strength that made me miss her even though I had never known her.

The men of my grandfather's generation, like the women, were beset by forces greater than themselves. In the old country they had toiled like beasts of burden, trapped in a grinding poverty, victimized by landlords, tax collectors, and military press gangs. Having fled to the crowded tenements of New York, they found they had a little more to live on but sometimes less to live for. My mother's father, Vincenzo, came to the United States in 1887. He spent his working days in East Harlem carrying 100-pound bags of coal up tenement stairs, a profession that left him permanently stooped over. My father's father, Giusseppe, arrived in 1909; a landless peasant who had worked for one of the great estates in Puglia, he was fleeing military conscription. Like many of the immigrant men, Grandpa Giusseppe worked as a ditch digger and day laborer in New York, helping to build the city's tunnels, subways, and bridges (as he seldom let us forget), managing to raise an enormous family on subsistence wages.

These immigrant laborers were the paragons of the humble, thrifty toilers to whom some people like to point when lecturing the poor on how to suffer in silence and survive on almost nothing. In truth, the immigrants were not all that compliant—at least not originally. In fact, they had taken the extraordinary measure of uprooting themselves from their homelands in order to escape the dreadful oppression of the Old World. Rather than suffer in silence, they voted with their feet. We may think of them as the virtuous poor (although in their day they were denounced as the swarthy hordes), but they saw themselves as lifelong victims who were somewhat less victimized in the New World than the Old. Even if life in New York meant trading off certain human amenities (as life in New York still does), it was better in a basic way, for now they worked only twelve hours a day instead of fourteen, earning three dollars a day instead of three lire a week. And here they were better able to feed their children.

Still, in their hearts, most of the first-generation immigrant men nursed a sentimental attachment to Italy. Many of them, like Grandpa Giusseppe, never quite accepted their economic exile in the new land. And as the years wore on they idealized the past and "the old country" all the more. In time, Italy for them became Paradise Lost. A common expletive among the old men was *"Manaccia l'America!"* ("Cursed be America!"). To them the new land could be heartless, money mad, and filled with the kind of lures and corruptions that turned children against their parents. Giusseppe remembered the air in Italy as "sweet" while New York was "not fit for dogs to breathe," a judgment delivered many years before an environmental consciousness took hold in this country. The first-generation immigrants always spoke respectfully of Italy and would never think of exclaiming *"Manaccia l'Italia"*; nor were they prone to express any patriotic devotion to their adopted country. What kept them in the United States was the fishes and loaves, not the stars and stripes. The popular movie and radio character of that day, "Luigi" (played by an Irishman, J. Carrol Naish), the tearful immigrant who spent his time gratefully kissing the ground and exclaiming "Mama mia, I'm-uh love-uh deese-uh bootifullah countree, Amerrreeca!" was a cartoon conjured up by Americans for the gratification of the Great American Ego. Had such a silly fellow made his appearance in East Harlem, the old men would have smothered him with scorn.

The immigrant men drank wine made in their own cellars and smoked those deliciously sweet and strong Italian stogies (to which I became temporarily addicted in my adulthood). They congregated in neighborhood clubs, barbershops, and the backs of stores to play cards, drink, and converse. They beat their children occasionally, and their wives rarely. They exercised a dominant presence in the home, yet left most domestic affairs, including all the toil of childrearing, to the women, who exercised a greater day-to-day influence over the children and over the domestic scene in general.

Religion was also left to the women. The immigrant males might feel some sort of attachment to the saints and the church but few attended Mass regularly and some openly disliked the priests. In the literal sense of the word, they were "anticlerical," suspicious of clergymen who did not work for a living but lived off other people's labor, and who did not marry but spent all their time around women and children in church.

The Italian American community was deeply divided over Mussolini. The first-generation immigrants tended to think of *Il Duce* as a strong and admirable leader who supposedly brought order and prosperity to the old country. Their view was no different from one widely reflected in the American press throughout the 1920s and early 1930s. Through his exploits in Africa and by "standing up" to other European powers, Mussolini won "respect" for Italy and for Italians everywhere—or so the immigrant men believed. Of the many opinions I heard about the dictator, the most amusingly self-deluding was that "after Mussolini came along, the Americans stopped calling us 'wop.' "

The second generation, that is, the American-born children of the immigrants, usually spoke of *Il Duce* with scorn and derision, especially after the United States entered World War II. I recall bitter arguments in my grandfather's house between the older and younger men. (The women rarely voiced opinions on such matters.) As the war progressed and Mussolini showed himself to be nothing more than Hitler's acolyte, the old men tended to grow silent about him; but in their hearts, I believe, they never bore him any ill feelings.

The military performance of Italy's legions in the war proved to be singularly lacking in anything that might resemble heroism and was an embarrassment to those East Harlem supporters who had been anticipating Benito's version of the Second Coming of the Roman Empire. One of my younger uncles gleefully told the story of how the entire Italian army landed one evening in Brooklyn to invade the Navy Yard, only to be routed and driven into the sea by the night-shift maintenance crew. When Italy switched sides and joined the Allies in the middle of the war, there was much relief and satisfaction among the American-born and probably even among many of the immigrants.

Contrary to what we have heard, the immigrant Italians were not particularly loving toward their children. They sent their young ones to work at an early age and expropriated their earnings; or they had them toil long hours in the family business for no wages. For most of the immigrants, there was little opportunity to face the world with ease and tenderness. Of course, infants and toddlers were hugged, kissed, fondled, and loved profusely, but as the children got older it would have been an embarrassment, and in any case was not the custom, to treat them with much overt affection. Besides, there were so many of them, so many living and so many dead, and after a while each new child was either an additional burden or an early tragedy but seldom an unmitigated joy.

"*La famiglia, la famiglia,*" was the incantation of the old Italians. The family, always the family: be loyal to it, stick with it. This intense attachment to the family was not peculiar to Italians but was—and still is—a common characteristic of almost any rural people (be it in the Philippines, Nigeria, India, or Appalachia) where the family has an important survival function. Much has been said about the warmth, closeness, and vitality of Italian family life—but only some of it is true. More than anything, the family was one's defense against starvation, the *padrone,* the magistrates, strangers, and rival families. As any combat unit, its strictures were often severe and its loyalties intense. And betrayals were not easily forgiven.

If the Italian family was a support unit, it was also a terrible battleground. "Nobody can hate like brothers," the saying goes, especially brothers (and sisters) who had hard childhoods, working long hours when they should have been in school or at play, handing their pennies over to immigrant parents who themselves saw life as a series of impending catastrophes (not always without cause). I remember the many squabbles, grudges, and hurt feelings that passed between my father, his brothers and sisters, and their respective spouses. The series of shifting alliances and realignments among them resembled the Balkan politics of an earlier era. One particular feud that split the family down the middle lasted long after the initial *causus belli* could be recalled. In time everyone wanted it to end, but no one would make the first move. Finally, my father had me invite the son of one of the opposing sisters to come and play with me. She in turn had her son

183

invite me over to her house the next day, and within a week everyone was on speaking terms again. But the rapprochement had involved all the touchy, diplomatic overtures and reciprocal gestures that transpire between sovereign states.

Years later, as the various brothers and sisters put the deprivations and insecurities of the immigrant family behind them and mellowed with time and the advent of children and grandchildren of their own, they tended to get along much better with each other.

Like everyone else, I had two extended families, one on my father's side and one on my mother's. There was less feuding in my mother's family and a larger circle of cousins to enjoy. I loved the nourishing encompassment of the big family gatherings (whichever side it was), the summer outings at the beach, the picnics, the parties, and the holiday dinners. When times were good, we ate well.

When times were bad, we still ate well but only on special occasions. The Italian feast was a celebration of abundance with its platters of antipasto, spaghetti, the variety of seasoned meats, the bowls of thick, tasty soups, the green salads seasoned in olive oil, the crisp crusty bread, fresh fruits, roasted nuts, rum pastries, and the endless bottles of homemade red wine. I wonder if these feasts were a kind of ritual performed by people who had long lived in the shadows of want and hunger, a way of telling themselves that at least on certain days the good life was theirs. Whether or not there was any larger meaning to them, the feasts were enjoyed for themselves.

I have a special fond memory of my maternal grandfather, Vincenzo, a stooped, toothless, unimposing man who was my closest ally in life. During his last years, suffering the defeat of childhood for a second time around, and finding himself relegated to the edge of the adult world, he entered wholeheartedly into my world, playing cards with me, taking me for walks around the block, watching with undisguised delight as I acted out my highly dramatized cowboys-and-Indians games. He could speak no English and I no Italian, but we communicated effortlessly. He always took my side, and despite his infirmity was sometimes able to rescue me from the discipline of my parents—which is the God-given function of grandparents.

At the age of seventy-five or so, Vincenzo, a widower of many years, was discovered to have a girlfriend, a woman of about fifty-five years. She would steal into the house when no one was home and climb into bed with Grandpa. The discovery of the tryst plunged the family into a state of panic and rage. My relatives denounced the woman as a *putan'*, a whore of the worst sort, whose intent was to drive Grandpa to an early grave by overexerting his heart. (He died when he was eighty-seven.) Under the threat of collective family reprisal, the poor lonely woman dared not see Vincenzo anymore. And my poor grandfather, after being scolded like a child, was kept under a sort of house arrest. In those days, the idea that elderly parents might have sexual desires caused a furious embarrassment among their grown children.

In any case, Italian grandfathers were frequently made captives by their families after passing a certain age, as the sons, daughters, older nieces and nephews competed to put the old man under their protective custody. If a car came too close for comfort while the grandfather was crossing the street, as might happen to any pedestrian, the family would try to keep him from taking unaccompanied strolls, convinced that he could no longer judge traffic. If he misplaced his hat or scarf, as might anyone, he would be judged no longer able to care for his personal articles. At the beach, if an Italian grandfather waded into the water much above his knees, one or another of his self-appointed custodians could be seen jumping up and down on the shore, waving frantically at him and shouting: "Papa's gonna drown! Somebody get him!" I read somewhere that this phenomenon of grandfather captivity still exists in parts of Italy.

I saw the protective custody game repeated with my paternal grandfather, Giusseppe, who in later years presided in silence at the head of the table during holiday meals, a titular chieftain whose power had slipped away to his sons and sons-in-law, those who now earned the money and commanded their own households. While a certain deference was still paid him because of his age, more often he found himself, much to his annoyance, a victim of overprotection—which was a sure sign of powerlessness. Years later, in 1956, when an adult, I had occasion to have a few long talks with him and discovered that he was a most intelligent and engaging man although he did have a number of opinions that were strange for that time, namely that country air was better for one's health than city air, canned and packaged foods were of less nutritional value than fresh foods, and physical exertion was better for you than sitting around doing nothing. Giusseppe also believed that doctors and hospitals could be dangerous to one's survival, automobiles were the ruination of cities, too much emphasis was placed on money and material things, and the simple life was best. We treated such views as quaintly old-fashioned, having no idea that Grandpa was merely ahead of his time.

After my birth, the doctors warned my mother that another pregnancy would be fatal. So I went through life as an only child. My mother tended to spoil me, for which she was criticized by her older sisters. More than once she mentioned to me how sorry she was that I had no brothers and sisters to play with, and she encouraged my playmates to come spend as much time as they wanted at our house. But I entertained no regrets about being an only child, for why would I want to share my lovely Mama with some other little brat?

As a mother, she was far from faultless. Often her fatigue

from working long hours in a sweatshop and her disappointment about the conditions of our life got the better of her and she would snap at me in an irritated way or take a swing at me with her open hand if I became too impossible. Her knowledge that she was living with a congenital heart disease probably did not help matters. Even so, Mama was nice to be close to. She had a smooth, soft face to kiss, and she was the only person who knew how to tie my shoelaces without making them too tight. What more could a child ask for in a mother?

My father played a more distant role than my mother, as was the usual way in Italian working-class families—and in just about any other family where the division of labor is drawn along gender lines. He labored long hours for meager sums, sometimes two jobs at a time. Papa was born in Italy and transported to this country at the age of five, spending almost a month on a crowded, ill-ventilated, infested boat. He attempted to throw himself overboard during the voyage but was caught at the railing by his uncle—a story I listened to with a sense of relief.

My father did not do well at school, mostly because of the demands the immigrant family imposes on its first-born son. When he was ten years old, his day went something like this: up at 6:00 A.M. and working on his father's ice truck until 8:00 A.M., then to school, then back to work until 7:00 P.M. to complete a thirteen-hour day. On Saturdays he worked from 6:00 A.M. to midnight, an eighteen-hour day. On Sundays he labored from 6:00 A.M. to 2:00 P.M., eight hours; that was supposed to be a half-day.

Papa was probably the only child in America ever to have failed kindergarten—twice. He was left back again in 1A because he could hardly speak English. By the time he made it to 5B he was fluent in English but he was fourteen and still a poor student. As he put it: "I was too damn tired to learn to read and write very good." His fatigue often overcame him, and he would fall asleep in class. On one such occasion a teacher dumped water on him. He retaliated by taking the inkwell out of the desk and throwing it at her. That was 3B. After that, the teachers labeled him "a bad kid." Kicked out of school at fourteen, he went to work full-time. More than fifty years later, shortly before his death, I talked with him about his youthful days and recorded his thoughts. The things he remembered most were the toil, the humiliation of not being able to speak English, and the abuse he received from teachers. There was one bright spot, as he tells it:

> The only teacher that cared about me was Miss Booth because she saw me carry ice a few times on 110th Street and she asked, "How come you're carrying ice at your age?" and I said, "I got to work. My father can't afford a man. There's seven of us at home to feed." So she saw I wasn't really a bad kid. She saw I was no good in school really on account of I had to work. That Miss Booth, she got around me in every way. She got me to wash the blackboard. Anything she wanted, I did because she showed she cared about me.

When I was five or six, Papa would take me out to the park on Sundays—as so requested to do by my mother—but we invariably ended up at the local saloon. There I had the pleasure of sitting at the bar next to him, sipping ginger ale and eating pretzels while he and his cronies drank beer and conversed. This was in the days before television when neighborhood working people relied on conversation as a source of diversion and social sustenance to a greater extent than they do today. My father's friends were all men. Cross-gender friendships were not a common thing in those days (nor really are they all that common today among working people). The women in a man's life consisted of his mother, his wife, his sisters and other female relatives. He might know various women in the neighborhood and stop and chat with them briefly, but there was no occasion for sustained socializing. It would have been considered inappropriate.

To illustrate the patriarchal mentality of my father's world I might recall the time he informed me in troubled tones that Uncle Americo, while drunk one night, had started beating his wife, Aunt Fanny. Americo's son, my cousin Eddie, forcibly intervened and wrestled his father to the floor. What shocked my father was not Americo's behavior but Eddie's. "I don't care what happens," he concluded, "a son should never raise a hand to his father"—a pronouncement that left me wondering what I would do if ever in Eddie's place.

Hovering over us was the Great Depression, a mysterious but palpable phenomenon that seemed to explain everything we did: why there was never enough money, why Papa was away working all the time, why I couldn't have this or that toy. I remember during one unusually difficult period my mother bought a small steak and cooked it for me as a special treat. She sat watching as every morsel disappeared into my mouth. When I offered her a piece she declined, saying she wasn't hungry. Only years later did I realize with a pang that she very much would have wanted some.

None of my relatives talked of "careers"; I don't think the word was in usage among us. But everyone talked about jobs—or the fear of being without one. A high school education was considered an unusual accomplishment, and the one uncle who had graduated from high school was considered something of a celebrity. My mother's dream was that I would someday get a high school diploma, for then all doors would be open to me and the world would be mine. As she said, I would be able to "dress nice every day not just Sundays" and "work in an office," a fate that sounded more like death than salvation to a spirited street boy.

Toward the end of World War II, things improved for my family. My father got steady work driving his uncle's Italian bread truck and my mother found a job in a neighborhood dress shop, sitting at a machine all day sewing buttons on children's clothes. I pledged to her that someday I would earn lots of money so that she would never have to set foot in that sweatshop again, a vow that heartened her more because of its expression of loyalty than because she believed she would live to see the day. As it happened, she died when I was seventeen, still employed by the same shop.

When Papa was not driving the bread truck, he was driving a taxicab—as remained his situation even through the years I attended graduate school. Indeed, while getting my Ph.D. at Yale University, I recall going to a party and being introduced to a young man who said in a crisp resonant voice, "I'm Henry Lee Adams"—or some such patrician name—"My father's in oil." Not knowing exactly how to respond, I answered, "I'm Michael Parenti. My father's in transportation." Had I been more explicit about Papa's occupation, I believe young Mr. Adams would have suffered an even greater embarrassment than I.

From time to time during my childhood I would wonder about the world outside East Harlem, about the strange American people who inhabited parts of Manhattan we passed through on rare occasions, the tall, pink-faced, Anglo Protestants who pronounced all their r's, patronized the Broadway theater, and went to Europe for purposes other than to locate relatives. I would think of other equally strange people and unexplored worlds with anticipation. This "intoxication of experiences yet to come" left me with a feeling that East Harlem was not my final destiny in life, a feeling that would grow with time.

When I was about twelve or thirteen, I chanced upon a copy of *Life* magazine that contained an article that mentioned East Harlem, describing it as "a slum inhabited by beggar-poor Negroes, Puerto Ricans, and Italians," a sentence that stung me enough to remain in my memory. Some time later, I mentioned to my father that we lived in a slum. He asked "What's a slum?" I said, "That's where there's a lot of crime and dirt in the streets and the people are as poor as beggars." Upon hearing this, he scowled at me and said, "Shut up and have respect for where you live." This got me to thinking that my neighborhood was not really a slum.

Slum or not, we abandoned East Harlem in the late 1950s. Most of the Italians—including all my relatives—moved to what sociologists call "second settlement areas," leaving the old neighborhood to the growing numbers of more recently arrived Puerto Rican immigrants. The money the Italians had saved during the relatively prosperous war years and postwar period became the down-payment passage to the mass-produced housing tracts of Long Island, Staten Island, and New Jersey, where as proud homeowners they could settle down to a life that better resembled the one in the movies. The few surviving old immigrants were taken along in this exodus, often reluctantly, now in the isolation of suburbia to regret the loss of both Italy and East Harlem. For Grandpa Giusseppe, who spent his last few years in Lindenhurst, Long Island, not even the magnificent vegetable garden he grew in the back of his daughter's house could compensate for the sense of double displacement he now endured.

The new prosperity and lifestyle took its toll of the second generation too. One uncle who used to have huge "open house" parties for friends and relatives in his home on Third Avenue, complete with mandolins, accordions, and popular and operatic songs—drawn from the amateur talents of the guests themselves—now discovered that no one came to visit him in the outer edge of Queens. An aunt of mine, who had lived all her life within shouting distance of at least three of her sisters, tearfully told my mother how lonely she was in Staten Island, "out in the sticks where there's nobody but the crickets."

In time, I went off to graduate school and saw far less of my extended family, as they did of one another. Years later, in

1968, I got a call from my cousin Anthony: "It seems we only get together these days for weddings and funerals," he said. "And there have been too many funerals and not enough weddings. So we thought we might have a family reunion."

It took place in Anthony's home in Queens, a crowd of cousins and their fourth-generation children, the latter being youngsters whom I was meeting for the first time, and for whom East Harlem was nothing more than a geographical expression, if that. Time had brought its changes. The women wore coiffured hairdos and stylish clothes, and the men looked heavier. There was much talk about recent vacations abroad. There was a slide show of Anthony's travels to Europe, and a magnificent buffet of Italian foods that made the slide show worth sitting through. And there were a lot of invitations to "come visit us." Much to my disappointment, the older surviving aunts and uncles had decided to stay away because this was an affair for the younger people, an act of age segregation that would have been unthinkable in earlier times. In all, we spent a pleasant evening joking and catching up on things. It was decided we should get together more often. But we never did have another reunion.

In the late 1970s I began to have recurring dreams, one every couple of months or so, continuing for a period of years. Unlike the recurring dreams portrayed in movies (in which the exact same footage is run and rerun) the particulars and fixtures of each dream in real life—or real sleep—differ, but the underlying theme is the same. In each dream I found myself living in a lovely, newly done apartment; sometimes it had spiral stairwells and bare brick walls and sometimes lavish wood paneling and fireplaces, but it always turned out to be a renovation of 304 East 118th Street, the old brownstone in East Harlem where I had spent most of my life. We might think of recurring dreams as nightmarish, but these were accompanied by sensations of relief and yearning. The life past was being recaptured and renovated by the life now accomplished. The slum was being gentrified. The working-class Italian youth and the professional-class American academic were to live under the same roof. I had come home to two worlds apart. Never quite at home in either, I would now have the best of both. Once I understood the message, the dreams stopped.

Joseph Bruchac is best known as a poet, storyteller, and authority on Native American writing. His 1983 anthology of contemporary American Indian poets, *Earth on Turtle's Back*, is one of the most comprehensive of its kind. He is the founding editor of the *Greenfield Review Press*. His poems, stories, and essays have appeared in hundreds of journals. He is the author of over twenty books of poetry, fiction, and American Indian folktales including *Return of the Sun*, *Dawn Land*, and *The Girl Who Married the Moon*.

Grampa's Indian Blood

Joseph Bruchac

Joseph Bruchac's grandfather Jesse Bowman "passed" for French Canadian as a way of surviving. Native Americans, in what was to become Vermont, dispossessed of land and life, needed to become "invisible." Jesse Bowman, an Abenaki Indian, taught Joseph Bruchac about social consciousness, especially as it applied to those who had little power over their lives: children and the poor. The influence of his grandfather led Bruchac "to seek equality in my words and in my life."

My grandfather Jesse Bowman passed for white. Although I did not say it then, that is how I see it now. A dark-skinned man of Native American blood, he never referred to himself as Indian. The birth records of his father, Lewis Bowman, who came down from Canada, showed that he was born at St. Francis, Quebec. So my grandfather would always say, "We is French Canadian." He would not mention that St. Francis was another name for the Abenaki Indian reserve of Odanak.

Grampa's face, though, and the way he did and thought about certain things, showed his ancestry. Behind his back, other people in our little Adirondack foothills town of Greenfield Center, New York, would say "Jesse Bowman is as black as an Abenaki." After his death, people would come to me and, in a kind of tentative way, say just that and then be surprised that I knew my grandfather was Indian. But there was no way I couldn't know.

Prejudice against Native Americans, a prejudice (and an accompanying violence) that still exists in far more corners of America than most people admit, was one of the major reasons for so many Native people taking my grandfather's path—seeking to blend in or at least be ignored. It didn't always work.

To be French Canadian was a way of surviving. Surviving not only the stereotypes and the deeply held prejudice against Indians in the Northeast but physically surviving, not being killed as an Indian—an easy target. We see that in the histories the Abenaki people did not write. The histories they did not write, but held in oral tradition. The histories they did not write, which were written by non-Indians.

There were no Indians here. That is what was said in the histories of the state of Vermont, from Samuel Allen on down into the second half of the twentieth century. No Native people. Perhaps they passed through, wanderers and nomads on their way elsewhere, but they had no claim on this land. Thus, in the state of Vermont, the histories spoke of raids by the fierce and bloody "St. Francis Indians" from Canada. The histories did not speak of dispossession, of treaties or even land sales, where at least the fiction of legal transfer of land from Native to immigrant hands took place—as in nearby New York State where the Seneca Nation lost its reservation of Buffalo Creek in the early 1800s through a land sale that was held valid by the courts even though every Seneca Indian name signed to it was a forgery.

There were no Indians in Vermont? Even Hayden Carruth,

the twentieth-century Vermont poet, says so in one of his poems. That was the official history. What happened was infinitely more complex. In the seventeenth century, when the great influx of Europeans into this part of the continent began, all of the current Maritime provinces of Canada and northern New England, including the area now known as the Adirondack region of New York State, was inhabited by Abenaki people. Speaking similar languages, following similar cultures, these people included the Micmac, the Maliseet, the Penobscot, the Passamaquoddy, and the many other groups living in the area of New Hampshire and Vermont that became known as the Western Abenaki.

Unlike the French, who made alliances—both politically and through intermarriage—with the Abenaki, the English approach to what later became known in America as "the Indian problem" was to attempt to drive out or kill off the indigenous people of New England. This extirpation of the Native people was attempted in a number of ways over the centuries following the arrival of the first European settlers at Plymouth Colony. Although the greatest number of Native American fatalities would come from European-introduced diseases (which wiped out as much as 75 percent of the Indian population of New England in 1617), more direct measures were often taken. In 1637, the Plymouth Colony passed a resolution to exterminate the nearby Pequot Nation and followed it up with a military campaign that ended with the deaths of nearly all the Pequot people.

A little more than a century later, the following Proclamation regarding the Penobscot Indians was "Given at the Council Chamber in Boston this third day of November 1755 in the twenty-ninth year of the Reign of our Sovereign Lord George the Second by the Grace of God of Great Britain, France and Ireland, King, Defender of the Faith" stating that "I do require his Majesty's subjects of the Province to embrace all opportunities of pursuing, captivating, killing and destroying all and every of the aforesaid Indians."

As an incentive, at a time when one English pound was the equivalent of $100 today, a bounty was offered:

> For every scalp of a male Indian brought in as evidence of their being killed as aforesaid, forty pounds.
>
> For every scalp of such female Indian or male Indian under the age of twelve years that shall be killed and brought in as evidence of their being killed as aforesaid, twenty pounds.

But it did not end in the eighteenth century, the nineteenth, or even the twentieth. In Vermont, where my grandfather had relatives and friends, there was a eugenics project in the early part of the twentieth century. Just as in Hitler's Germany, its aim was to identify those who were genetically undesirable and then sterilize them. A major part of those identified as genetically undesirable in Vermont were those who had any American Indian blood. Sponsored by the state and coordinated through the University of Vermont, the eugenics project sterilized a good number of people before it was terminated prior to World War II. The records still exist, as does the fear of being identified as Indian among many Vermonters of Native American blood.

A good friend of mine is, like me, a storyteller who draws on his Indian ancestry. A native of the state of Vermont, where he and many of his older relatives still live, he was the first person in his family in generations to stand up and publicly acknowledge his Abenaki blood. Known by his Indian name, Wolf Song, he has performed all over the United States in schools and colleges and storytelling festivals to appreciative audiences. But he still remembers the phone call he received from one of his aunts in the late 1980s when an article about him had just appeared in a newspaper. She was terribly upset as she spoke to him. "Why did you tell them about us? Why did you tell them we were Abenaki? Now they are going to come and get us," she said.

One of our family rituals was to go south each summer to

visit my grandmother's brother, Orvis Dunham. Orvis ran a small tourist hotel in Warm Springs, Virginia. My grandmother, my mother, my sister Mary Ann, and I would be the ones to go on that pilgrimage. We'd drive down through the Delaware Water Gap, pass through Gettysburg and Washington D.C., go along the Skyline Drive, and after several days of travel in those times before four-lane highways, we'd reach Warm Springs at last.

Warm Springs must have been a very special place for my grandmother. My grandfather, years after his wife's death, would tell me how her parents had sent her down there to stay with her brother. They had done it to separate her from the dark-skinned hired man that she had taken such a fancy for—my grandfather. But Grampa had followed her down there, gotten a job from Orvis—who was then working in the big Warm Springs Inn, a large hotel. Grampa's job had been to work in back as a teamster, driving the teams that delivered food, loading and unloading the wagons. That way he was out of sight of the guests, whose only glimpses of brown-skinned men and women were the waiters and the maids. Shortly after my grandparents came back north from Warm Springs, the tactic of separating them having failed, they were married. From that day on, the only time they were ever apart were those times when we traveled to Virginia. My grandfather stayed home and "watched the station," running their general store—Bowman's Store—by himself. In all those trips that we made, summer after summer, I remember only one time when Grampa came with us. I remember the awkwardness that was almost palpable when we crossed the Mason-Dixon Line and began to see the first bathrooms labeled *Colored* and *White Only*. I remember my grandmother and grandfather filling the gas tank as full as it would go before crossing into the South. With my grandfather alone, they didn't want to have to make too many stops. There might have been, I now realize, the chance of a misunderstanding.

That one time when Grampa was with us, Orvis didn't give us the same third-floor rooms in his little tourist hotel that we had been given the year before. Instead, we were placed in a small windowless room in the hotel basement, a room that was entered from a cellar door. It was right next to the boiler. Next year, and in all the following years, when we went to Virginia, we went without my grandfather.

Yet it was not only on my mother's side of the family that issues of equality affected my life from my youngest years. Jesse Bowman was my mother's father. My father, whose name I bear, had immigrant parents. They came from the Slovak town of Turnava, not far from Bratislava. Years later, as an adult, I would hear from my father some of the stories of his growing up. I would learn of the prejudice he encountered, how the Slovak kids were called "brownheads," beaten up and made fun of by the other children. Ridiculed when they spoke English with an accent like their parents, they were made to feel ashamed at times that they came from families where people "couldn't talk right."

"An outcast," my father told me, many years later. By then I was a father myself. "An outcast was what I was. All I had to wear to school in the winter was an old brown fur coat of my mother's. The other kids said that it smelled like a dead horse. The only friend I ever had in grade school, aside from my brothers and sisters, was a Negro boy named Ed." Hearing his stories, stories that still made him clench a fist as if getting ready to fight sixty years after those painful days had happened, I began to understand the roots of the anger that had always made me fear my father. Perhaps it was because of that shame and anger that he hit me so many times when I was a small child.

I believe it was because of that anger that my grandparents kept me from my parents' house. Until I was three years old, my mother and father lived with my grandparents. When my grandparents gave them the piece of property we always called "The Farm," my parents and my little sister moved there without me. I stayed with my grandparents. Although they lived less than half a mile from my grandfather's general store, I never lived with my mother and father again.

One of the things I remember clearest is that my grandfather never raised a hand to me. No matter what I did— even when I set fire to the curtains in their bedroom—it was never call for my grandfather to hit me. It was the way he had been brought up.

"My father never struck me. I done something wrong, he'd just talk to me."

And it was only as an adult that I learned that that kind of child-raising, a nonabusive way, was always deeply part of Abenaki Indian culture. The rights of children were implicit. It was one of those unspoken things that my grandfather always carried with him, deep as his blood and the earth tone of his skin.

"Grampa," I would say to him, "if you're French, why are you so dark-skinned?"

He'd laugh then. "Us French is always dark," he would reply.

"Well, if you're French and Gramma says she's English and Dad is Slovak, what does that make me?"

He'd laugh again. "Why you're a mongrel. Jes like me. But that's all right. Mongrels is tough!"

Although Grampa Jesse was often more given to silence than to speech, he was also a man never afraid to express his feelings. I have strong memories of both his laughter and his sorrow, all through the twenty-eight years that we shared. In my teenage years, after my grandmother died, his despair and mine echoed each other. We both cried many tears in a house that never lost its emptiness until my wife, Carol, and our first son, James, returned from my years of volunteer teaching in Africa to live there with him.

For a good part of his adult life, my grandfather worked for the road crews with the town of Greenfield. He plowed the roads in the days when horses pulled the snow plows and could handle an ax or a shovel better than any man he ever worked with. He took pride in the fact that he knew how to lay out a dirt road so that the crest of it was just right and it wouldn't wash out with the heavy spring rains that came down the hilly slopes of our town in the Adirondack foothills. Perhaps if he had gotten an education he would have been a civil engineer. But his formal education, his "book learning," ended for him that day in fourth grade when he flattened one of the other kids who'd been calling him names, jumped out the window, and went to work for a man named Seneca Smith.

"Why'd you do that, Grampa," I said.

"They kept calling me an Indian," he said. And that was all he would ever say about school.

I went to school in nearby Saratoga Springs, New York. Unlike most of the upstate New York towns of that time, Saratoga Springs was cosmopolitan in its mixing of people. Because of its healing springs, it was long a place of pilgrimage for Native people and was a crossroads place between the Indian nations of the Mohawk, the Abenaki, and the Mahican. Because of those healing springs, Saratoga was a place of truce between sometimes warring tribal nations. Just north of where the Mohawk— the river that was the gateway to the west—runs into the Hudson, it quickly became a crossroads area for European people as well, their trade routes and their war trails bringing them to Saratoga. Runaway slaves made their way through our area on their way to Canada, and a good-sized community of African Americans existed in Saratoga from the early 1800s on. One of the more famous slave narratives was written by a well-educated African American freeman who was kidnapped from his home near Saratoga Springs and taken in chains to the South.

The mineral springs, whose waters attracted an international clientele, and the Saratoga Race Track, resulted in such a yearly influx of tourists that many great hotels were built along the main street, which was predictably named Broadway. The track and those hotels also contributed to the black population of Saratoga, as hundreds of African Americans found employment there, bought homes, and raised families. Congress Street, which ran south from Broadway, next to the gigantic, opulent Grand Union Hotel, marked the beginning of black Saratoga. In the summer, there were so many bars and nightclubs in operation on Congress Street that it was like stepping into Harlem.

So it was that I grew up with an awareness—from a briefer distance than many—of an African American community. Perhaps it is only my innocence or the blurring of memory, but I do not recall strict lines being drawn between the kids of different races and religions when I was in high school. I remember interracial dating. I remember sitting in the same high school classrooms and being on the football team and the wrestling team with kids who were Anglo or Jewish or black and never thinking that it was a strange thing that we should be there, treated as equals and seeing each other as equals. After football games, I would sometimes walk with Jimmy, who was African American, over to his house in the black section of town just behind Congress Street. We'd stop in the nearby Italian section of the town and buy a submarine sandwich, then a group of us—black and white—would go over to his house where we'd listen to records and dance. It was Jimmy's sisters who taught me how to do the grind.

My grandfather came to all of my wrestling matches. He wasn't quiet at the wrestling matches. I was an awkward first-year wrestler, even though I was in my senior year. I wrestled heavyweight and somehow, more through luck and strength than skill, I usually won. You could hear his voice louder than any other, yelling out, "Pin him, Sonny!" After the wrestling matches, Grampa and I usually went out to-

203

gether. He was the only seventy-five-year-old man in the crowd of kids who always went for pizza to DeGregory's Restaurant, our main high school hangout in those days, but he fit in. He never drank, but he was so relaxed around young people and so playful that people sometimes asked me, laughing as they did so, what he'd been drinking. One night he saw Cuzzo, one of my friends, on the other side of the restaurant.

"Hey," my grandfather shouted, just before he used his spoon to flip a meatball across the room. It hit Cuzzo right in the chest.

One of my friends in high school was named David. In my senior year, he and I both played tackle on the Saratoga Streaks football team that won the conference championship. During the wrestling season that followed, David wrestled at 145 pounds and I was the heavyweight. David's nickname was "Jumpy," and my nickname was "Jumping Joe." When I went off to college the next fall at Cornell University, my grandfather came out to visit me and watch one of my wrestling matches at the college. It was too long a trip for him to drive himself in his gold, fish-finned Plymouth, so two of my friends came with him to help him drive. David was one of them. His family didn't have the money for him to go to college, and he was soon to join the navy. All three of them stayed in my room. Grampa slept on the bed and the rest of us slept on the floor. David had the same kind of sense of humor that my grandfather did, and it was a memorable experience. One night, when we had been making too much noise, the dorm resident came to our floor to ask us to be quiet. Jumping out from behind a door, David hit the resident with a pillow and said, "Come on, join in."

We all held our breath for a minute until the resident burst into laughter and picked up a pillow.

Wherever we went, I introduced them. "This is my grandfather," I would say.

Then Grampa would smile and say, "This here is David. He's Joe's brother."

"That's true," David would say.

And then people would look at my grandfather and then look at David and then look at me. Then they would look at my grandfather again. I knew why they were doing that. I also knew why, a few weeks later, when the fraternities began their rushing season, inviting potential pledges to visit their houses, only a very few of Cornell's fifty-two fraternities extended an invitation to me. It was because my grandfather was brown-skinned and my friend David—who really wasn't a blood relation—was a very dark-skinned African American.

Eight years later, coming home to my grandfather's house after five more years of college and three years of teaching in West Africa, my grandfather couldn't wait to tell me something.

"Heard about Jumpy?" he asked.

"No," I said.

"After he got out of the navy year fore last he went to school at that there Florida A&M. He's down there now. He's the captain of the wrestling team." Then my grandfather laughed. "Heard he's the president of his fraternity, too!"

As I look back now over the years, I realize at last how much of my awareness of the world began with my brown-skinned grandfather. It was, at least in part, Grampa's Indian blood that led me to be involved in the civil rights movement, to teach as a volunteer in West Africa, to coordinate a college program in a maximum-security prison, to work with the Abenaki Indian Nation in asserting identity and preserving culture and language, to be a writer and a teller of stories from once despised or ignored traditions, to seek equality in my words and in my life.

William Winter is one of those vanishing Americans, a news analyst. In 1941 he became a war correspondent for CBS Radio. Since 1957, he has presented his very popular extension course on "Today's World Headlines" as a lecturer for the University of California. His twice-monthly newsletter, *William Winter Comments,* was in its thirty-fourth year when it ceased publication in 1996.

———————

Prejudice Is a Curable Disease

William Winter

*William Winter grew up in Newark, New Jersey, near the begin-
ning of the twentieth century. Although he spent his early years in
a poor, ethnically diverse neighborhood, he did not experience racism
and bigotry until his family moved to a middle-class community.*

*Winter practiced law in North Carolina during the Great De-
pression. Later, he became a war correspondent in Asia during
World War II and the Korean War. He believes that changing laws
is the best way to reduce or eliminate prejudicial behavior.*

Nearly nine decades ago, I was born and raised in a factory
neighborhood in Newark, New Jersey. My closest friend,
Jimmy King, lived in a tenement next door. All of us kids
liked Jimmy because he could pitch. It happened that he was
black, but we kids were color-blind. Most important question
was how well he could play baseball on the corner sandlot
every Saturday morning. Two houses down the street lived Peter
Balsamo. His father was a wrestler, a big, burly man who used
to buy us ice-cream cones when he got a wrestling assignment.
Sometimes when we were playing ball in the street, a

woman would stick her head out of her fifth-story window of the tenement building across the street, and yell: "*Vladek! Itch taw domu, spatch!*" Or at least, that's how it sounded. Her son, Walter ("Vladek") was a sickly boy, and she would call him home to take his afternoon nap. She always talked to him in Polish, just as my parents would talk to me in German.

My parents had moved to Newark from Vienna just a few years before I was born. They spoke English but with a distinct German accent, and decided to teach me pure German at home and let me learn English properly in school rather than have me imitate their German pronunciation. I can still remember that on my first day in kindergarten I didn't understand a word the teacher was saying. Conversation with classmates was impossible. So I watched what the others were doing, picked up blocks when they did, and joined them in drawing crayon sketches on the paper the teacher gave us. After the first few days, I could begin to understand some of the teacher's instructions.

On the day I entered the third grade, my mother accompanied me to school to ask my new teacher whether my English was satisfactory. The teacher told her, "I didn't know the child spoke another language." No need for bilingual classroom education. I continued to speak and write English in school, conversed effortlessly with my friends, while I always spoke German at home. That's how I got my bilingual education.

At home I never heard belittling comments about our neighbors. The parents of Jimmy King, very dark-skinned blacks, were as welcome in our home as were the Poles or Italians. As was young Chan, whose father ran the laundry down the street. People were people, and my father rated them according to intelligence, personality, character, but never mentioned ancestral roots or skin color. That's how I grew up. In a factory neighborhood completely devoid of racial or religious prejudice.

That factory neighborhood continued to influence my life

through the first two years of high school. At Barringer High, I befriended classmates of various ethnic backgrounds. The big question always was whether they could play baseball on our corner sandlot after school.

My father, a mirror manufacturer, became successful in business and decided that we'd better move to a "nicer neighborhood" where I could attend a "better" high school, Southside High. There I was introduced to an entirely new world. This kid was a "dago" or a "wop," the other was a "nigger" and I, being Jewish, was called a "sheeny" or "kike." I got into fist fights nearly every day. This was strange talk from my new classmates. I couldn't understand how skin color or the parents' national origin could make the slightest difference. And when I happened to develop a crush on a young black girl, I was ostracized. "Nigger lover!"

It was that experience, moving from a poor section of the city to an upper-middle-class area, that made me a lifelong, determined, and active "liberal." My father, who, like my mother, always seemed to be buried in a book, recommended that I read John Locke and learn about "liberalism." That was my teenage introduction to the meaning of democracy.

Another childhood influence emphatically shaped my future life, decided my career. During the First World War, our nation became so shamefully paranoid that nothing German was permitted. Everyone was warned not to speak German in public, not even to listen to the music of German composers. Beethoven, Wagner, Bach were never performed. Everything German was virtually outlawed. Every Sunday afternoon my indoctrinated mother would prepare for a *"kaffee klatch"*—a traditional Germanic coffee break. She baked a *Kugelhupf* coffee cake, a big round cake with a big hole in the middle. And the inevitable coffee. My father would invite a group of his friends to sit around the dining-room table, one of those old round ones with no square corners so everyone faced everybody else. And everyone was free to express opinions, even in German. The friends included, as I remember, our German-born letter carrier who felt free to side with the kaiser when they discussed the war. He argued that "England" had imposed the war on the kaiser "for commercial reasons," because of jealousy over German trade competition. I was too young to understand what that meant, but old enough to follow the war talk around the table, and tall enough to have my nose just above the table top as I watched the fingers outline the latest battle area in France. My father provided a big map of Western Europe, on which he and his friends would point out towns and cities in the week's war news. I would watch with fascination and listen to the talk by the German letter carrier, and then the very chauvinistic American principal of my Robert Treat Elementary School, and the others, who included men of different ancestral origins. Each brought his own interpretation of the war news. The Italian wrestler, Balsamo, was most belligerent about his convictions, I remember, and one man, a Scot, spoke with an endearing brogue. And always quietly, in contrast with the Italian.

I learned about the war each week, and then joined in the rejoicing over the Armistice on November 11. I also learned about Woodrow Wilson and his "Fourteen Points." The letter carrier thought they were a sinister plot to enslave poor Germany, while the Italian was sure this would be the beginning of a new order in Europe. Each week I would follow the arguments pro and con, and then one day, heard that "thirty-three willful men" in the U.S. Senate had turned down Wilson's League of Nations proposal. By that time I knew more about the League of Nations, its advantages and disadvantages, than any of my schoolmates. Indeed, I knew more about the world than any of them because I had been taught by the open discussions around that Sunday afternoon coffee table.

Years went by and my father was disappointed that I wouldn't succeed him in the mirror manufacturing business. I had little interest in business, in money, in profit making. My major interest was international politics, which had become my boyhood fascination. After being admitted to the bar in North Carolina in January 1928, I practiced for about a dozen years. But then I quit, when a new career in radio broadcasting was offered. The decision to change professions was not very difficult because, for one thing, I couldn't choose my clients. In my early law years, I accepted retainers indiscriminately, without regard to political or sociological opinions. I needed the money. In order to offer services gratis to indigent defendants in criminal trials, most of whom were poor, illiterate blacks, I represented some well-paying corporations with whose policies I happened to disagree.

In those days, from 1928 through the 1930s, prejudice was still a way of life in North Carolina. The state had a higher education level than most other southern states at the time, yet prejudice against people with black skins was no less rampant than elsewhere in the South. When a black man approached a white man on a sidewalk, he was required to remove his hat and get off the sidewalk into the gutter, so the white man could walk by. In the courts, prejudice was commonplace. A black defendant in a criminal trial was always tried before a white jury. Blacks were not allowed to serve on juries. So the defendant was denied the right of trial by an "impartial jury," as guaranteed by the Constitution. It seldom happened that one of the parties in a civil action was white and the other black, since the black man would hesitate to sue a white. And if the white had a cause of action, he'd usually find some way to gain satisfaction without reducing himself to the indignity of a lawsuit.

I learned about this southern racism soon after I began my law practice. Like most young lawyers, I accepted debt-collection assignments. I'd write a letter to the debtor, inviting discussion about the debt and its repayment. One of my early clients, a local hotel owner, had me write a letter to a black man who owed the hotel some money. I addressed the letter to "Mr." Sam Jones, and included the usual salutation, "Dear Mr. Jones." Because I was a very young lawyer, and was writing my first letters on his behalf, the hotel owner asked to see my letter before I mailed it. He became furious. "Never call a nigger 'Mister!' " he exploded. "Niggers are niggers. Just call him "Sam Jones." And never, but *never,* call a nigger "Dear." That's not the way we do things around here. And don't use his last name. Just say 'Sam.' "

Shamefully, I submitted. Keeping the hotel as a client was more important to me than principle, unfortunately. But whenever opportunity arose, I was glad to represent an indigent black client without any fee. Before long, I was told by a friendly colleague that some of the other attorneys in the law building referred to me as, "that Yankee nigger-lovin' Jew lawyer."

So one reason I wasn't reluctant to give up the law practice was the feeling that I was like a prostitute, selling my services to anyone who paid. Furthermore, law practice was too confining, too narrowly concerned with single clients rather than with history. Too little to do with the outside world about which I had begun to learn while I was growing up.

So it was that when a local radio station offered me a job as news commentator, I accepted eagerly. Radio was not a strange experience at the time. It happened that I'd worked my way through law school as a radio announcer on Station WWNC ("Wonderful Western North Carolina") in Asheville. My parents had moved there with me in the early 1920s because my father had been diagnosed as suffering from tuberculosis. Mountainous Asheville was believed to offer the ideal climate for curing the disease. The radio experience, my law practice, and my early exposure to international affairs every Sunday afternoon all helped me into the career I had always wanted, discussion of current world affairs.

After Asheville, I moved to the "big city," Charlotte, North Carolina, where one day the local CBS radio station, WBT, signed me on as its attorney. In the mid-1930s, the station found itself involved in a national dispute with the Musician's Union, and that happened to lead to my subsequent career in international journalism. The Musician's Union story bears recalling at this late date as a matter of minor historic interest.

In 1935 the American Broadcasters Association was confronted at its annual meeting by the head of the Musician's Union, whose name, I remember, was Petrillo. He argued that the recently formed radio networks were displacing local musicians and called for "stand-by charges" to be paid by both the networks and the local radio stations. Each station should be required, he contended, to employ local musicians in an orchestra to be maintained by the station. And the networks must pay for the musicians displaced by broadcasting music. Also, every time a local radio station would broadcast music records, it was "displacing live music" and therefore should pay fees to the Musician's Union. Moreover, when a virtuoso musician, a noted pianist or violinist, gave a concert, the local station must pay "stand-by" fees to a local musician!

After much discussion, the broadcasters agreed, in principle. The networks would set aside a certain amount each year, and their local radio outlets would establish a fund to employ local musicians. The details, including agreement on the precise amounts, were to be negotiated with the networks.

Petrillo decided to negotiate the first network contract, not with attorneys for one of the networks in New York City, but with the attorney for some local network-owned station somewhere "in the boondocks." Obviously, he felt it would be easier to negotiate with some small-town lawyer than with

213

a high-powered network law firm in New York. Somehow, he decided to negotiate with the CBS-owned station in Charlotte, North Carolina, which had retained me as its attorney. A contract with WBT would be as binding on the network that owned the station as a contract with the Columbia Broadcasting System in New York. And that contract would serve as the standard for the entire industry nationwide.

Petrillo sent an attorney from Chicago to negotiate with me. Each day I would telephone the head of the CBS legal staff in New York for detailed instructions. The negotiations went on for weeks. Eventually we reached a compromise acceptable to both parties.

One of the CBS vice-presidents, Meff Runyon, came down from New York to sit in on the talks I was having with the Musician's Union attorney. One evening we went to dinner in a local restaurant where a newsboy came in, hawking the latest headline: *Il Duce Invades Abyssinia!* Runyon: "What the hell is all that about?" I was happy to show off: "Abyssinia is Ethiopia, in Northeast Africa. Mussolini has attacked Ethiopia." Runyon said he couldn't understand what I was talking about. I told him about Mussolini, "Il Duce," about the League of Nations and how Haile Selassie had been humiliated, laughed off the stage, when he pleaded for collective action. When I related all I knew about the Ethiopian invasion, Runyon said that he kept busy reading the trade journals—*Broadcasting, Variety, Radio Daily*—and didn't have time to follow all the world news in the daily papers.

"But," he said, "you explain the story so clearly, it makes it easy to understand." When he learned about my early interest in world affairs, he suggested that I "go on the air" to "explain the news to people." "Ever hear of that fellow Kaltenborn?" he asked. It so happened that I had not yet heard of the one important pioneer world news commentator on network radio in those early days, Hans von Kaltenborn. "Well, anyway," he continued, "you ought to go on the air and explain the news."

Soon, I was "on the air" three times weekly with a fifteen-minute news commentary on WBT. After just a few days, I had my first sponsor, Chatham Mills. It quickly became apparent that preparing those radio commentaries took time away from my law practice. I'd have to give up one or the other. Quick decision: I gave up the law.

But one doesn't just walk out on a law practice. Clients can't be neglected. So, I joined a law firm, Flowers & Carter. We became "Flowers, Carter & Winter." Over the next two years, while I continued my new radio career, I would introduce clients to one of my new partners and gradually Flowers or Carter would take over, as I phased out. For the two years we were associated, I tried to prevail on Carter to change his name to Blum. Had he agreed we'd have had a unique law firm: "Flowers Bloom 'n' Winter." Mr. Carter was not amused.

When the manager of WBT, Linc Dellar, moved to San Francisco to become manager of a San Francisco radio station, also affiliated with CBS, he called me to join him, which happily brought me to the West Coast. Within a few months, the United States was at war. Eventually, I became a war correspondent, joining General MacArthur's headquarters in Australia, and then moving "up North." That experience introduced me to the Asian reaction to what was considered "America's racism."

The Japanese, at the time, still occupied the Dutch East Indies down in the South Pacific. The big island of New Guinea had been largely recaptured by American forces, and as a correspondent there I learned about Asian attitudes toward American prejudice. A sympathetic Indonesian led me to the secret hideout of Indonesian leaders who were plotting a war of independence against the Dutch. They had agreed to receive me, having listened to my shortwave broadcasts from

San Francisco, which seemed to convince them that I "was on the side of people, not governments." Ahmed Sukarno was their leader. (He would be independent Indonesia's first president after the war.) With him were his colleagues, Sharir and Hatta. They were glad to discuss their plans for publication ("because by the time you get printed in American newspapers, we will have started our fight, and the Dutch will know all about our plans anyway"). I asked Sukarno whether he expected any help from the United States in his independence efforts. "No," he replied. "Americans will be sympathetic with the European imperialists after this war. Only because they are white men. They won't want to help us because we're Asians."

Sharir added that America went to war to stop the Japanese from building an empire in Asia, "but America didn't go to war against the British and French and Dutch empires in Asia! No, it's all right for white Europeans to have empires in Asia, but not Asians!"

When I remonstrated, Sukarno went on, "We hear that you have put all your Japanese-Americans in concentration camps."

I protested that they were "internment camps" not to be compared with Hitler's concentration camps. Also, that many of us had protested loudly when the internment was announced. That made little difference.

"I am talking about the actions of your government. That's what we're talking about. What the American government will do to help us. And that is a racist government. You didn't put your German-Americans and your Italian-Americans into camps, did you? I have read in the Australian newspapers that your movie stars in Hollywood entertained some Italian war prisoners in their swimming pools. But I have never read in the papers that your movie stars entertained Japanese war prisoners in their swimming pools. What is the difference? The Japanese do not have white faces!"

Trying to reason with Sukarno got me nowhere. He was convinced that America was a racist country and that the American government would side with the Dutch after the Japanese were ousted. Sukarno, it turned out, was very wrong. It was President Franklin Delano Roosevelt who led the United Nations into supporting Sukarno and his Indonesian rebels after the Japanese defeat. And it was Roosevelt who pressured the government in Holland to grant independence to the new Indonesia. Further, after Sukarno had become president of the new Indonesia, he was invited to Washington where he was welcomed at the White House and invited to speak before a joint session of the U.S. Congress. The United States has never acted prejudicially against Indonesia because of racial differences.

But it remains that Sukarno's sensitivity was not uncommon in Asia. After American forces landed on Leyte in the Philippines, in October 1944, I interviewed Philippine President Sergio Osmena, who had assumed leadership in his newly liberated country. He told me frankly that many Filipinos had welcomed the Japanese when they first arrived in 1942 because of their "Asia for Asians" propaganda. They had felt mistreated by the Americans who lived in the Philippines before the war. For one thing, the American Army and Navy Club in Manila had been open to all military officers of Britain, France and Holland, but not to Filipinos. Filipinos were admitted to the club only as servants—cooks, waiters, busboys. Not as members. "We didn't say anything," Osmena added. "But it hurt."

Of course, we Americans weren't unique in our arrogant behavior toward Asians. The British had put up a sign in a park they controlled in Shanghai, prior to the war, which read: *Dogs and Chinese Not Allowed.* Dogs, it was quickly noted, came ahead of the Chinese in the British lexicon.

After leaving the Philippines, I was assigned to the China-

Burma-India "theater" (as the military call a region of operations). One day in Bombay I saw three British Army officers walk three abreast along the sidewalk. An Indian man came toward them. One of the British officers pushed the Indian off the sidewalk into the street with his swagger stick. That brought back memories of North Carolina racial arrogance of the 1930s.

But prejudice was a raging sickness in India. Hindus would look down their noses at Hindus of a lower caste. And those who were of no "caste" were "Untouchables." No Hindu would ever associate with an Untouchable. Indeed, orthodox Hindus would go to extremes. When the shadow of an Untouchable happened to cross their garment, the Hindu would rush to the nearest bath and soap and scrub to wipe the contamination of that shadow from his hallowed body.

In time, Mahatma Gandhi changed the rules. By example and through his preaching, he elevated India's Untouchables to equality status. After some years, Hindus came to accept the new reality and Untouchables, like blacks in America, were elected to public office and often became respected leaders in their communities.

In the 1950s, I was a correspondent in the Korean War. One day a Korean Army officer with whom I had become friends, pointed to a U.S. Army latrine that had two entrances. One was marked, both in English and Korean, *Men.* The other, *Koreans.* "You see," he said, "in the eyes of the Americans we Koreans aren't Men." I tried to explain that the signs indicated that special Oriental-style toilets were available for Korean men so that they could squat, Oriental fashion, and not sit as Westerners habitually did. He understood that, but insisted that at the very least, the language sounded condescending. "But we're used to that," he shrugged.

All this is certainly not to suggest that all British Army officers were coldly disdainful of Indian people, nor that all

Hindus mistreated "Untouchables." And certainly all Americans were not racist. Racial prejudice is evidently a disease that is transmitted by parents at home. Not through genes, but through parental conduct. Young children raised in the Old South were exposed to the demeaning of black servants by their parents. They even learned that ugly word "denigrate," which had been coined in the pre–Civil War South to mean "downgrade to the level of a nigger." The word is used innocently today, with little understanding of its etymology.

But happily, race prejudice is a curable disease. Over half a century ago when I lived in North Carolina, I joined groups of public-spirited compatriots who formed committees to deal with civic issues. In our committees we included several black men. But they were always highly educated professionals like the president of Johnson C. Smith University, a Negro school, a prominent local attorney, a doctor, a school principal. We felt noble in serving on the same committees with them, something many Charlotteans at the time would never do. We frequently discussed the question of how to break down the existing prejudice, and we would find ourselves dividing into two groups.

Some insisted that racism could be cured through education. When the prejudiced whites are properly taught to avoid "label thinking," committee members argued, then they would understand that it is wrong to generalize about people on the basis of their skin pigmentation. But while we all agreed that social understanding could be taught, we eventually recognized the difficulties. First, who would do the teaching? And, how would those who need the education agree to receive it?

The argument for education was, of course, not new. All through history, social reformers fell into two groups, similar to our committee divisions. One, which we might call "the Behaviorists," believed that individual behavior should be changed in order to change society. Argument was that society is made up of individuals, and once its members change their behavior pattern, the society will change. This was the argument of religionists, for example. Teach individuals to become God-fearing worshippers, and you'd have a moral society.

Unfortunately, while religion has effectively guided the individual's identification with the Deity, it has failed in producing a moral community. The most devout worshipper who attends prayer services every Sabbath, who prays fervently out of the printed page in the prayer book, could be the community's worst crook the very next day. Clearly, there are two distinct aspects of religion. One deals with man and his God, the other, with man and his fellow man. The former does not necessarily influence the latter.

The other groups of reformers, which several of us identified with, insisted that instead of trying to correct the attitude and behavior of each individual in a society, it is more practical and infinitely more effective to change the rules of society. A convincing example of this approach to curing the disease of race prejudice is found in our own recent American history.

When the U.S. Supreme Court in 1954 ruled in *Brown* v. *Board of Education* that separate school facilities are not equal, it changed the behavior pattern of everyone in racist regions of the country. Recently I revisited my old neighborhood in Charlotte, North Carolina, and saw black schoolchildren playing ring-around-the-rosy with white schoolchildren. Because they were attending the same classes, they learned to play together. The white youngsters no longer thought of darker-skinned schoolmates as "niggers." That was because the rules of the society had changed, and people had learned to adjust.

As the civil rights movement progressed, we found black citizens elected to city, state, and national offices. And white voters joined in electing them. So much so that a black mayor or a black member of Congress no longer stands out as unique.

A far more dramatic alteration in the prejudicial attitudes of whites is the story of South Africa. Who would have expected, as recently as a decade ago, that white Afrikaners would welcome black voters and even elect a black man as their nation's president?

When the rules change, people learn to change accordingly. Since it is now illegal to restrict occupancy of a dwelling on the basis of skin color, the discrimination is no longer attempted. In recent years, we have adopted new laws against racial discrimination and they have changed people's behavior patterns.

Prejudice as it was manifest just a few decades ago is no longer taught to children by their parents. That's because we now live under new rules. Private clubs no longer bar membership on the basis of racial or national origin, or because of the way an applicant chooses to worship his Deity. Women are no longer barred from public places, nor are the doors closed to their pursuit of professional or business or political careers. (As this is written, California has two women U.S. senators!) Sexual harassment has become illegal, and its incidence dramatically reduced.

Therein lies the cure for the disease of prejudice. Don't waste time trying to remake each individual member of a community. Change the rules, and society will change with them.

Alice Brooks is an instructional computing consultant at California Polytechnic State University, San Luis Obispo, where she is completing a degree in computer science. She was recently selected as one of the California State University Trustees Outstanding Achievement in Scholarship winners.

———————————

A Dream Deferred

Alice Brooks

Alice Brooks grew up in poverty in Chicago. She experienced physical and sexual abuse from an early age. At the age of eighteen she left Chicago and joined the navy. Her story is one of facing and over-coming the hurdles of racism, sexism, domestic violence, and alco-holism. It is clear that the concept of equal opportunity has little relationship to the life Alice Brooks has led. Now, at fifty-four, Ms. Brooks is a college student. She is studying computer science. Her life has truly been a "search for equality."

Grandpa

I suppose the stories about my grandfather had a lot to do with my determination. After all, I was the granddaughter of a hero. I had to live up to that. My grandfather was a tall, muscular man, well over six feet tall, with shiny black skin and a shaved head. He had an affinity with the land. He grew crops where crops failed all around him. The Ku Klux Klan came to his home in Alabama in the dead of night and forced him and his family to leave so that they could

223

take his land and crops. When he was able to relocate and replant, they came again, but they were not going to profit from my grandfather's green thumb a second time. My grandfather and his sons hid the smaller children in the trees and exchanged shots with the Klansmen until morning. In the morning, they set fire to the fields, packed up the family, and moved to Louisiana.

Setback

My mother told me that I was very ill just after I learned to walk and started talking and that the illness was so severe that I did not talk or walk until a year later, when my brother, one and a half years younger than I, started to talk. She would never say what the illness was. I later discovered that I was sexually molested. A baby, molested in her own house.

Church

A woman by the name of Katie Booth knocked on our door one day and asked my parents if they had any children who wanted to come to Sunday school. I was pretty small, but I was curious, and pretty obedient. My mother sent me alone at first, then my brother when he was about three. We learned to read at Sunday school. We learned that no matter what, we were equal to everybody in God's eyes, and that prayer and hard work would give us anything we wanted. My mother never went. She claimed that her experiences as an orphan being raised by her grandmother and her vicious Baptist minister husband soured her on church. He threw a rock and broke my grandmother's leg (my mother's mother) when she was young because she didn't move fast enough for him. She had polio when she was younger and it left her with a limp. The break never healed properly. He had married my great-grandmother after her first husband died. The first husband was an Indian and the children were pretty, with straight hair and chiseled features. Their stepfather, Mr. Charlie, found reasons to hit them daily. Mama told me that her mother tried to walk to my great-grandmother's house when it was time for my mother to be born. Her husband was a tinker and was away, and my great-grandmother was the area root doctor and midwife. My grandmother fell and was unable to get up until someone drove by in a wagon the following morning. She had the baby (my mother), but pneumonia killed her nine days later. Her sister and brothers, my Aunt Gussie, Uncle Martin, and Uncle Benny went to my great-grandmother and told her that either the baby (my mother) had to come with them or Mr. Charlie had to leave. They blamed him for my grandmother's death and felt that he would mistreat my mother just as he had mistreated them. My great-grandmother sent him away. When my mother's father came for the baby, they refused to give her to him and threatened to shoot him if he came back. They blamed him for not being there when their sister needed help. My mother grew up without her father or grandfather. She never trusted ministers, especially Baptists. Later in my life, she would be supportive of my becoming a member of any religion I wanted, except Baptists.

Runaway

I ran away from home for the first time before I was old enough to go to school. I emptied my piggy bank, made a sandwich, put on my warm coat, and left. I went to the bus stop, caught a bus, and rode to the end of the line. I got off and got on the IC train headed out of the city and rode it to the end of the line. By then it was dark. There were no more trains or buses at the end of the line, so I started to walk. By now, it was dark and scary. I lost my courage when the distance between houses got pretty long. There were big fields and no lights. When I finally saw a house, I ran to the front door and knocked. The residents were afraid to open the door. When they asked who was there, I answered, "A little girl. I'm lost." I was deep in the suburbs though, and nobody was going to let a little black girl in. They told me how to get to the downtown area where there were lights. I went there and walked down the street, entranced by the beautifully decorated store windows. Nothing like that in my neighborhood. Eventually, the police came and put me in the patrol car. They knew I didn't belong there, but they couldn't get me to tell them my address or name. I kept insisting that if I told them my name, they would know where I lived and take me back there. No amount of bribing, bullying, or trickery would get me to give up my name or address. They kept checking Chicago for missing children reports, and finally my parents discovered that I was missing and called the Chicago police.

I ran away frequently, either because I was being beaten or because I woke up and found my father in my bed. I never stayed away very long, I always went to school, and I always called my mother. My friends at school would always tell me which gate my father was waiting at, and I'd scoot out one of the others. If he caught me, I'd get beat up again, but if I stayed home, I'd get beat up anyway. I was pretty young when I decided I was going to get hit for something every day, so I might as well do things my way. The treatment was the same. I remember running away one day and hiding at my friend Mary Chandler's house. Her father was a drunk and didn't even know I was there. Someone told my father where I was, and he came looking. He didn't believe them when they told him I wasn't there and pushed his way in to look. I ran into Mr. Chandler's bedroom and slid under the bed. I still remember lying there terrified, with the dust under the bed choking me and being afraid of rats. I could hear them in the wall. I could see my father's feet as he walked in Mr. Chandler's room and looked around. Mr. Chandler was so drunk, he never woke up. He tossed around and mumbled enough so that my father left without finding me.

He went looking for me once at Nathaniel Jones's house. Nate had five brothers, and they more or less adopted me. Nathaniel thought I was so dumb I needed a keeper. My father accused me of sleeping with one of the Jones brothers. Mrs. Jones told him that I was a nice girl, and she didn't understand why he didn't know that. She also told him never to come back and that the next time she saw me with bruises or a swollen face, she was calling the police. It was Nathaniel who made him stop hitting me. When I was fourteen, I ran outside one day after he started to hit me. He was right behind me. Nate stepped between us and said, "No more, Mr. Young. You can't hit her out here or anywhere else anymore. If you do, you have to deal with us." My father talked real crazy to him, but he didn't hit me.

Ignorant

When I was about seven, my mother sent me to the store across the street for toothpaste. I got the toothpaste and started home. Just after I crossed the street, a man stopped me in front of Nate's building and told me to show him what I had. I told him I just had toothpaste. He pulled a knife and pulled me into the lobby of Nate's building. He told me to show him what I had or he would cut me. I kept trying to give him the bag with the toothpaste in it, but he kept pushing it away. "That's all I got," I kept crying. He kept repeating himself and finally grabbed me by my shirt and shook me roughly. I cried out and someone came into

227

the lobby. He ran. I ran home and told my parents. I still didn't understand why he wouldn't take the bag with the toothpaste and change in it. My dad got his gun and went looking for him. He never found him.

Fighting Back

I was always tender-hearted. I didn't want anything to hurt. I hated hitting and name-calling or anything else hurtful. As a result, someone would always push me around, and I would run home crying. I learned early that to back away from a fight for any reason was interpreted as an invitation to fight by a bully. Once, when I was about eight or nine, my upstairs neighbors Laverta and Barbara were playing with my brother and me in the backyard. As usual, they started a fight, and I went upstairs, crying because my feelings were hurt. My mother stood at the top of the stairs and told me I could not come upstairs crying, that I had to turn around and go back and fight. I cried that I didn't want to fight. It wasn't nice to fight. My mother gave me a Hobson's choice. I could go back down and fight or I could come up and fight her. I was furious. I screamed at her, "Nooo." She didn't budge. She stood at the top of the stairs with her hands on her hips. I cried harder, and angrily went back downstairs. My mother told my brother that he better not let both of the sisters hit me without helping me. I was so angry with my mother that I literally flew into the sisters, my little arms making a windmill, I was swinging them so fast. After the dust settled, they were going upstairs crying. Their mother was pretty mad, but she didn't say a lot to my mother. Pearl was a player, a good-time girl, with an easygoing nature. My mother was Mrs. Housewife and SuperMom, but she was mean. From that time on, if I had to fight, I fought hard and quickly. I never had to fight often because

I would totally commit to it. If you made me angry enough
or frightened enough to fight, I was enraged.

Nate, Brock, and Me

Nate and Brock were my best friends. We were inseparable.
We were all misfits. Nate went to the Franklin School for
Disturbed Boys. When he was very young, his baby brother
had been killed by a retarded white boy who suffocated him
and tried to bury him. Nate went looking for his baby
brother; he asked the white boy if he had seen him, and the
boy couldn't lie very well. Nate made him take him to the
sand dunes where they had been playing and found his
brother half buried in the sand. He took the shovel and
bashed the white boy's head in. He was too young for jail
or the reformatory, so he was sent to Franklin. He hated
white people. He used to stand on the corner of 16th Street
and wait for the buses to stop. If some white person had his
or her arm hanging out the window, Nate smashed it with a
bat. He'd go from bus stop to bus stop. Once I followed him
and begged him to stop, but he just chased me away and waited
for the next bus. Everybody in our neighborhood was afraid of
him, except me and Brock. We were afraid too. We just knew
he wouldn't hurt us and he wouldn't let anybody else hurt us.

Brock was the next-scariest guy on the block. He was an
albino with reddish straight hair. His father was a mean
white man who beat Brock's mother unmercifully. Brock
stayed away from home as much as possible. He and his father fought like two strangers whenever he did go home.
Brock looked white, but if you mentioned the words "white
boy," he'd be on you like "white on rice." He was small and
slight, but he was a dirty fighter, and he held a grudge
forever. Once Nate made him shake hands and make up with
another guy on our block. When the guy stuck his hand out,
Brock held it and beat him over the head with a steel pipe in

his left hand that he had hidden behind his back. Brock taught me how to be an effective street fighter. We practiced in the park. He never pulled punches. If I didn't get out of the way, I got hit, hard. He tried to teach me how to be ruthless, but it never really fit. I wanted to love everybody. I would fight if I had to, but if you let me, I just wanted to be friends. When I was gang raped, Brock helped me locate one of the guys that the police didn't catch. We broke the light in his hallway and waited for him. When he came, I jumped into the hall and hit him with this iron pipe. I remember hating the sound it made when it connected with flesh. I stopped, and Brock made me keep hitting him, harder. When I absolutely refused to hit him again, he told me that if I didn't, he would. I was afraid he would kill him, so I continued to hit him. I was sick on the way home. . . .

One time I went to the movies with Brock and a younger kid we called "Dooges." On the way back, we stopped at Brock's house. He had Dooges help hold me so that he could rape me. For some insane reason, he thought that I would still be his friend. He knew how badly I had been hurt before, and he still thought that I would just be angry for a while, then forgive him and be friends. He cried, but I had no compassion. I was utterly and completely devastated. It was the worst kind of betrayal. I never forgave him. Later I discovered I was pregnant. I never told anyone. I went into labor one night at six months and the baby was born breech. When I came home from the hospital, Brock came to see me. I refused to talk to him. I never told him what happened to the baby, nothing. I never again talked to him. The next year I was gone.

The Gang Rape

When I was fifteen, my mother let me go to my first party. My dad was off gambling and she thought he wouldn't find out. My girlfriend and I went without my brother. Some rough guys led by a thug named "Crip" came and asked us to dance. We refused. The people who were giving the party made them leave because they weren't invited and they were causing trouble by harassing the girls who wouldn't dance with them or talk to them. After they left, Andrea and I thought we'd better go home in case they came back with more of their gang members. When we crossed the alley a few feet away, they were in it. They made a ring around us. When Andrea started to run, Crip hit her with a cane, and knocked her down. I started swinging when they grabbed me. Andrea promised to cooperate if they didn't hurt her. I fought until they beat me unconscious. When they let her go, Andrea ran for our parents. They found me beaten and bloody in another alley hours later. An ambulance took me to the hospital. They were cutting my clothes off when my father came into the emergency room and started strangling me on the gurney. When they forced him away from me, he stood there yelling and calling me names until the police took him away. When I left the hospital, my mother went to the police station. The detectives accused me of everything from prostitution to getting my kicks by having rough sex with groups. I was speechless. The D.A. tried to get me to admit that I had been involved with the guys all the time. When we left the station, my mother told me that they offered her money from Crip's father if she would drop the charges, but she refused. He was out on bail pending another rape, and his father was sure he would get time when a second set of charges were filed. The next day, my parents told me I had more questions to answer at the Children's Shelter. When we arrived, I was told to go have lunch with the girls in the next room while my parents filled out some papers. After lunch, I turned to leave, and the doorway now had bars. I was told that my parents had turned me over to Juvenile Detention for being sexually wayward and a chronic runaway. My father was stamped all over this. He spoke and my mother obeyed. I went into a rage. I refused to get undressed and put on the uniform. I refused to shower, and when the matron tried to force me, I started fighting. It was useless. Her big fellow matron walked in, threw me down, and put her foot on my chest. I couldn't move.

Social Services came to get information the next day. I told her why I ran away. I told her about the molestation, the beatings, the bizarre behavior at the hospital. I referred her to my neighbors, my teachers, my girlfriend. She promised to look into it. I thought I would be living there until I was eighteen, but she came back in a couple of weeks and told me that her investigation had established that I told her the truth. She also told me that my teachers had suspected that I was being physically and sexually abused but that they were unable to get me to talk to them. She told me that I could not go home again and asked if I had relatives that I could live with. I went to stay with my Aunt Gussie and her daughter.

It was hilarious. My Aunt Gussie was an alcoholic and my cousin was a heroin addict. Things have to be pretty bad when this is the best placement Social Services can make for a bruised teenager. Talk about no choices. My aunt's house was full of the worst influences, but they loved me. They never touched me and they never let anyone else. My aunt showed me her collection of meat cleavers and her .45 revolver to make sure I knew I was protected. My dad called and threatened to bring me back home. I hid in the bathroom, shaking. When my aunt came home, she made me come out and tell her why I was so frightened. After assuring me that my dad was never going to come to her house for any reason, because he knew she would kill him, she called him up and told him that if he ever frightened me again, she would come to get him. Life was never dull there. My cousin would buy me clothes on Monday and steal them and sell them on Wednesday. She pierced my ears and bought me diamond earrings, which she stole back the first time I took them off.

I lived there comfortably until my mother would call crying and convince me to come home to visit. My mother had been a closet alcoholic for most of my life. It was apparent to everyone now why her moods constantly changed: now vicious, now apathetic, now tearful. Once while I was there, she went to the store. My father came in while I was washing dishes in the kitchen. He started working up an excuse to hit me. He was talking and making himself angrier and angrier. When he started to walk toward me, I knew he had convinced himself to beat me, but I wasn't going to take a beating that day. When he swung, I ducked and countered with a cast-iron skillet. When he started to fall, I gripped it with both hands and kept hitting him. I didn't stop until he stopped moving. I was sure I had killed him. I went downstairs and sat on the front porch. When the police came, they told me to stay put while they went upstairs. As soon as they went inside the door, I poised to run and a policeman stuck his head back out the door and told me to stay put or get handcuffed. They went upstairs and talked to my father for a while. When they came out, they told me I had no business there, that the court placed me with my aunt to protect me and that I needed to stay away from my parents' house. I knew he was right, but I was only sixteen and I missed my mother.

The Navy

I was only seventeen when I graduated from high school. I wanted to go to college, but there was no money and no interest at my house in sending me to college. When I graduated from elementary school, my grades qualified me to go to Austin High School, which was a college prep high school. The counselor told my mother that I would be unhappy there

because I "wouldn't fit." There were no black students at
Austin. That did it for Mom. No matter that I had never fit
in our neighborhood, or at our house. I found a scholarship
for veterans' children and asked my father to sign and furnish
proof that he was a veteran. He refused and told me that I
was only going to get married and have babies. I needed to
stay home and help my mother with her kids. My brother
needed college to support a family. Not only was I not going
to get any help, I was also tagged as selfish because I wanted
to go to college. I found a navy recruiter and signed up. In
1960, on my eighteenth birthday, I was sworn in and left
Chicago for Bainbridge, Maryland.

I was pretty naive. I really thought I was just like everybody else. There had been some racial strife at school, but the
Chicago racism was subtle. You were excluded socially and
snubbed or discriminated against in a covert fashion. When I
got into the navy, I learned about overt racism. My best
friend from Chicago joined the navy four weeks after I did.
She and another woman from Chicago, a friend of my
cousin's, who had disappeared after stealing a large package
of heroin from my cousin's dealer and pimp, were the only
two black women in my battalion. The only friend in my
company was Beverly, a Jewish woman from New York. They
didn't like either of us, but Beverly and I were the smartest
women in the company and they couldn't change that. The
officer in charge of our company hated me. She followed me
around, looking for chances to make my life miserable. Once
outside, I lifted my cap to wipe my brow. She gave me ten
demerits for being uncovered; when I tried to explain that I
never removed my cap, she gave me another ten. I got excel-
lent marks at school, so she couldn't get me removed for
grades. She just rode my back. My company commander,
Chief McCaffrey, knew what was up and tried to keep me out
of her way. One day before inspection, I snuck into a vacant

laundry room to iron my cap. She caught me in there and ordered me to attention. She told me to wipe the smile off my face, then to wipe the frown off my face. Being totally unaware of how my face looked, I struggled to look neutral. She took off her coat and threw her hat and coat onto the bench and stepped close to me with a snarl on her face and her hands raised. Wrong combination. That signaled physical abuse to me. I sidestepped and caught her with a right to the jaw. She totally collapsed, out cold. I went back to the barracks and told Chief McCaffrey what happened. She confined me to my room. Later she came and told me that there would be a hearing at the Battalion Office first thing in the morning. We walked to the hearing together. I stood at attention for over two hours. She came out and put me at rest and went back in. I stood there for another two hours before she came out. The decision was to give me enough demerits to set me back for two weeks, but not to discharge me. I kept a low profile until I was accepted for aircraft electronics school in Memphis, Tennessee. . . .

Memphis

I left for Memphis, Tennessee, by train. I thought I was feeling fine, but after a night of drinking with some other service personnel on the train, I took a bottle of aspirin. It only gave me a stomachache when I woke up the next morning. I spent the next day babying my stomach and refusing to drink. When we arrived in Memphis, it was midmorning and I didn't have to check in until midnight. I'm in my dress blue uniform. I decided to go to the movies. I found a movie theater and waited in the ticket line. When I got to the front of the line, a man came out of the theater to the booth. I slid my money into the little opening, but he didn't take it. He looked at me and asked me if I was there to make trouble. I said no, I just wanted to kill time and watch a movie. He asked me where I was from and I told him. Then he explained that "Negroes" bought their tickets at a booth in the alley. No problem. I go to the alley, buy a ticket, and go upstairs to the balcony. The balcony is enclosed in chicken wire. No, thanks. I go down the stairs to the white booth and wait. Sure enough, here he comes. "You *are* here to make trouble." "No—I just want my money back. You didn't tell me I would have to watch the movie through chicken wire." He gave me my money back and told me there was a nice "colored movie," the New Daisy, in town. I went to the taxi stand on the corner and waited. And waited. And waited. Finally, a taxi pulled up. As I walked toward the door, the driver leaned over and told me that he couldn't pick me up. He just stopped to tell me that I was standing at a white taxi stand and nobody would pick me up there. I needed to go across the street to the colored taxi stand. I'm pretty sick of Memphis by now, but I went to the colored taxi stand and took a colored taxi to the colored movie.

When the movie was over, I took a taxi to the bus station for the shuttle to the base. I went inside and there were benches labeled *White* and *Colored.* There were four bathrooms, *White Women, Colored Women, White Men,* and *Colored Men.* There were even *White* and *Colored* drinking fountains. I was incredulous. I backed out of the bus station and waited outside. When the bus came, I got on and sat in the "safe" seat for unaccompanied women at night. Right behind the driver. Wrong seat for a woman of color. He told me I had to sit in the back. I refused to go. I was fed up with Memphis. He refused to start the bus. The sailors and marines on the bus promised to thrash him if he made them late back from liberty. He relented. When we got to the base, I checked in and an MP drove me to my barracks. Forty women were standing on the steps. As I got out of the truck and walked toward the steps, one shrill voice called out. "We ain't never had no niggers in this barracks and we ain't gonna start now." There was a loud "Yeah, you're right" chorus. For about twenty seconds, I saw bright red and yellow. I watched the crowd until I identified the two loud mouths. I put down my bags and my hat and went straight for the biggest loud mouth. I gave her the opportunity to keep me out. We fought for about five minutes before the MP broke up the fight and the Wave rep came. She was pretty ticked off. She read us the riot act, then told us we were going to learn tolerance, whether we liked it or not. She assigned the three of us to the same room. There was a bunk bed set and a Hollywood bed in the cubicle. Normally, the junior person slept on the top bunk, the next senior the bottom bunk and the most senior slept in the Hollywood bed. Since neither of them wanted to sleep that close to me, I got the Hollywood bed.

My previous dealings with the South were in Grambling, Louisiana, which is a primarily black college town. It was full of my relatives, and I could go anywhere I wanted. With the exception of one incident when I was about nine or ten, I'd never been uncomfortable there. That time, we'd gone to Ruston to shop. While my mother and aunt were shopping, my cousin Ray took us for ice cream. While we were walking, this policeman walked up to us and kicked Ray off the wooden sidewalk into the dirt, calling him a nigger and bawling him out for blocking the sidewalk. I went nuts. Ray was my hero. He was eight years older. Not only was he also interested in science, he was soft-spoken, gentle and patient. I kept screaming at the policeman and tried to kick him and bite him. My brother ran for my mother. Ray apologized to the policeman and kept telling him that I didn't live there and I didn't understand. When my mother and aunt got there, the policeman told my aunt that she needed to train us better before she let us come to town. Then she starts apologizing. I didn't get it. I kept telling my aunt that I didn't do anything wrong. The man kicked Ray, and Ray wouldn't even hit him back. My mother made me shut up and gave me the lecture about being seen and not heard for the rest of our visit.

I was totally unprepared for life as an adult in the South. On the Tuesday following my arrival in Memphis, I was sitting on my bunk reading a novel when my cubicle mates got dressed to go to the movies. As they walked out the door, Ruby called out, "We're going to the movies, nigger, and you better have this cube cleaned up by the time we get back or we're kickin yo' ass." It was so bizarre, I started to laugh. I couldn't believe she actually thought I would clean up the room because I was afraid of them. The next day was inspection, and we would all be in big trouble if we failed it, but Ruby's threat was a guarantee that I wouldn't be doing any cleaning. I read and did my laundry while they were gone and about twenty minutes before lights out, I put my book and glasses in my locker. I heard them coming down the hall, laughing. When they got to the entry into the cubicle, they were amazed to see that it looked just the way they had left it. The next shock was when I slammed the locker door into Ruby's face right in the middle of the "N——" she started to say. When the barracks master at arms broke up the fight, she told us we were all crazy. Back on report. Nobody was going to the movies that month and we had various areas of the barracks to scrape wax off the floors with a razor blade during our spare time. I was never sure whether it was the arrival of my friend Mamie from boot camp or the wax detail that was most responsible, but that was our last fight. We still talked crazy to each other, it just didn't erupt into violence anymore.

School was fun. I was a good student and my electronics instructor, Randy Mason, became a friend of mine. During the first week, we introduced ourselves to the class by name and home town. There was a southern marine by the name of Baker who sat right behind me and taunted me. "I never heard of no niggers who didn't come from the South." I ignored him, but every time I stood in response to a question from the instructor, he had something foul to say, setting off a wave of snickers behind me. The last time he did it, I snatched my book from my desk, turned around and slammed the side of his head with the book as I kicked the chair from underneath him. I kept slamming him with the book and kicking him so fast he couldn't get out of the way. Mason told one of the guys at the back of the room to close the door. A few minutes later, he said, "That's enough, Young." Then he told Baker that if Baker would let the matter go and not attempt any retaliation, he (Mason) wouldn't tell the marine corps that a skinny girl had kicked Baker's ass in full view of the entire class. Baker let it drop. . . .

Memphis was turbulent during that time. I participated in sit-ins. I went to town and tore down *Colored* and *White* signs wherever I found them. I hung with a pack of black and white "malcontents." We went to a restaurant just outside the gates that wouldn't serve Mamie and me hamburgers. Arthur, a white sailor from New York, pitched a big boulder through the plate-glass window. We went to Beale Street to the W.C. Handy club, home of the blues. Whites were not allowed to go to Beale Street. We went in a group and fought the police when they tried to take Arthur or Tony. We were lucky they never killed anybody. One black sailor by the name of Oliver was a favorite target of the police. If they caught him in town, they arrested him and kept him hidden from the navy for a couple of days while they beat him. The attorney from the JAG (Judge Advocate General) office was sympathetic. He came for us immediately whenever we were arrested. No navy charges were ever filed against us for demonstrations. The base captain was a different story. He was furious with our "outlaw" attitude. Once he asked us what he could do to be supportive. We knew he had to be under orders even to say that. When we told him that the mural in the chow hall of slaves "lifting that barge and toting that bale" and dancing for pennies at the docks on the waterfront was offensive and asked him to have it painted over, he went nuts. He told us that we may not like it, but it was history and it was true. He had no intention of removing it, just because we didn't want to be reminded of our inferior backgrounds. We had to pull Oliver out of his office to keep him from getting court-martialed.

I discovered that I could drink most of the sailors I knew under the table. I was a young alcoholic. I didn't know it yet, but I had the family disease. I didn't get stumbling drunk or loud or rowdy; I just drank until I passed out quietly. I had several blackouts in Memphis, and every time I tried to commit suicide. I never recalled it or even remembered why I tried to hurt myself. I decided that the safest thing for me to do was stop drinking before I actually succeeded in killing myself during a blackout.

Leaving Memphis

Shortly before I completed Aircraft Electronics "A" School, I received orders for my next duty station, Corpus Christi, Texas. I was devastated. I couldn't take another eighteen months in the South. My friend Mamie had been ordered to Pensacola, Florida. She wrote back stories about the segregation on the base. There was a rope down the middle of the snack bar that separated black servicemen from white ones. Incensed, I wrote the Bureau of Naval Personnel and pointed out that I felt that sending black military personnel to bases in the South where we were exposed to brutality and mistreatment by the civilians as well as segregated conditions both on and off the bases was grossly unfair. I pointed out the particular unfairness of taking me from Chicago, Illinois, where racial bias was a little more covert and sending me to Bainbridge, Maryland, and Memphis, Tennessee, was bad enough, but to send me to yet another duty station in a place where I was a second-class citizen even within the base was unconscionable. I told them about the indignities I had suffered in Memphis, including the fact that I was forced to eat in a dining hall with the walls covered with pictures of black men and women with exaggerated eyes and lips picking cotton, carrying bales to and from ships docking, and dancing at the docks. I told them how I had to fight my way into the barracks and how it felt to be unable to walk to the hamburger stand outside the base gates and order a hamburger or unable to go to a movie in town that wasn't labeled *Colored.* People laughed at me and said the bureau wasn't interested in my feelings; that I'd given up my rights when I joined the navy. I got to laugh the following month when I got new orders for NAS North Island at Coronado, California. YES!!

Coronado

I was a Petty Officer 3rd class by the time I arrived at Coronado, so I had responsibility for one duty section at the Wave barracks in addition to one duty section at work. I was assigned to the aircraft electronics shop and the ARC-27 bench. The senior person on the ARC-27 bench was a 2nd Class Petty Officer by the name of Zuscar. . . .

Zuscar was pretty nice. He had the reddest hair I'd ever seen. He told me that the only other black people he'd ever been close to beat the daylights out of him in Harlem just for being there. He thought I would know why they wanted to beat him up, even though he never hurt any black people in

241

his life. I thought just being condemned to life in Harlem made people mad enough to want to hurt somebody on a daily basis. I told him about the last white girl in my neighborhood, Patsy. Somebody beat Patsy up every day of her life, just for being white. They weren't mad at Patsy. They were mad at poverty and discrimination and lack of opportunity. Patsy was worse off than anybody on the block. Her mother was an invalid, living off Social Security. No way did Patsy symbolize the ruling class, but she got hit because she shared skin color with them. Anyway, Zuscar graciously decided not to punish me for the transgressions of the people in Harlem who shared my skin color. . . .

The Okie

A year later, I was the bench chief, and Zuscar was gone. One morning, Chief Cleary brought in a seaman recruit who had been aboard ship for a year. He wanted to "strike" for a rating as an aircraft electronics technician. "Strikers" didn't have high enough placement scores to qualify for schools, but could apply for an apprentice position and earn a rating with good performance in on-the-job training. If he did poorly, he'd have to return to "black-shoe" (nonaviation) navy, probably as a boatswain's mate aboard ship. When the chief introduced me as his immediate superior and trainer, this kid looked me in the eye and said, "I ain't never took orders from no woman or no nigger in my life, and I ain't gonna start now." The chief and I were shocked both by what he said and by the vehemence with which he spoke. The chief recovered first. "This is your assignment, sailor. You have six months to either learn a trade or go back aboard ship. You decide which. Young is first in your chain of command. Report to her every day." The chief literally vanished. He did not deal with strong emotion at all. This kid was my responsibility. The chief was finished with it. I told the recruit that if he decided he wanted to be trained, he should let me know. Until then, he should muster for duty and sweep down the hangar and dump the trash every day. After about two weeks of sweeping down that long hangar, first furiously, later resigned, he apologized and asked me to train him. Several of the guys in the shop had stopped to tell him that he was lucky he hadn't smarted off to them. He'd be back aboard ship by now. Some told him that I was a pretty good technician and that he could learn a lot from me.

I didn't rub his nose in it. I felt like I had been successful in that shop because Zuscar went out of his way to help me, even though he was bitter about his treatment at the hands of the black men he met in Harlem. By his actions, he proved to me that he was a better man than they were. I owed Zuscar. I had an opportunity to repay him by being a "better man" than this kid and by both accepting the apology and training him without rancor. I did it. When I signed off on his training report, he apologized again and told me that he appreciated the fact that I hadn't held his ignorance against him. . . .

The Terminal

On the days that we stood watch, we were on duty for twenty-four hours. We worked in the shop from eight to five, broke for dinner, then went back to the shop until the following morning when we were relieved. The storekeeper on duty in my section was a guy by the name of Gray. Women were still fairly new in the aviation rate, so there was no women's bathroom in the shop. We had to go to the air terminal, which was about a mile away. One night, I locked the shop, passed by the storeroom to let Gray know

I was going to the terminal, and left. There were three guys working in the terminal when I went in. No planes were in, so they were just sitting around. I went into the bathroom. When I came out of the stall and started to wash my hands, I heard the door open. When I turned around, there was one of the guys from the terminal standing with his back to the door. I just looked at him. He was nervous. He told me that he had just come in to get my panties. He wasn't going to hurt me. I could go back into the stall and take them off and give them to him. I didn't move. I just stared at him. I had a long Phillips screwdriver in the tool kit on my belt. I had decided that if he got close to me, I would stab him with it. I never felt frightened, just furious. He started getting insistent. He told me that he would take them if he had to, that he couldn't go back out without them. He had to have them to prove to the other guys that he had sex with me. I promised him that I'd kill him if he touched me. It was a standoff. I couldn't get out of the door, but he didn't dare get close to me. After a while, I heard Gray calling me outside. I called out to him that I was trapped in the bathroom. He came into the terminal and tried to get into the bathroom. It was locked. He screamed that he had called the Shore Patrol and if the door wasn't opened immediately, he was going to break it down. It was quiet for a minute, then Gray opened the door with a key and pushed his way past the kid. He asked if I was all right and after I nodded yes, told the kid that he was writing the incident up. As we left, he yelled at the other two guys. The next day, the terminal chief came down to the shop to talk to Gray and Chief Cleary. He told us that there was no one working at the terminal that fit the description we gave him. The two men on duty that night thought some transient passing through must have been the culprit. When I got back to the barracks, I went to see a Wave I knew who worked at the terminal. Millie was from Memphis and had been a civilian when I was stationed there. She used to come to the dances and ask me about navy life. She finally got her courage up and joined. When I got to Coronado, she had been there for several months. Millie told me that the guy I wanted was named Shezzby. When I took the name to the Shore Patrol, they pulled his picture from the base records and I verified that it was him. After he was arrested, the chief who didn't have an employee fitting that description came to see me again. He pleaded with me to drop the charges because a court-martial would ruin the life of a basically nice young man, who was afraid to stand up to two older and more malicious sailors. He asked me just to listen to the guy before I made up my mind. I said that I would. I was angrier at the chief and the two instigators than I was at Shezzby. I had never felt in danger in that restroom. He had been frightened. He had also been the one in danger. I was totally prepared to kill him. When I looked in his eyes, I could tell that he would stand at the door forever if I wasn't fearful enough to cave in and hand over my underwear. I couldn't get to the chief or the two instigators by punishing Shezzby. The black NCOs on base wanted me to hang him because they were sure that a black sailor in the same situation would get lynched. I wanted to decide for myself. I finally decided not to press charges, in spite of the chief, in spite of the opportunity to punish somebody white. I let Shezzby off the hook because I felt it was the compassionate thing to do and because I hadn't been hurt by his behavior. He came and thanked me afterward and told me what I already knew—that he would not have touched me or otherwise harmed me, he just wanted to get those guys off his back. He said that he gained from the incident, that he'd never again risk so much, just to belong. I listened, but I didn't believe it. . . .

Brooks

Brooks was the jet mechanic with squadron VX-5 from China Lake. They were regulars at our air terminal. The jet mechanic is the crew chief. When the plane was ready to leave, he had to turn the completed checklist over to the pilot. He was hard to work for. He was a perfectionist. He was always joking. He was good medicine. We dated for about a year, visiting back and forth. When he proposed, I was so overwhelmed, I didn't notice a couple of very important things. The first was that he had gotten orders to WestPac, a six-month tour of duty aboard ship. The second was the fact that he wanted me to leave the navy after we were married. This was not about love, it was about possession. Brooks wanted to marry me before he went to WestPac so that he didn't have to worry about my finding another boyfriend while he was gone, and he wanted to isolate me from everything and everybody I knew. We moved to San Francisco. My parents had moved to Richmond, across the bay. Actually, my father had moved to Richmond with his girlfriend, leaving my mother in Chicago with two small children and a teenaged son. When he got an attack of conscience, he kicked Thelma and her kids out and sent for my mother.

I loved San Francisco. While Brooks was away, I shared an apartment with a woman I met from Texas. Pat and I were to stay friends for the next twenty years. We were both interested in the sciences. She was a student then at UC Berkeley, a chemistry major. She was the first black woman I met who didn't think I was a freak because I was more interested in books than men. We hung out with a crowd of young black intellectuals. We spent weekends having long discussions about civil rights and politics. I loved it. . . .

During this time, I started to have nightmares. Every night before I went to bed, I pushed a dresser in front of the door.

Pat got disturbed about it because she thought I would be trapped in my room in the event of a fire. I wasn't sure why I did it; I just didn't feel safe until I did. One night, I asked if she thought I might have been molested when I was a child. Her answer made a lot of sense. "If not, why did the question even come up?" People don't normally wonder if they had been molested and they don't normally barricade the bedroom door every night. I started trying to remember.

I found out that I was pregnant in the summer of 1963. I was excited about it. I walked two miles every day in order to be able to eat ice cream from Kirby's. I was enrolled in San Francisco City College for one class. The baby was due in March. As it turned out, baby Everette was induced in January just after the semester ended. Brooks sent me flowers and called. He said the navy would discharge him early if I needed him, but he would rather go back to Whidbey Island with the squadron and be discharged at the end of January. I told him I could manage. He called at the end of the month to say that he had to be hospitalized for a couple of weeks.

When he did come home, Brooks was different. Cold, angry, and domineering. Several women called him from Vancouver and from Washington. One of then sent him nude and seminude pictures of herself. He didn't bother to hide them. One of them even flew all the way to San Francisco to see him, believing that he was unmarried. I let her in to wait for him. My esteem hit rock bottom during this time. He would disappear for days at a time and come home and start hitting me without a word. He worked for Western Electric during the day and as a bartender on Haight Street at night. I thought it was ironic that he could have a job with no electronic or electrical training that I couldn't have because I was a woman even after one year of training and two years on the bench actually repairing equipment.

One day I asked Brooks for cigarettes and nylons. He refused, telling me that I was going to have to stop smoking and go barefoot. The next day I got a job at the telephone company. They refused me a job as a repairperson or technician, as usual, but they did give me an operator's job. Brooks was furious. When I got my first paycheck, he demanded that I turn over all paychecks to him. He would give me an allowance every week and credit cards. I agreed. I never spent the $100 weekly allowance. I saved it and used credit cards whenever I needed to buy anything. I worked short hours, which were six-hour shifts starting at 4:00 P.M. We were paid for eight hours and sent home in taxicabs after our shifts were over. This way, someone was always home with the baby. Brooks still went out and stayed whenever he felt like it, but I stayed home. One night he started hitting me while I had the baby in my arms. Initially, I was afraid that I would drop the baby, so I didn't even try to get out of the way. Then the baby started to cry, and I became enraged. I put the baby on the floor between my feet and started to fight back. Brooks was amazed. He told me I was crazy and that I might hurt the baby. From that day on, I fought back. I didn't get hit as often, but I still got hit. Usually at night when I got home from work. If the taxi was five minutes later than he thought it should be, I got beat up. I showed up at work frequently with a black eye. The women I rode the cab with started asking the drivers to take me home first, no matter what the written rotation was. One night, one of the women told me that they were going out for drinks after work and they were not going to invite me. Not because they didn't like me, but because they didn't want me to get beaten.

I was ashamed. I had called the police for help, but they only took him for a walk or cautioned him. I started hunting for an apartment during the day. I found one to share with a woman from the telephone company with a baby the same age as mine. She worked from seven to four, and I still worked the short hours. One Monday morning while Brooks was at work, I moved. I hired a process server to serve him with divorce papers. After he attacked two process servers, I couldn't hire another one. I finally got a friend of mine from the telephone company to serve him. Somehow, he found out my address. One night I was awakened by the sound of breaking glass as he broke into my apartment. I ran next door and called the police. He was gone by the time they got there. The following week, while I was working, my supervisor plugged into my board. "Alice, you have to get your timecard and punch out. We just had your husband arrested for trying to force his way into the building. We're sending you home in case he comes back." I went to family court and was awarded the whopping sum of $10 weekly for child support. When Brooks came to bring it, he attacked me verbally and then started hitting me. My landlord asked me to move. When we went to court, the judge issued a restraining order against him. He wouldn't pay child support unless he could visit, and I refused to give my address. For $10 weekly, I was not going to risk another beating. I could probably beg that much money and not get a black eye. Brooks stalked me all over San Francisco. He snatched me off the street as I got off the bus and took me to his house and raped me. He broke into my house at night and threatened to kill me. He broke my windows. The police were no help. One day they came to ask me if I would sign some commitment papers, so they could hold Brooks for mental health evaluation and get him some help. He had attacked his bosses at both Western Electric and his next job at Hunter's Point Naval Shipyard. He had even attacked a fellow passenger on the bus crossing the Bay Bridge and been thrown off the bus by the other passengers. I couldn't believe it. Nobody cared when he was beating up his wife, but attacking strangers rated concern and possibly help. No protection for the defenseless, but protect the male citizens at any cost. I refused. Two days after he got out of wherever, he'd be on my doorstep. Nobody was going to commit him for beating me. My friend Pat moved to Los Angeles. When I complained to her after Brooks got me evicted yet a second time, she urged me to come to Los Angeles. It made sense. I arranged for the baby to stay with my mother while I hunted for a job and an apartment and headed for L.A.

Los Angeles

I got a job at Union Bank's computer center. Initially, I worked in the auditor's office and attended classes at night. My boss was a very nice man. When the IRS attached my wages because I was not entitled to claim the head of household exemption as an abandoned spouse unless I was actually divorced, he got a friend of his to file for my divorce. The attorney told me I could pay him in raindrops. I paid him in cash, over time. I loved my job, but I was an oddity there. The black workers at the bank didn't like the fact that I wore a short Afro. Afros weren't in fashion then. Young, upwardly mobile blacks were embarrassed by the "natural" look. My white coworkers thought I was arrogant and standoffish. I supervised the "Due to Banks" area. I was pretty good friends with the bookkeeping supervisor, Lorraine, but her assistant didn't like me. They hired a Mormon missionary student for the summer in bookkeeping. She was sweet, but she was slow, primarily because she was so friendly. One morning, I told her that she had to bring me the completed charges by 10:30 without fail. She had been getting later and later and I still had to balance and make my deadline to call totals to the Federal Reserve Bank. She went ballistic, called me a dirty nigger, and said she hated me. My response was that the word "nigger" stopped exciting me a long time ago and that she still had to produce the charges by 10:30. My boss came out of his office and ordered her back to bookkeeping. When I went to bookkeeping to take the Federal Reserve figures, Lorraine apologized for the student and promised me that when she returned the following day, she would apologize in person. I told her not to bother, I wouldn't believe any apology she made, anyway. Her assistant, who was also Mormon, told me that I was evil, not because I was black, but because I didn't care about people. I reminded her that she knew squat about my feelings, that however evil I was, I never had the nerve to pass myself off as a missionary of God, taking my racial prejudices to foreign countries, and that her gripe with me was the fact that I didn't curl up and die when someone who did started calling me names. She shut up.

There was also a guy in our office, Pete, who bragged about the fact that his father got the last Nazi funeral in Germany. Pete and I locked up about once a week over his racial and ethnic slurs. After the explosion, he'd always look puzzled and ask, "What did I say?" When he was promoted and got his own office, in Beverly Hills, we went down to celebrate the opening. (Why would anybody give a Nazi sympathizer an assignment running an office in Beverly Hills?) While we were eating cake and drinking coffee, I noticed an old woman standing in line. She had a cane and had been standing there a long time. I went over and asked if I could help her. Since our group audited branches for procedure, we all knew what teller procedure was. This woman took one look at me and drew back and spit on me. We were all in shock. Pete came over to the counter and asked one of the women standing there to get a towel and help me clean off my suit. He told the woman that her business was not welcome there if she could not respect the employees, all of them, without regard to race. Now I was really in shock. Racist Pete, standing up for a black woman? Unreal.

On Fridays, I used to walk to Crenshaw to treat my son, Everette, to a hamburger. On the first Friday after the riots started in Watts, I was amazed to see National Guardsmen in tanks riding through my neighborhood with bullhorns, ordering us off the streets by 8:00. Even though the riots were happening in South Central and we lived northwest of that area, a good half hour away, they included every area with a substantial number of black people in the curfew zone. Everette was at an awkward size, too big to carry comfortably and too little to walk fast. We started for home barely ten minutes before curfew. The tank rode by several times ordering us off the street. Everette was walking as fast as his little legs would carry him. Finally I yelled at the tank to give us a ride, shoot us, or shut the hell up. Later, I thought about how stupid that was. Those were a bunch of scared weekend warriors. They might well have thought the preferred solution was to shoot us. I certainly did not smart off at the soldiers at the barricade when I went to work at night. They stopped cars with weapons pointed at your head. Several people were shot and killed for trying to "crash the barricade." I was sure that some of them were just rushing and didn't see the soldiers until they started shooting. . . .

JDL

I switched to working at night and going to L.A. City College during the day. I got to see Everette between 1 and 4. I slept from 4 to 11 and went to work at midnight. I was pursuing a math degree. I wanted to teach. I was doing well in school. I even tutored some engineering students who were having trouble with calculus. That led to problems with the Black Student Union. They felt that I should tutor them. The school paid for BSU tutors as well as general math department tutors. I felt that most of the tutees in the BSU were having problems because they spent more time politicking than studying. I told them I preferred to stay with the math department. They called me an Aunt Jemima, but I didn't care. They started invading my tutoring sessions and harassing me. The guys in my tutoring session, black and white, started throwing them out when they barged in. At the end of the semester, the BSU boycotted finals. I couldn't believe it. Who was going to be hurt if these guys didn't go to their finals? Surely not LACC. I went to take my final exams and discovered that they had set up barricades all around to prevent people from reaching the entrances. I tried to step over the barricades and one of the BSU members pushed me away. I kept trying and he kept pushing. Finally, in frustration, he snatched my books and threw them down, then pushed me down. Then came a bunch of white guys with black armbands. They punched this guy out, tore up the barricades, gathered my books and helped me up. While the others ran over to the next barricade, I thanked the guy who helped me up and asked him who they were. He told me they were from the Jewish Defense League. As I walked to class, I kept pondering on it. Imagine—blacks who should be sympathetic to my desire to get an education willing to hurt me to keep me out of school and young Jewish men willing to fight them to protect my right to go to school.

Back to the Bay

In 1974, I went to work at Chevron, U.S.A., Richmond Refinery. I earned a good salary as a process computer systems analyst and was able to take care of my son and myself, but my emotional life was still a mess. My mother was constantly undermining my authority with my son. She railed at me for making him do chores. She belittled me constantly. One evening, I'd had enough. I told her that I was an adult who was entitled to the same respect that any other human being was entitled to and that I would not come back to her house until she could treat me with respect. After about two days, she called me, screaming abuse. I hung up. I was determined to draw hard lines for the people in my life. If they cared about me, they wouldn't cross them out of concern for my feelings. If they didn't, they wouldn't cross them out of concern for their own feelings. Finally, my mother called and apologized and invited me to her house. For the first time in my life, my mother started to treat me as if she valued our relationship.

So, for the next ten years, my biggest abuser was my employer. In our first meeting, he told me that I looked just like the pickaninnies in the Bahamas. I informed him that in the United States, black men and women didn't like the term "pickaninnies," especially used to describe them. To a bigot, that was like waving a red flag. He harassed me continually. Luckily, I only had to see him periodically. My office was usually near the computer I was responsible for and was located at the process unit. His office was in the main office building. I kept myself safe by being effective at my job, but he always found some reason not to promote me. He'd even tried to fire me for being AWOL while I was on Reserve Duty. When we were all moved to the tech center, I was faced with him daily. There was always some kind of verbal fireworks. Finally, I'd had enough of him. His behavior was obvious to everybody around us. I got letters of evaluation from all the departments that I was in service to and went to his supervisor. My boss went ballistic. I showed his supervisor the letters I had received and a copy of the department resource list that showed myself and a black man proficient on every system in the refinery, but having the lowest rank and the lowest pay. After the meeting, my boss followed me into the copy room, closing the door and barring my way out.

He started screaming at me and walking toward me with his hands curled into fists. Initially, I was shocked and frightened, then angry, then enraged. In a quiet voice, I told him that if he didn't drop his hands and move out of my way, he'd regret it.

He complied. I was so angry, I felt dizzy. When I went to the doctor, my blood pressure was so elevated, he put me on sick leave for six weeks. When I went back to work, my boss had been replaced by a guy that I'd worked with successfully for a long time. When I checked in with the medical clinic, I had to check in with a corporate psychologist who told me that my former boss claimed to be in fear that I might make some attempt on his life. I laughed as I told her about the harassment and unfairness over the years. If he lived through all that, he was safe. She told me that he painted a picture of a violent, hostile woman and that she had been surprised at how soft-spoken and thoughtful I was. Before I left, she told me that she was Jewish and gave me some advice she'd gotten from her grandmother. "Live well and defeat your enemies. Just be successful. It hurts them worse than anything else you could do." . . .

One night in 1988 my sister called me, crying. My mother's heart had stopped. She'd been taken to surgery. I left for Richmond right away. The doctor told us that her liver was enlarged and she had congestive heart failure as a result of all the years of secret drinking. When my leave was up, I went back to work. I was back to days that started at 5:30 and ended at 8:00. At night, I couldn't go into my mother's room to talk to her. She had called me in one night and told me that she was sorry for all the things that had happened to me and sorry that my life had been ruined and that she loved me. She told me to make myself happy and not to let anyone else use me. I didn't want her to start talking to me about my childhood. It was too frightening. When she came home from the hospital, I could make her meals and take care of her at night, but she was at the mercy of my brother and sister during the day. My brother was doing drugs, stealing from everyone in the house. I had to sleep with my money pinned to my nightgown in order not to be a victim as well. I needed to leave there in the worst way, but I couldn't leave my mother. She wouldn't let my older brother and me move her away. When she started walking around in the house, I thought she was going to get better.

I felt safe enough to go to Monterey to take advantage of the weekend that Digital gave my project team for successful completion of a factory automation project. The night before, she started having trouble breathing. I took her to the hospital and talked softly to her in the waiting room so that she wouldn't panic. I kept reminding her to breathe slowly and to breathe deeply. When they finally took her into the room to see the doctor, her heart stopped again. From that point on, I was afraid constantly. I couldn't sleep at night or relax during the day. After she was stabilized, she came home again. This time she seemed to get progressively weaker. One day, while I was at work, she was taken back to the hospital. I took another week off from work and visited with her every day. On the Monday morning I was to go back to work, I went to the hospital and explained that I had to complete the class I started before she got sick and that I had to stay in Santa Clara until the weekend in order to avoid being caught in the traffic. I promised to call daily and come back on Friday. She had an oxygen mask on and couldn't answer me, but she held my hand tightly for a minute, then let go. I kissed her good-bye and left. When I arrived at class, they told me to call my supervisor. When I called, she told me that my mother had died shortly after I left. She sent me home in a limousine. The limo had a bar. I remember drinking brandy and watching the rain. I was glad that there was no sunshine. It was as if the heavens were crying with me.

I went back to Santa Clara after the funeral, but I couldn't shake the depression. I couldn't stop thinking about my mother's short life. I don't ever remember her being happy about her life. She had lived and died without ever achieving any of the things she wanted in life. She was intelligent, pretty, a good homemaker, and a good mother. She had all the qualities that women were supposed to possess for a happy, successful marriage. Yet, she died a bitter and unfulfilled alcoholic with none of her ambitions or dreams realized. I had to find out what my real needs were and start trying to meet them. I didn't even know what they were. I was becoming my mother. My son, Everette was in the army, my mother was dead. I didn't know how to live for just me, so I was committing suicide, one drink at a time. My whole life had been a response to someone else's needs. . . .

East Palo Alto

I moved to East Palo Alto in search of an identity. I had been surrounded by white people for the last ten years. Maybe if I got in touch with my roots, I could find out who I was and what I wanted. I was totally out of my element. I was a walking target. I gave a ride home to a girl who snatched my purse as she got out of the car. I let a woman stay in my apartment when she lost her ride home to Fremont. When she left, she took my checkbook. Somehow I lacked the energy even to defend myself. I starting drinking myself to sleep again. At work, I was locked in another struggle with my immediate supervisor. I actually had to get the salesmen I worked with to put their impressions of my skills in writing and send them to her supervisor. My customers were totally happy, but she kept looking for something to hang me with. This time, my preoccupation with self-discovery preempted everything. I had fought and struggled my entire life, but I didn't have anything to show for it. What was so wonderful about the right to go to work every morning and spend eight hours watching my back? I was a zombie. I went to work, I came home, I drank. I had no friends, no life, really. I stopped answering the telephone. I wouldn't leave the house. I wouldn't even open the mailbox. I only went out when I ran out of alcohol. One Saturday morning, on my way to the store, I was stopped by the police.

What started out to be a nightmare was actually a blessing in disguise. I was arrested. Since I stopped going to work, my supervisor reported the car stolen. I was under the influence; there was a controlled substance in the car. I was released after arraignment on Monday. I went home to brood. East Palo Alto was full of people who were in trouble with the law. Now my neighbors stopped trying to hustle me and started trying to help me. "Help" in the form of offers to front me drugs to sell, offers to show me how to rob people who were silly enough to come to East Palo Alto searching for drugs or women. One night, I woke up about 3:00 A.M., packed an overnight bag and caught AMTRAK to Fresno. It was the last place I remembered being healthy.

A Dream Deferred

I took stock of my life. I had a little money and a desire to get free of alcohol. I needed people to care for and to have them care about me. I wanted to complete college. I started from there. I joined a twelve-step program for alcoholics. I joined the Powerhouse Church. I was court-ordered to a drug and alcohol diversion program, the Olive Street Bridge. I enrolled in Fresno City College. I started to volunteer at the Good Samaritan House for Battered and Homeless Women and Children. Since I worked the graveyard shift, I got free room and board. Later, when they got a budget, I got paid as well. I completed my diversion program. I went to court several times with help from the Powerhouse Church. Eventually, I was sentenced to two months in jail, community service, and probation. Since I was in school, they let me serve during summer vacation. I stayed six weeks. I survived. I continued to volunteer at the Good Samaritan, even though I moved to Fresno.

During my stay at the rehab hospital, at the twelve-step meetings, and at Olive Street Bridge, I had started to probe my feelings about my childhood. I learned of a center for childhood sexual abuse survivors called Healing for Survivors. I didn't have enough money to pay for sessions, so I applied to the State Department of Rehabilitation for help. They paid for one workshop and ten sessions.

Those were some intensely painful feelings, but they were very freeing. I started to come alive as a person. I loved the Good Samaritan. I felt great washing dishes, mopping floors, and being in service to women who needed someone to care about them and let them know they were important. Loving them was like loving myself. Those women *were me.* I had gotten part-time work at Fresno City College in the Enabler's Office, the Disabled Student Services Office. That helped me continue the sessions at Healing for Survivors. I started to become energized. I volunteered to work as a group counselor at Healing for Survivors. I spoke to women's groups about domestic violence, childhood sexual abuse, and alcoholism. I held Bible study groups for women in crisis. I gave up the graveyard shift at the Good Samaritan, but I became a member of the Board of Directors. I started to work as a legal secretary/paralegal in a law office. All of a sudden, I was graduating from Fresno City College.

San Luis Obispo

One of the transfer counselors suggested that I visit San Luis Obispo before I made a decision on a four-year school. I came down for a tour and fell in love with the campus. I started school in winter quarter 1994. I applied for scholarships for the 1995–96 school year and was invited to apply for the CSU Trustees Outstanding Achievement Award. I applied and to my surprise, I was one of the winners. I still have trouble believing that I'm a student. Here I am, a fifty-three-year-old woman, in the midst of students whose average age is twenty-two, studying computer science. Delayed by thirty years, but I'm here. Dreams can come true.

Index

Philip L. Fetzer received his B.A. from Princeton University and his Ph.D. from the University of Oregon. He is an associate professor of political science at California Polytechnic State University, San Luis Obispo. His essays have appeared in the *American Indian Law Review,* the *South Carolina Law Review,* and the *Thurgood Marshall Law Review.*
